Dialogues on
Migration Policy

Program in Migration and Refugee Studies

Dialogues on Migration Policy

Edited by
Marco Giugni and Florence Passy

LEXINGTON BOOKS

A division of
ROWMAN & LITTLEFIELD PUBLISHERS, INC.
Lanham • *Boulder* • *New York* • *Toronto* • *Oxford*

LEXINGTON BOOKS

A division of Rowman & Littlefield Publishers, Inc.
A wholly owned subsidiary of The Rowman & Littlefield Publishing Group, Inc.
4501 Forbes Boulevard, Suite 200
Lanham, MD 20706

PO Box 317
Oxford
OX2 9RU, UK

British Library Cataloguing in Publication Information Available

Library of Congress Cataloging-in-Publication Data

Dialogues on migration policy / edited by Marco Giugni and Florence Passy.
    p. cm. — (Program in migration and refugee studies)
 Includes bibliographical references and index.
 ISBN-10: 0-7391-1097-7 (cloth : alk. paper)
 ISBN-13: 978-0-7391-1097-3 (cloth : alk. paper)
 ISBN-10: 0-7391-1098-5 (pbk. : alk. paper)
 ISBN-13: 978-0-7391-1098-0 (pbk. : alk. paper)
 1. Emigration and immigration—Government policy. 2. Emigration and
immigration—Government policy—United States. 3. Emigration and immigration—
Government policy—Europe. I. Giugni, Marco. II. Passy, Florence. III. Title.
IV. Series.
JV6271.D53 2006
325—dc22
                                   2005029931

Printed in the United States of America

∞™ The paper used in this publication meets the minimum requirements of
American National Standard for Information Sciences—Permanence of Paper
for Printed Library Materials, ANSI/NISO Z39.48-1992.

Contents

Part III: Determinants: Ethnicity or Political Channeling?

Part IV: Influence: Members or Challengers?

Acknowledgments

Some of the chapters included in the present volume are revised drafts of papers that were originally discussed at an international conference convened by the two editors and held at the University of Geneva in October 2000. The conference, titled *Explaining Changes in Migration Policy: Debates from Different Perspectives*, gathered a number of leading scholars of immigration politics, both from Europe and the United States. Its purpose was to have academic experts in the field confronting each other on some fundamental issues concerning migration policy as if the gathering was a series of dialogues among people with different, sometimes quite opposed, viewpoints. Then, we asked other experts to comment on the dialogues in order to put the different positions into perspective and single out the implications for the study of migration policy, as well as to point to directions for future research in the field.

Although we could not reach our goal of having all of the papers presented at the conference included in this volume, the following chapters still reflect the spirit of that event. The book also includes two reprinted chapters (by David Jacobson and Galya Benarieh Ruffer, and by John Rex), that we thought were particularly well suited for the present purpose. It has taken a long time, but eventually the fruitful discussions we had at the conference have materialized in an edited volume which we hope will be of use by students of immigration politics and, more generally, by all those who are interested in both migration policy and in policy change.

We thank the institutions and foundations that financially supported the Geneva conference: the Swiss National Science Foundation (in particular

Rosita Fibbi, Director of the National Research Program 39), the Swiss Academy of Humanities and Social Sciences, the Academic Society of Geneva, the University of Geneva (in particular Paolo Urio, Director of the Plurifacultary Program on Social Exclusion), and the Department of Political Science (University of Geneva). We also thank all the participants in the conference. A special thought among them goes to the late Hans Mahnig, a colleague and friend who did much for the study of immigration politics in Switzerland.

Chapters 1 and 5 have been published previously and are reprinted here with permission. Chapter 1, Jacobson, David and Galya Benarieh Ruffer. "Courts Across Borders: The Implications of Judiacial Agency for Human Rights and Democracy." Human Rights Quarterly 25:1 (2003), 74–92. © The Johns Hopkins University Press. Reprinted with permission of the Johns Hopkins University Press. Chapter 5, John Rex, "The Nature of Erthnicity in the Project if Migration," pp. 269–83 in *The Ethnicity Reader: Nationalism, Multiculturalism and Migration,* edited by Montserrat Guibernau and John Rex, Cambridge, Polity Press, 1997. It is reprinted here with permission of Polity Press.

Introduction:
Four Dialogues on Migration Policy

Marco Giugni and Florence Passy

Issues relating to immigration and ethnic relations are central to public debates and political decision-making in the contemporary Western societies. As a result, migration research has witnessed a great expansion in recent years. The amount of scholarly work and international conferences is increasing at a very high pace. Much of this work focuses on explanations of policy-making in this field, that is, migration policy. Broadly speaking, migration policy covers the following three aspects: (1) the regulation of immigration flows (i.e., immigration control); (2) the management of ethnic relations and the integration of minorities living in the host society (i.e., minority integration); and (3) antiracism and anti-discrimination policies (including state intervention against the extreme right).

What accounts for variations in migration policy across nations and over time? How has policy evolved since World War Two? Is there a general trend toward more restrictive and exclusionary policies or rather a trend toward more liberal and inclusive policies? Do we observe policy convergence and a Europeanization of this field, or do national states keep their strong imprint on these matters? These are some of the crucial questions that scholars have tried and still try to answer. They do so from a variety of approaches and theoretical perspectives: class and economic theories, political economy and liberal theories, theories stressing the role of ethnicity and race relations, institutional channeling and political opportunity theories, neo-institutional theories, post-national theories, and so forth. This variety of perspectives is certainly beneficial to the study of migration, but it sometimes leads to different or even opposing results.

1

In addition to such a variety of perspectives, underlying the research efforts of students of immigration and ethnic relations politics are a number
of theoretical concerns. Let us mention three that seem to us as crucial ones
on which scholars often cannot find a consensus. The first one is related
to the *role of the national state in a globalizing world*. After the path-
breaking contribution of Rogers Brubaker (1992), who has stressed the crucial impact of national citizenship traditions on migration politics, many
authors have produced informed studies supporting this argument (Birnbaum 1998; Favell 1998; Joppke 1999; Koopmans and Statham 1999; Safran
1997; Schnapper 1994). At the same time, other analysts have put forward
an opposed argument, stressing that in the postwar era immigration has
changed the nature of modern states considerably and, specifically, undermined national sovereignty (Jacobson 1996; Sassen 1998; Soysal 1994). In
this view, the main driving forces behind policy changes are not to be seen
at the national level, but rather at the supranational level. These opposing
perspectives on the role of the national state lead to different views on the
question of policy convergence or divergence in the migration field (Mahnig and Wimmer 2000).

A second theoretical concern regards the *determinants of policy change*.
Some analysts have stressed the impact of economic factors for explaining
changes in migration policy. For example, during periods of economic
growth, states can be open to the inflow of immigrants, whereas in phases
of recession they need to regulate transnational immigration flows and at the
same time enact policies aimed at the integration of migrants (Straubhaar and
Weber 1994). Other analysts, in contrast, point to the role of political factors
in defining and bringing about changes in migration policy (Freeman 1995).
Still others argue that the nature and form of policy-making largely depend
on the national or ethnic origin of migrants (Rex 1996). For example, post-
colonial states have enacted different policies than new immigration countries (such as Southern European countries). Finally, several authors stress
the impact of national institutions on the political responses to immigration
flows and settlements (Ireland 1994).

A third theoretical concern bears on the *role of collective interests* for migration policy. Several analysts point out that political parties and their ideological orientation do not impinge fundamentally upon policy definition.
This is the thesis of the "hidden consensus" between leftist and rightist parties that would strongly influence immigration politics (Hollifield 1994; Weil
1995). However, while established parties do not seem to affect migration
policy significantly, less institutionalized extreme-right actors have been
shown to have a more important impact (Schain 1987). More recently, some
scholars have stressed the growing role of the judiciary (courts) for the regulation of immigrant flows and especially for the implementation of anti-
discrimination laws (Joppke 2000; Guiraudon 2000b).

Of course, this way of presenting the literature is exceedingly simplistic. Often existing theories combine more than a single explanatory factor. For example, Hollifield's (1992a) argument about the impact of "embedded liberalism" combines political and economic factors. Similarly, it is difficult to find a purely "globalist" view of migration or a scholar who denies the impact of global changes on policy-making. However, for analytical purposes it is helpful to frame these issues in terms of opposing perspectives, each one stressing a major explanatory factor or a type of actors having the greatest impact on policy. This book addresses the general theme of why and how migration policy is brought about through a series of informed debates on the different perspectives that scholars have developed to understand the development of migration policies adopted in receiving countries (specifically, in Europe and North America).

Following this simple but unconventional format, the contributions to the volume are divided into four parts, each dealing with one of four theoretical debates or "dialogues": (1) the *scope* of migration policy; (2) the relationship between migration, politics, and *economy*; (3) the relationship between migration, politics, and *culture*; (4) and the *impact* of certain collective actors on migration policy. Each "dialogue" is made up of two main chapters and a commentary chapter. In each "dialogue," two authors working in different theoretical traditions and with divergent views on the subject matter confront each other on a specific topic of relevance to the general theme of the book. Then a third author gives a commentary based on her/his reading of these authors' views.

While some of the approaches and theoretical perspectives mentioned above can be seen as complementary, others are clearly opposed. As we said, however, we think that such opposition of views is fruitful rather than detrimental to the study of immigration and ethnic relations, for it helps us to highlight both the strengths and weaknesses of each theory. Next, we briefly address each of these four issues as a way to introduce the eight chapters and four commentaries that follow. In the final section of this introduction, we shall outline the contours of a research agenda for the future.

THE SCOPE OF MIGRATION POLICY: GLOBAL OR NATIONAL?

The first debate concerns the scope of migration policy and is addressed in Part I of the book by the chapter of David Jacobson and Galya Benarieh Ruffer, the chapter of Adrian Favell, and the commentary provided by Saskia Sassen.

Although migration was by no means a new phenomenon, the decades following World War Two have been characterized by important population movements. In this regard, however, we must distinguish between two periods: before and after the economic crisis of the mid-1970s. For the former period, Castles and Miller (1998: 67–68) mention three main types of migrations that led to the formation of ethnic minorities in advanced industrial countries:[1]

- "migration of workers from the European periphery to Western Europe, often through 'guestworker systems'
- migration of 'colonial workers' to the former colonial powers
- permanent migration to North America and Australia, at first from Europe and later from Asia and Latin America"

As far as Western European countries are concerned (especially those that do not have a colonial past), labor force from Southern Europe represents the main stream of migration during this period.

These migratory movements shared a number of typical features (Castles and Miller 1998). The most important is perhaps that they were motivated mostly by economic reasons. This holds both from the point of view of the migrants who moved from the European periphery to Western Europe to escape economic hardship ("push" factors) and from the point of view of the receiving countries who needed cheap labor for their growing economies ("pull" factors). A second, less important feature, but which is more characteristic of the post-1973 period, is the growing diversity of areas of origin as well as the increasing cultural difference between migrants and the populations in receiving countries.

The oil crisis of the mid-seventies and the economic restructuring of the world economy produced many changes to this traditional migratory pattern. Castles and Miller (1998: 79) mention the following main trends:

- labor migration to Western Europe has declined
- family reunion has become a major source of immigration, and new ethnic minorities have formed
- certain Southern European countries have shifted from the status of emigration countries to that of countries of immigration
- the economically motivated migration to North America and Oceania has continued, but the areas of origin and the forms of migration have shifted
- new migratory movements have emerged relating to economic and social change in newly industrializing countries
- mass movements of refugees and asylum-seekers have developed
- international mobility of highly qualified personnel has increased

Some of these changes can be seen as a result of what we may loosely call "globalization." Indeed, globalization (i.e., broadly defined, the increasing interconnectedness of economic, social, and cultural relations in time and space across the world) challenges the traditional patterns in a least two ways. On the one hand, immigration flows are increasing in intensity, scope, and diversity. On the other hand, the normative bases for policy-making in various political domains—including migration—are increasingly found at the supranational level. With regard to the latter aspect, two positions can be discerned in the literature that are quite opposed, although this opposition is slowly giving place to more balanced statements. As a shortcut, we may call them, respectively, the post-national thesis and the nation-centered perspective. Let us examine each of these two aspects in some more detail.

Boldly stated, the *post-national thesis* maintains that the post–World War period has witnessed a broadening of the scope of migration issues and policies beyond the national level as well as the emergence of a post-national citizenship based on the transnationalization of migrant communities and on the growing importance of supranational organizations and conventions. Among the most well-known proponents of this thesis are David Jacobson (1996), Yasemin Soysal (1994), and Saskia Sassen (1996). Soysal, in particular, has perhaps made one of the boldest statements of this position and has largely contributed to its popularity in the scientific community. She argues that the basis of legitimacy of human rights—including those of migrants— is increasingly found at the transnational rather than the national level. More specifically, she maintains that the traditional concept of national citizenship is being supplanted by the emergence of what she calls a post-national citizenship, which is no longer anchored in the national state. As she remarks, in the postwar period the discourse on human rights has taken on a universalistic dimension and crystallizes around the idea of personhood: "[i]n a world within which rights, and identities as rights, derive their legitimacy from discourses of universalistic personhood, the limits of nation-ness, or of national citizenship, for that matter, become inventively irrelevant" (Soysal 1998: 210–211). Discourse on human rights as well as its institutionalization into social norms and practices form the normative basis for an expansion of citizenship. Therefore, if the organization of the incorporation of immigrants in the host society still depends on the national state, its legitimacy is increasingly located in international institutions and conventions on human rights (Soysal 1994). With respect to our subject matter, this shift in the basis of legitimacy of human rights would result in a loss of power on the national state in policy-making on migration issues and a transnationalizing of immigration policy.

David Jacobson (1996: 8–9) points to the same direction when he states that "[t]ransnational migration is steadily eroding the traditional basis of national state membership, namely citizenship. As rights have come to be predicated on residency, not citizen status, the distinction between 'citizen' and 'alien' has eroded" (Jacobson 1996: 8–9). Not less than Soysal, Jacobson stresses a post-national citizenship based on the transnationalization of migrant communities and on the growing importance of supranational organizations and conventions. In this regard, he underscores the role of the European Convention of Human Rights as an international legal basis to which individuals and non-governmental organizations can refer to claim their rights. In his view, these "rights across borders" bring a fundamental challenge to the traditional basis of national membership, that is, citizenship.

Against this view, a number of authors have put forward a *nation-centered perspective*, maintaining that it is much too early to speak of a loss of significance of the national state in this policy area, as dynamics inherent to national politics still affect the saliency and extent of international and transnational developments (Dummet and Nicol 1990; Heisler 1992; Hollifield 1992a, 1992b; Joppke 1999). Human rights are a constitutive principle of liberal democracies that have a legal-domestic source (Joppke 2001), and changes in the political culture of liberal democracies have brought about rights-based politics that, in turn, has impinged upon international norms, rather than the reverse (Hollifield 1992a). In a similar vein, other authors have stressed that citizenship provides the best framework for analyzing relationships between immigrants and host societies (Schmitter Heisler 1992), and that states tend to regulate international migration following their national interests (Weiner 1985).

An important piece of work in this respect is Rogers Brubaker's *Citizenship and Nationhood in France and Germany* (1992), in which the author points to the cultural foundations of national states and how present-day formal definitions of citizenship reflect deeply rooted understandings of nationhood. The author distinguishes Germany's *jus sanguinis* legal tradition based on a conception of the national community in ethnocultural terms and France's *jus solis* rule, which stems from a republican, contractualistic, and political definition of the state, and explains this difference with the divergent history of state formation in the two countries (see Weil 2002 for a criticism). Brubaker points to the cultural foundations of national states and how present-day formal definitions of citizenship reflect deeply rooted understandings of nationhood. He has made a strong statement in favor of this perspective in his book, which is worth reporting here (Brubaker 1992: 3): "[D]efinitions of citizenship continue to reflect deeply rooted understandings of nationhood. The state-centered, assimilationist understanding of nationhood in France is embodied and expressed in a expansive definition of citizenship, one that automatically transforms second-generation immigrants into citizens, assimilating them—legally—to other French men and women. The ethnic-cultural, differentialist understanding of nationhood in Germany is embodied and expressed in a definition of citizenship that is remarkably open to ethnic German immigrants from Eastern Europe and the Soviet

Union, but remarkably closed to non-German immigrants."[2] Following the way paved by Brubaker, a number of comparative studies have shown that the modes of incorporation of immigrants are largely dependent on national configurations of citizenship (Castles 1995; Favell 1998; Giugni and Passy 2004; Joppke 1999; Koopmans and Kriesi 1997; Koopmans and Statham 1999, 2000a; Koopmans et al. 2005; Safran 1997; Smith and Blanc 1996; Soysal 1994).

Thus, this debate focuses on the significance of the concept of national citizenship following the emergence of a post-national citizenship. It also deals with the degree of autonomy and determination that the national state, as well as nation-based actors and processes, have on the political process and policy-making in the field of immigration and ethnic relations. With regard to this second aspect, the state-centered model can be opposed to the multi-level governance model. According to proponents of the multilevel governance model, the political impact of national states is eroding, as they are increasingly forced to share their decision-making power with supranational institutions as well as with other states and subnational organs and actors.

This distinction applies to the debate on EU migration policy, which opposes two positions that reflect the controversy outlined above: a state-centric approach that stresses sovereignty and national interests, according to which the lack of a unified European immigration policy stems largely from the reluctance of national states to give up their sovereignty (together with a stress in national differences in migration policies and inter-governmentalism in European coordination), and a society-centric approach that points to the increasing interdependence of national situations, globalization, and the impact of transnational institutions (Ugur 1995).

From the point of view of immigration control, the latter approach underscores policy harmonization through the creation of power centers and institutions located above the national state. For example, Soysal (1993) argues that, despite the lack of formal EU authoritative rules and structures, there is much standardization at the European and national levels in terms of both policy-making and policy outcomes. Such standardization as well as the expansion of the EU agenda to include various new issue areas, which contributes to the creation of a common discourse and understanding, would point to the Europeanization of immigration policy, not simply the aggregation of national agendas. This view has been challenged by a number of authors who are more skeptical about the process of Europeanization in the migration political field (Favell 2000; Favell and Geddes 2000; Giugni and Passy 2002).

In sum, this first dialogue engages those who believe that, at least in the field of immigration and ethnic relations, the national state is becoming overwhelmed by emerging actors, structures, processes, and normative standards brought about by globalization and the acceleration of European integration to those who think that the state remains the main frame of reference in this field. While the former stress the emergence of a post-national citizenship, the latter underscore the continuing relevance of the traditional bases of (national) citizenship. Now, many of the statements for the continuing relevance of the state's autonomy and prerogatives in this field have been made in the 1990s or even in the 1980s. Yet globalization and especially European integration have accelerated since, and therefore, we need to reassess this question in light of the new developments.

DETERMINANTS OF MIGRATION POLICY: ECONOMY OR POLITICS?

Another matter of discussion among specialists of migration studies is whether and to what extent policy-making in this field is driven by economic motives rather than by political forces. In terms of the traditional distinction between immigration policy and immigrant policy (Hammar 1985), this debate deals above all with the former, that is, with immigration control and the regulation of flows of immigrants, in particular of immigrant workers. This debate is addressed in Part II of the book by the chapter of Etienne Piguet, the chapter of James Hollifield, Valerie F. Hunt, and Daniel J. Tichenor, and the commentary provided by Gary Freeman.

As we mentioned earlier, one common feature of the population movements of the post–World War Two period is the predominance of *economic reasons* for migrating. The bulk of the first waves of immigration, both in the traditional countries of immigration (basically, Australia, Canada, and the United States) and in Western European countries (most notably, Belgium, France, Germany, Great Britain, the Netherlands, Sweden, and Switzerland) was made of people looking for a job or, in any event, a better situation than the one they had in their homeland. In the European context, this kind of immigration has been subsumed under the guest-worker model, as migrants were considered temporary "guests" in search for work, not as permanent settlers.

In the scholarly literature, this view has been translated in an approach and explanatory framework derived from economics and stressing the political economy of immigration. According to this approach, which has become dominant in migration theories, migration stems from a combination of "push" factors that incite people from poor countries to look for a job in richer countries and "pull" factors that makes host countries willing to use foreign workers to fill the needs of their economies. In other words, immigration is understood mainly in terms of supply and demand of labor. Among the push factors in homelands, one can mention demographic growth, weak standards of life, and a lack of economic opportunities, but also political repression. Pull factors in host countries include demand for labor, land availability, and economic opportunities, but also political freedom. Thus, labor has become the principal concern of immigration policy in industrial democracies during the postwar period (Hollifield 1992a).

Explanations of migration policy—specifically immigration control policies—have reflected this push/pull perspective. The dominant framework for analysis has followed such an economic perspective (see Castles and Miller 1998 for a review). Explanations inspired by neoclassical economics have stressed the importance of economic equilibrium, self-regulation through the (labor) market, and the law of supply and demand for understanding changes in migration policy.

Push/pull theories have been criticized for being individualistic and largely ahistorical, for relying on a doubtful assumption of the maximization of utility by both migrants and policy-makers, and for being too simplistic and incapable to explain and predict migration flows. Furthermore, these theories often conceive the state as a distortion of the correct functioning of the market, while it can easily be shown that the state plays indeed a big role in formulating and implementing policies, both in the field of immigration control and minority integration.

More specifically, push/pull theories have been questioned on the basis of a simple observation. If international migration is driven mainly by economic reasons and can be explained through a push/pull framework, one should expect immigration flows to reduce and even reverse in times of bad economic conditions and a tight labor market in the host societies. In such a situation, host country governments should stop immigration and foreign workers should go back to their homelands. This has not occurred, at least not to the extent that this explanatory framework would have predicted and policy-makers in host countries societies would have wanted. Why is it so?

Political scientists have stressed the importance of *politics* to explain why the regulation of immigration has largely failed (e.g., Hollifield 1992a; Joppke 1998a; 1999). James Hollifield (1992a), for example, has stressed the role of political factors to explain the persistence of immigration in spite of the willingness of host countries to diminish it in times of bad economic conditions, when, therefore, foreign labor is no longer needed. In his view, the persistence of immigration in industrial democracies—and therefore, the failure of these countries to effectively control immigration—comes above all from political liberalism and the emergence of a rights-based regime. Political liberalism provides for the extension of civil, political, and social rights to every member of the society (including migrants). This has made the use of the foreign labor force as a "shock absorber" difficult and has increased the impact of both family reunification and asylum-seeking as a source of international migration in recent decades.

More generally, migration policy must be viewed both in terms of economic liberalism (i.e., the creation and protection of relatively free markets)
and in terms of political liberalism (the extension of rights). Hollifield has
nicely summarized this argument as follows: "The confluence of open (un-
regulated) international markets for labor and rights-based politics in domestic regimes explains the surge in immigration in the postwar period, and
it has created the conditions for the emergence of international migration
regimes. Such regimes, which are evolving at a regional level in Europe and
North America, are confronted with the task of resolving the liberal tension
between rights and markets. In these regimes, legitimacy is derived both
from ideas of justice and from the legal protections of due process and equal
treatment guaranteed through the judicial systems of liberal democracies"
(Hollifield 1992a: 28).

DETERMINANTS OF MIGRATION POLICY: ETHNICITY OR POLITICAL CHANNELING?

If the economy versus politics debate concerns immigration policy, another
very important debate deals above all with immigrant policy, that is, the
management of ethnic relations and the integration of minorities living in the
host society. Indeed, this is perhaps the crucial issue relating to immigration
today. This debate is addressed in Part III of the book by the chapter of John
Rex, the chapter of Patrick Ireland, and the commentary provided by Paul
Statham.

The population movements that have occurred since the end of World
War Two have contributed to the formation of ethnic minorities in Western
countries. As we said, furthermore, especially in recent periods, the diversity of migrant groups has increased. This has forced the governments—
and the public opinions—of these countries to deal with ethnic diversity.
The question is how they did so. Thus, the crucial question here is what
explains the approaches and policies that states have followed in order to
deal with ethnic diversity and to integrate immigrants in the host society.
This is the question of citizenship and membership in democratic societies,
which includes not only the legal definition of who is entitled to become a
citizen but also issues relating to assimilation, ethnicity, race, and culture.

Existing theories to explain minority political integration in Western countries can be divided in three broad categories (Ireland 1994; Welch and
Studlar 1985): class theories; ethnicity and race theories; and institutional
channeling theories. Each has its own view about the ways in which Western countries have dealt with the integration of migrants and ethnic minorities, and each stresses a specific explanatory factor. Class theories stress socioeconomic factors and sees integration policy as a result of class conflict.

Accordingly, policy stems above all from the need of the state for a cheap labor force and, therefore, migrants suffer from a lack of incorporation when the state does not need foreign workers. This brings us back to the discussion above concerning the role of the economy. Ethnicity theories stress sociocultural factors. Here integration policy is explained in terms of the (national) origin of migrants and in terms of ethnic diversity. Therefore, the state enforces different measures according to the origin and statute of migrants, their number and variety. Finally, institutional channeling theories stress political and institutional factors. In this view, migrant incorporation depends on the institutional context of the host country, regardless of the type of migrants.

The most interesting distinction for our present purpose is that between ethnicity and institutional theories. These two theoretical perspectives represent perhaps the two main competing theories explaining integration or immigrant policy. Most important, they lead to contradictory predictions concerning the incorporation of migrants and ethnic minorities in Western countries as well as their political participation in the host society. According to *ethnicity theories*, the main driving force of integration is not class interests (as maintained by Marxist approaches to immigration; e.g., Castles and Kosack 1985) but ethnic and racial identities (e.g., Miller 1981; Moore 1975; Rex and Tomlinson 1979; Richmond 1988; Royce 1982). In this perspective, the immigrants' ethnic identity is of fundamental importance. Immigrants' interests are organized and articulated along ethnic or racial lines. Therefore, each ethnic group has its own mode of participation and integration in the host society, which has developed from socialization processes and in response to discrimination (Ireland 1994: 7). As a result, this theory predicts that migrants of the same national origin or coming from the same region will have similar forms of political participation and integration.

Institutional channeling theories make completely different predictions. They maintain that the incorporation of migrants in the host society is context-sensitive. In other words, there are important cross-national variations in the ways the state engages in activities aimed at improving the integration of immigrants, and such variations explain fundamental differences in the degree and forms of integration as well as in the degree and forms of the political participation of migrants in the host country. In this view, migrant incorporation stems not from class interests or ethnicity but from the characteristics of the institutional context as well as from the interaction between such context and migrants, which expresses itself through the political process (Koopmans and Statham 2000a).

When it comes to the political participation and mobilization of migrants, this perspective stresses the role of political opportunity structures, a concept that has been developed by students of social movements and contentious politics. Political opportunities refer to "*consistent—but not necessarily formal, permanent, or national—signals to social or political actors which either encourage or discourage them to use their internal resources to form social movements*" (Tarrow 1996: 54; emphasis in original) and can be summarized in the four following aspects: (1) the relative openness or closure of the institutionalized political system; (2) the stability or instability of that broad set of elite alignments that typically undergird a polity; (3) the presence or absence of elite allies; and (4) the state's capacity and propensity for repression (McAdam 1996: 27). To these general aspects of opportunity, other authors have added aspects concerning more directly the specific framework of immigration and ethnic relations. One of them is Patrick Ireland (1994: 10): "[t]he political opportunity structure includes the immigrants' legal situation; their social and political rights; and host society citizenship laws, naturalization procedures, and policies (and nonpolicies) in such areas as education, housing, the labor market, and social assistance that shape conditions and immigrants' responses." In addition, this approach also stresses the role of national actors other than the state: "[I]ndigenous trade unions, political parties, and religious and humanitarian 'solidarity groups' have acted as institutional gatekeepers, controlling access to the avenues of political participation available to the immigrants" (Ireland 1994: 10).

Given their stress on contextual factors, institutional channeling theories have paved the way to a truly comparative perspective. Specifically, recent comparative work on national regimes for the incorporation of migrants has stressed the importance of citizenship rights in this context, often following a neo-institutional framework of analysis (e.g., Brubaker 1992; Castles 1995; Favell 1998; Giugni and Passy 2004; Koopmans and Statham 1999, 2000a; Koopmans et al. 2005; Smith and Blanc 1996; Soysal 1994). These works stress the existence of at least three basic institutional approaches through which states deal with immigration, which can be see as three distinct types of integration or immigrant policy (e.g., Altermatt 1999; Castles and Miller 1998; Soysal 1994). They correspond to models or configuration of citizenship, that is, dominant conceptions of what it is to be a citizen and what the rights and duties attached to it are (Koopmans et al. 2005). The ethnic-based or differentialist approach is characterized by a virtual absence of any substantial integration policy. Immigration, following a guest-worker model of immigration control, is considered to be a temporary matter. Germany and Switzerland are often taken as examples, although the former country has recently moved away from a strict differentialist view of immigration through a softening of its citizenship regime. The pluralist or multicultural approach is, in a way, the opposite of the differentialist model. It is more open regarding both the individual citizenship rights (i.e., the formal rules for the acquisition of citizenship) and the cultural group rights (i.e., the recognition of ethnic and cultural difference). The recognition and promotion of ethnic difference is what best distinguishes this approach from the other two. The old immigration countries (Australia, Canada, and the United States) and, in Europe, countries such as the Netherlands and to some extent the United Kingdom are often-cited examples. Finally, the assimilationist or republican approach stands somewhere between these two extremes, as it is relatively open regarding the formal access to citizenship, but very close regarding the recognition of ethnic difference, which is largely denied to the benefit of an assimilationist view of citizenship. France is perhaps the paradigmatic case of this kind of approach, but Italy, Spain, and other new immigration countries seem to follow a similar model.

What we should keep in mind is that each of these three institutional approaches entails a distinct way to deal with immigration and, in particular, the incorporation of migrants, and that such differences have important implications for the current debate about the pro and contra of a more active integration policy in order to deal with the problems caused by the presence of a growing migrant population in Western European countries.[3] In other words, each approach provides a different answer to the fundamental issues of citizenship and multicultural democracy.

INFLUENCE ON MIGRATION POLICY: MEMBERS OR CHALLENGERS?

Policies, in the end, are made by actors, not by institutions or economic trends. To explain migration policy, therefore, we must look at the behavior and impact of those actors who are involved in this field. This debate is addressed in Part IV of the book by the chapter of Triadafilos Triadafilopoulos and Andrej Zaslove, the chapter of Marco Giugni and Florence Passy, and the commentary provided by Hanspeter Kriesi.

If the three dialogues discussed so far confront sometimes divergent views (especially the first one between "globalists" and "nationalists"), this one is less contentious and deals with the issue of influence of collective interests on migration policy. Which (collective) actors are influential and have an impact on legislation and policy measures in this field? Obviously, *legislators and policy-makers* ultimately take the decisions—except in a situation of direct democracy—and therefore have the greatest impact by definition. Among state actors, in addition, the *judiciary* emerges today as one of the most influential actors in this field (Joppke and Marzal 2004). We have mentioned earlier the role of supranational fora such as the European Court of Justice in the creation of a juridical and normative ground on migratory matters (Jacobson 1996; Soysal 1993). Such supranational fora often have a liberalizing effect on migrants' rights, functioning as a court of appeal to which they can resort when possibilities at the national level have extinguished. European integration, of course, strengthens the role of European tribunals. Yet national courts play a role as well, perhaps a greater one (Guiraudon 2000b). As we have mentioned earlier, policy-making in the field of immigration and ethnic relations still depends more on dynamics inherent to the national state than on transnational processes or supranational structures. Among such national dynamics, state courts can sometimes have a substantial impact. Their effect, of course, varies according to the degree of separation from the executive and legislative powers but should not be underestimated. The counts have been shown to be instrumental in particular in pushing forward migrants' rights even when the governments are more inclined to follow restrictive policies (Hollifield, 1992a, 1992b; Joppke 1998a, 2001).

The most interesting point, however, lies perhaps in assessing the effect of collective actors other than state actors who have an interest in migration issues and who try to influence the decision-makers. In this regard, a cursory look at the existing literature yields a range of actors that potentially may have a big impact on migration policy. Here we may distinguish between three types of collective actors according to the main arena in which they intervene and their privileged—though not exclusive—form of intervention: political parties, interest groups, and social movements. Parties act primarily in the parliamentary (and, for some of them, governmental) arena through legislative action, interest groups in the administrative arena through lobbying, and movements in the public domain through protest actions. Of course, both parties and interest groups sometimes also use the public domain and adopt more aggressive forms of action to make their claims. For example, unions engage in strike activities, especially so when institutional channels are closed. Yet each of these three collective actors (or forms of representation of collective interests and identities) has its own privileged arena.[4]

The specific literature has more often dealt with the role of parties and interest groups than social movements. As far as *parties* are concerned, most of the existing studies look at extreme-right parties (e.g., Minkenberg 2001; Schain 1987; Schain et al. 2002), largely neglecting the impact of other parties, especially those of the left side of the political spectrum. This is quite astonishing if we think of the central place this type of organization has in liberal democracies, not only for migration politics. Parties are the main organizational form between the citizens and their representatives within the polity. As such, they play a crucial role in transforming societal demands into political decisions and measures, including those demands that concern immigration and ethnic relations.

Although some have argued that mainstream parties, for a number of reasons, tend to manage this issue rather consensually and on the backstage (Freeman 1995; Hollifield 1994), immigration is today a major issue on which parties confront each other and compete for public (electoral) support. This is certainly true for extreme-right parties, which in recent years have made the immigration issue one of their favorite battlegrounds, one in which they try to distance themselves from mainstream parties. If the effectiveness of this demarcation strategy seems clear in terms of electoral breakthrough and voting gains (Schain 1987), much less clear is whether extreme-right parties have actually succeeded in influencing policy-making in this field. Take the Swiss example. Here the major party of the right (the Swiss People's Party) has made frequent use of the direct democratic instruments (popular initiative and referendum) to strengthen the existing legislation on both immigration and immigrant policy. Most of the time, the party's proposals were defeated by the popular vote, which suggests a lack of effect. However, if the major changes for which it asked (such as, for example, limiting the number of foreigners living in the country) were not accepted, they succeeded in pushing the governmental agenda toward more restrictive policies.

Apart from the importance of parties, the migration field is often governed by interest-based politics, and *interest groups* are crucial actors in this field (Hollifield 1992a; Freeman 2001). The two most important such type of actors are employers' associations and trade unions, which are among those intermediary organizations that have high stakes in immigration control. These organizations have a specific interest in relation to the presence of foreigners on the labor market. Obviously, seen like that, employers' associations and unions have divergent interests in this respect. While the latter usually push for more liberal policies to the extent that foreign workers often represent a cheap labor force, the latter often ask for more restrictive measures as they see foreign workers as contributing to a deterioration of the situation of the labor market, both in terms of wages and unemployment. The success of these actors in opening up the nation's doors, respectively in protecting the indigenous labor force, is likely to be highly contingent on the state of the economy in the host country, as we discussed earlier.

Where research is less advanced is on the impact of *social movements* and protest activities on migration policy. This applies more generally to the study of contentious politics. Indeed, the consequences of social movements only recently have come to capture the attention of scholars in a systematic fashion (see Giugni 1998 for a review). Previously, apart from a number of remarkable exceptions (most notably, Gamson 1990), scholars had paid much more attention to the origin and mobilization of movements than to their effects, including their policy effects.

Three collective actors have a particular interest to form social movements engaging in protest activities in the field of immigration and ethnic relations politics. The first and most obvious one is *migrants* themselves. The political mobilization of migrants has not been devoted the place it deserves in the literature (but see, among others, Blatt 1995; Fibbi and Bolzmann 1991; Giugni and Passy 2004; Ireland 1994; Koopmans 2004; Martiniello and Statham 1999), perhaps because often migrants are not considered political actors. This gap has also begun to be filled by an increasing number of studies that look at the political participation of ethnic minorities as a form of political integration in their host society (Berger et al. 2004; Fennema 2004; Fennema and Tillie 1999, 2001; Jacobs and Tillie 2004; Tillie 2004). Thus, the emerging debate on minority integration and the parallel interest shown by students of migration in this issue has contributed indirectly to the revamping of the study of the political participation and mobilization of immigrants and ethnic minorities. No matter how positive this trend is, however, it still does not tell us anything about migrants' impact on policies that concern them most directly. How effective are organized minority groups when they take the streets or act through other unconventional means and how responsive are the public and political authorities of host countries to these mobilizations? To give an answer to this question is all the more important to the extent that minorities are the less powerful actors among the three considered here and those whose lack of institutionalized channels of access to the polity is greater.

The interests and identities of migrants are most directly threatened by the mobilization of the *extreme right*. The main difference between this collective actor and migrants is that it often has a direct access to the parliament and sometimes even to the government. Indeed, the far right as a collective actor is characterized by the presence of a partisan form together with an extra-parliamentary form (i.e., a social movement), which often expresses itself through violent actions (for example, through racist attacks to foreigners and minorities). This, of course, is not to say that the two constitute a homogeneous actor. On the contrary, it may well be that extreme-right parties and, say, groups of naziskin have no ties to each other whatsoever and certainly have different constituencies. Yet they share a fundamental rejection of migrants and the willingness to push for more restrictive migration policies. Again, how effective they are in this effort and how responsive are governments to their demands are questions whose answers have important implications both from a scholarly and a political point of view.

If the extreme right carries an anti-migrant position—or at least a position that asks for more restrictive migration policies—there is a third collective actor that mobilizes on issues relating to immigration and ethnic relations but defends the rights of migrants and pushes for more liberal policies. This is what we may call the *solidarity movement*, which includes a range of organizations and groups going from general welfare associations and human-rights organizations to pro-migrant organizations dealing with particular aspects of this issue (asylum, specific minority groups, etc.). It also includes anti-racist organizations and groups. This movement clearly is an ally of organized migrants, attempting to improve their rights and living conditions. Yet often they do more than that. When migrants do not have the opportunity or the means to organize and form a social movement and engage in protest activities, solidarity organizations and groups take up the issue and mobilize on their behalf. Thus, this movement represents an important external resource for migrants, both to make their life in the host society easier and to put their claims on the political and public agendas.

In sum, the question of the influence of collective interests on migration policy can be narrowed down to the issue of the impact of *members* and *challengers* of the polity. In particular, both the role of political parties and that of other organizations such as interest groups and social movements mobilizing on migration-related issues (migrant, anti-migrant, and pro-migrant movements) need to be studied more thoroughly than has been done in the past.

A RESEARCH AGENDA

The four dialogues just outlined bring to the fore a number of theoretical and empirical issues that can be seen as avenues for future research. To complete this introductory chapter, let us briefly address those we see as the most relevant ones and which could form the basis for a research agenda for the future. They were inspired by the reading of the chapters and commentaries included in the present book. Therefore, they can also be taken as a conclusion to the volume after having read the other chapters.

1. *We need to distinguish between different groups of migrants.* Sometimes in the literature migrants have been treated as if they were a homogeneous entity, behaving in the same way and having a common identity. However, as works on ethnic diversity have shown, different groups of migrants can display diverse patterns of behavior. In addition, states can address different policies and measures to different types of migrants, the former aspect being strongly influenced by the latter. Much of the debate here, of course, is about how and to what extent ethnicity matters. Further research should pay a lot more attention to how migrants of different origins and entering the host societies with different statuses and identities are treated locally, nationally, and transnationally.

2. *We need to take into account actors other than state actors, institutional policy-makers, or political parties.* Studies of migration policy have focused on state actors and political parties. The role of the courts (both at the national and international levels) has recently been examined in a thorough way. It is important to broaden the scope of analysis to include other collective actors as well such as interest groups and social movements, who may become decisive in influencing migration policy. Interest groups have

received relatively much attention. What is still lacking, in our view, is a systematic investigation of the role of social movements and collective mobilizations. How can they impact migration policy? Which policies are they more likely to affect? In what ways can they have an impact? These are important questions that remain largely unanswered.

3. *We need to examine the crucial role played by politics.* Most, if not all, of the chapters in this book point to the importance of political factors in shaping migration policy. This seems quite obvious, almost a tautology. However, the state is often missing in migration studies. The role of politics is not always taken into account as it should be. Of course, culture, ethnicity, economy—all this matters. Yet all these factors are mediated or filtered by politics, in one way or another.

4. *We need to reconceptualize the national state.* The national state is central in most of the chapters in this book as well as more generally in the literature in migration politics. It frames the debates in this field and intervenes as a crucial actor. The study and practice of migration policy are still framed nationally. The national state, for example, defines the indicators for research immigration politics. The notion of the national state is so pervasive that it tends to constrain researchers into a sort of conceptual prison. We therefore should reconceptualize the notion of the national state, for example, by taking more seriously into account the impact of both global and local levels. Above all, we should study more thoroughly the interplay between these levels.

5. *We need to complement in-depth studies of single cases with broader conceptual and comparative approaches.* Many of the chapters in this book are comparative in scope. To be sure, in-depth qualitative case studies are both necessary and provide crucial insights into the mechanisms that account for changes in migration policy. However, we think that broader comparative frameworks have much to offer to an understanding of immigration politics. On the one hand, comparisons allow us to make a better sense of a given case and to avoid making a general rule out of a specific situation. On the other hand, comparisons across countries (or across other analytical units) permit control for various explanatory factors and hence allow for adjudication between competing theories, if need be.

6. *We need to ground the study of migration policy on a solid empirical basis.* Empirical evidence is the fuel of social science. Again, this is not to say that theory is not important, of course. Quite on the contrary, data make sense only if they are seen through the lenses of a theoretical framework. Yet, in our view, a large part of the dichotomies we find in the field of immigration politics might just disappear or at least be adjudicated if we ground our research on systematic empirical data. We are thinking, for example, at the debate between "globalists" and "nationalists," or the post-

national versus national debate. Often the ultimate verdict on opposing paradigms or perspectives can come only from confrontation with the "reality" out there. Good data (especially if comparative) are as necessary as good theorizing.

7. *We need to look at the processes and mechanisms underlying the formulation and implementation of migration policy.* Scholars often have a hard time in unveiling the mechanisms that account for changes in migration policy. Clearly, relations between variables are not enough; what we need is to look at processes, to disentangle mechanisms and dynamics. More specifically, it is important to look at the political process at work behind migration policy, which can be seen as the outcome of this process. Once again, taking mechanisms more seriously makes us less exposed to the risk of making hurried generalizations or, even worse, producing false results.

8. *We need to go beyond (supposed and/or false) dichotomies in the study of migration policy to integrate and complement different explanatory factors, theoretical perspectives, and methodological approaches.* This book is structured around a number of dichotomies or oppositions: global versus national scope, economic versus political factors, ethnicity versus political opportunity structures, and members versus challengers impact. Other dichotomies could be made and, indeed, emerge in the various chapters that form this volume. Some of these dichotomies remain and will remain such, at least insofar as there are authors of them who are willing to defend their position with nails and teeth. However, we think that what this book shows is not only that most of these dichotomies disappear once we look at migration policy through the lenses of sound empirical and, if possible, comparative studies that take mechanisms seriously into account but also that we will at the same time be encouraged to abandon some of our theoretical bastions in order to search for more integrated approaches.

However, some unresolved tensions remain. We think that, in the end, this book brings to the fore a fundamental tension within contemporary societies in regard to the management of ethnic relations and majority/minority relationships: It is what we may call a tension between *opportunity* and *rights*. This tension expresses itself in two ways. First, on a level more strictly linked to immigration politics, it is the tension between *group-specific policies* and *more general policies targeting the whole population*. This difference is institutionally crystallized, respectively, in the so-called multicultural (or cultural pluralist) and assimilationist (or republican) models of integration. The central problem is that of finding a good balance of measures targeting specific groups (of migrants) and measures that go to the benefit of the entire population, citizens and non-citizens. On the one hand, countries that have traditionally adopted a group-specific or multicultural approach (e.g., the

Netherlands as well as the extra-European immigration countries) are aware of the risk of segregation inherent in cultural pluralism and of the possible backlash, for example, by xenophobic and extreme-right milieus, who may react to this kind of policies. On the other hand, in a de facto multicultural society, traditionally assimilationist and universalist countries (e.g., France) have made some concessions to the republican model by moving toward group-specific policies.

Second, on the broader level of the relationship between citizens and the state, it is a tension between the *democratic principle* and the *equality principle*. Modern democracies entail two elements: a democratic element, whereby people must be granted full participation in the political sphere, and a constitutional element, whereby the state must guarantee fundamental rights to all individuals. Students of immigration politics cannot ignore this broader framework when studying the policies that states and other political entities (local, regional, supranational) enact and implement in order to deal with immigration and ethnic relations.

Thus, the challenge for migration research today is, on the one hand, to understand how de facto multicultural societies can best deal and actually deal with the tension of cultural pluralism versus assimilationism, where and how they find the right balance between the two approaches in the management of ethnic relations. On the other hand, the challenge is also to disentangle the complex relationship between democracy intended as social and political—and, we should add, cultural—participation, and democracy as the fundamental (constitutional) rights of individuals. In brief, the challenge is to better understand the relationship between opportunities and rights, both in the field of immigration politics and in social relations more generally. As far as the study of migration is concerned, our hope is that the following contributions can shed some light on this relationship as it expresses itself both horizontally within countries and vertically across different political administrative levels.

NOTES

1. In addition, Castles and Miller (1998) mention two other types of migration, which, however, did not contribute decisively to the formation of ethnic minorities: "mass movements of European refugees after the end of the Second World War" and "return migration of former colonists to their countries of origin as colonies gained their independence."

2. Later on, Brubaker (1999) has relativized the distinction between civic and ethnic conceptions of the nation, acknowledging that this distinction presents problems from both a normative and an analytical standpoint, and proposing to replace it with the distinction between state-framed and counter-state nationalism.

3. This model, for example, is questioned in the Netherlands today.

4. Where it exists, to these three arenas we should add a fourth one: direct democracy, which is available to all kinds of actors. This holds particularly for Switzerland, where the direct democratic instruments are developed and where they have been used extensively in the migration political field as well.

I

SCOPE: GLOBAL OR NATIONAL?

1

Social Relations on a Global Scale: The Implications for Human Rights and for Democracy

David Jacobson and Galya Benarieh Ruffer

INTRODUCTION

While our understandings of democracy have evolved within a particular conception of citizenship and nationhood, the emergence of new global structures, institutions, and modes of governance necessitate a recognition that democracy, as traditionally understood, is inadequate to conceptualize current modes of political engagement. The global expansion of human rights is often noted and, generally, is coupled with the assumption that this expansion is synonymous with the spread of democracy. The expansion of rights, domestically and internationally, however, is associated with a partial, but significant, shift in the mode of political engagement; from democracy, or republicanism, to the principle of the individual as "agent." The "decline" of the nation-state is symptomatic of an even more dramatic but hidden revolution, the emergence of agency.

Indeed, issues of *agency* have supplemented, and in significant part supplanted, dedication to the *democratic* and *republican* process. Agency implies the ability of the individual to act as an "initiatory" and "self-reliant" actor, and to be an active participant in determining his or her life, including the determination of social, political, cultural, ethnic, religious, and economic ends.[1] The foundational mechanism of agency is the dense web of legal rights and restraints, which are mediated or adjudicated by judicial, quasi-judicial, and administrative bodies of different kinds. In contrast to the past, no area of life today is beyond the potential reach of the law—its tentacles, for good and bad, reach into every sphere of life, from families to corporations to nation-states. Individual access to the dense web of judicially mediated legal rights and restraints has become the primary mechanism of individual "self-determination," rather than the traditional democratic route of voting, civic participation, and political mobilization.

The notion of collective "authorship," or deliberation, through the republican model fails to capture the force of the individual, as "agent," as a primary form of political engagement in current patterns of governance. The politics of rights is not about the politics of consent as such, and "agency," centered on the individual, is distinct from collective notions of national self-determination. Judicial and administrative mechanisms, as opposed to the legislature, become central in this process. Agency, in this context, rests in the implicit or explicit philosophical belief that individuals can shape the circumstances in which they live. Government and civil liberties are, or should be, in place to enable the individual's private "pursuit of happiness." Law, in this sense, is "enabling." In contrast, "collective authorship" rests in republican concepts of freedom, lying in the public and civic realm, where citizens come together (through civic participation, including but not limited to voting) to shape and form their commonwealth. Law, in the republican vein, is "constitutive."[2]

In the debate over the future of the European Union, Euroskeptics seem to have stumbled upon agency. Instead of recognizing it as a distinct mode of political engagement or studying it directly, however, they have cast it as yet another thorn in the decline of democratic legitimacy. Thus, they discuss the "democratic deficit" and complain about the lack of accountability; but, in fact, the nature of accountability has shifted (or become twofold)—from popular forms to one based on the rule of law or, more broadly, the "rule of rules." While popular accountability relies on things such as elections, national parliaments for the enactment of legislation, and a direct relationship between the people and government, the mechanism of accountability through "rule of rules" is more subtle and has not yet been fully explored. Indeed, the unpacking of "rule of rules" as a form of legitimate accountability challenges the deeply ingrained notion that courts function, and must be defended, within a democracy as a "counter-majoritarian" branch. "Rule of rules" differs, however, in that, as accountability is transferred to the legal realm with the individual as agent, states are increasingly held accountable for their actions through human rights norms and rules. (The European Union is of particular interest in this discussion as it is an acute representation of the movement away from republicanism towards judicial agency.)

Joseph Weiler has taken important steps in recasting the question of democracy in the debate regarding the European Union (EU).[3] According to Weiler, democratic deficit implies a given definition of democracy, which needs to be stated explicitly. He points out that it would be incorrect to judge the operation of the EU by the same normative criteria that are applied to ordinary nation-states.[4] He emphasized that it is important to recognize that different aspects of the EU may best reflect entirely new modes of governance.[5] Similarly, to ground our current understandings of "rule of rules" within traditional understandings of democracy, political engagement, and governance may prove counterproductive.

One can begin to unpack the logic of agency based on "rule of rules" by recognizing that certain political divisions are better categorized as disputes between claims for democracy, or republicanism, versus claims for agency, rather than a dispute over the general content of the rights at stake. Simply put, the advent of "rule of rules" has been challenging executive and legislative power. Agency places a strain upon executive and legislative power because individuals increasingly possess the capacity to assert their rights by accessing laws outside of the national structure and bringing them before the European Court of Justice (or, in the Council of Europe, before the European Court of Human Rights), or through new "cross-border" principles, such as direct effect, subsidiarity, harmonization, and proportionality.[6]

The threat agency poses to executive power became all too apparent as the United States and other governments throughout Europe quickly turned to extra-legal measures, outside of the web of laws, in reaction to the terrorist attacks of 11 September 2001, such as, notably, the establishment of military tribunals, "closed" removal proceedings, and interviews of 5,000 foreign nationals. Such measures are best characterized as strikes against agency. In the aftermath of 9/11, there was a perception among government officials and the general public that the Al Qaeda terrorist network had appropriated civil freedoms in forming their devastating attack.[7] The significance of the assertion of executive power is not its curtailment of the rights of those subject to government suspicion, but rather the stop it put on agency as a mechanism by taking security measures out of the realm of law altogether. In Germany and other EU member-states entrenched rights, such as the right of privacy, were not questioned so much as bypassed by executive power. Thus, for example, Berlin's Humbolt University gave information on twenty-three Arab students to the German government.[8] What we see is not a questioning of the right of privacy per se, but rather a questioning of agency and a reassertion of executive power.

While the generally accepted principle of, for example, a state's right of immigration control is not at issue (and is not subject to frontal challenge), the secondary "web of laws," such as rules of non-discrimination, empowers the individual, as agent, to affect how that immigration control is achieved. Thus, political divisions are played out, in important part, between claims for democracy, or republicanism, versus claims for agency. This creates interesting conjunctions on a policy level. Returning to the example of immigration control of asylees and refugees: The legal instruments of rights, specifically human rights, do not prohibit immigration control, just the form of regulation, that is, immigration control should be based on recognized universal, non-discriminatory criteria as defined by international human rights instruments. In principle, the flow of migrants, restrictive or liberal, is independent of human rights issues per se. Government authorities can interpret asylum laws in ways that meet the strict letter of international human rights law, while still severely limiting the flow of potential asylees.

Thus, we witness this interesting conjunction in border controls: In practical terms, because of internal pressures or because "host" societies feel asylum laws are being unfairly exploited, states may become more restrictive. But the question remains: Are those restrictions within the criteria of international human rights standards, as defined by the European Court of Human Rights, the European Court of Justice, and the like? Restrictive practices—*based on non-discriminatory criteria*—reflect the intersection of these different forms of political practices, of the executive or legislative branches on the one hand, vis-à-vis the judiciary on the other.

We see these conflicting forces between the judiciary and the executive in relatively recent decisions. For example, the European Court of Human Rights condemned the French government for trying to keep asylum seekers in "international zones."[9] These zones, though physically in France, were considered not to be in France for the purposes of the European Convention of Human Rights, which, in effect, placed people in indefinite detention.[10] Similarly, the United Kingdom was similarly unsuccessful in persuading the Court that a man, who was not formally admitted to the country but had been a resident for five years, was not, legally speaking, within the country.[11] Additionally, the Court has upheld the right of an individual not to be returned to a country where he would face degrading treatment.[12]

Conversely, the member-states have a "common visa list," maintained by the EU, that requires potential visitors of a specified list of countries to obtain visas from member-state consular officers in their country of origin before entering an EU member-state.[13] The list, which can change as countries are added or dropped from the list, catalogs countries that have a record of "sending" individuals seeking asylum. This is designed to bar individuals from ever reaching the European Union in order to request asylum. (It should be stressed that whether this actually violates international human rights law—which sanctions the right to leave a country but not a right, as such, to enter a country—is certainly open to question.) Thus the struggle between the judicial arms, which has the effect (in this regard) of promoting agency, and the state, which seeks to promote republican national self-determination, is evident in this process. Part of the contention here, however, is that the increasing density of the law, which promotes rights and prerogatives (and thus agency), is central to the growing role of the judiciary. It is the judiciary, at both national and regional levels, concerning both domestic and international law, which mediates and adjudicates this web of law. For example, the role of the judiciary in the newly emerging democracies, such as South Africa, differs significantly from that of the older liberal democracies, such as the United States or Germany. In the newer democracies, there is not just the acceptance of but the proactive vesting of power in the judiciary as a political body with a political function.

In the continuing evolution of the EU, there is an increasing shift of power toward formal commitment to human rights as well as mechanisms to enforce those rights within the member-states. The Treaty of Amsterdam formalized measures to extend the rights of citizens and sought to improve accountability and participation in the institutions of the EU.[14] In a significant departure from the past, the Treaty called for enforcement of non-discrimination principles within member-states, and opened the channels of communication not just to address issues such as gender inequality, discrimination, public health, and consumer protection but to enforce these rights through the European Court of Justice (ECJ).[15] In yet another significant departure, coordination of an immigration policy was transferred from the third pillar, where it was handled as part of justice and home affairs, to the first pillar.[16] Whereas legal provisions emanating from the third pillar are not part of community law but, rather, are norms regulated by public international law, legal instruments emanating from the first pillar become part of European Community law and are binding on each member-state. Moreover, given that individuals have the legal capacity to invoke first pillar laws and bring them to bear against member-states, the changes of the Amsterdam Treaty may give the judiciary, here the European Court of Justice, more control over immigration policy. Similarly, the now formal commitment under Amsterdam of the EU to human rights may enhance the ECJ's authority in such matters over member-states.

The extensive attention placed on the "democratic deficit" of the EU bespeaks a fundamental misunderstanding of the shift taking place in the very modality of politics. We need to turn more of our attention to changes in the institutional and organizational environments (within and across states), which facilitate "agency," in order to elicit more fully this relatively novel form of political engagement and governance.

THE LONG ARM OF THE LAW

One of the most remarkable developments of recent decades is the growing "density" of the legal milieu internationally, regionally, and nationally. Law is becoming more dense, not just in terms of the sheer number of laws created through the proliferation of administrative rules, legal institutions, and arbitration mechanisms internationally and, specifically, in Europe, through

the EU, the Council of Europe, the Organization for Security and Cooperation in Europe, but also on a national level, through the incorporation, or
tacit recognition, of the international human rights instruments into national
legal systems. In 2000, in the most recent case of note, the United Kingdom
incorporated the bulk of the European Convention of Human Rights into domestic law.[17] Internationally, there is a growing multiplication of multilateral
international treaties. Although the sheer increase in legal webbing, as a result of these developments, is significant in and of itself, more important are
the qualitative shifts.

International human rights law has relocated the individual as the object
of the law. This has affected national citizenship status in the Euro-Atlantic
arena as well as in other countries. We also witness the growing specialization of law in areas from intellectual property to the environment. In addition, there is the growth in importance of tribunals, arbitration mechanisms,
regulatory mechanisms, and other legal entities that deliberate independently of states and allow non-state actors to arrive at agreements and
arrangements independently of states, yet whose decisions carry the force of
law in many states. The rising importance and salience of international private law—akin to the increasing importance of civil law in industrializing
countries since the nineteenth century—are also of note. How has this proliferation of legal forms and mechanisms shifted or altered the nature and location of political engagement? It is through posing this question that the
emergence of agency comes to the fore.

The growing number of cross-border actors of different kinds, including
international nongovernmental organizations or corporations, also reinforces and emerges from this growing density and specialization of law. Administrative and judicial rules grow through arbitrating the kaleidoscope-like
complexity of a social world with an almost geometric increase in the number of actors with disparate social, economic, and political concerns. This
parallels the evolution of domestic law within nation-states where legal
mechanisms of control became tighter and denser with growing economic
and social differentiation, specialization, and complexity.

This growing legal density promotes, reinforces, and facilitates the phenomenon of agency. Indeed, agency itself presumes, by definition, universal and individualistic values as well as the concept of human rights. Agency
is embedded in this dense legal web, and the institutions that arbitrate this
legal framework—the judiciary and other administrative mechanisms—
grow in significance as a result. We see a growing density of law, including
law that "enables" agency, in issues that "cross borders," legally or in practice (for example, migration), where the courts are, in many cases, drawn
into transnational and international issues. Agency, in turn, reinforces that
legal framework.

Alongside the denser web of law is a related phenomenon, namely esca-lating litigation, nationally and in the European regional institutions. Litiga-tion activities are of interest because they reveal the extent of agency as well as how the law is facilitating that agency. This is revealed because litigation concerns arguments over rights and prerogatives. Growing litigation reflects a growing legal and social readiness and "recognition" of rights that inhere in, or are presumed to inhere in, the individual as well as other entities. Liti-gation reflects growing agency.

The growing legal density needs little elaboration, especially in the Euro-pean context. The scope, case-load, number of member countries, rise in the role of nongovernmental organizations (NGOs), and influence of the Euro-pean Court of Human Rights have grown substantially and to an extent un-dreamed of at its founding. The scope, caseload, and influence of the Euro-pean Court of Justice (as well as the "legal presence" of the EU generally) likewise has grown significantly and needs little elaboration. In terms of in-ternational law, we witness a similar picture. At the end of World War I, there was a steady accumulation in the number of multilateral international legal treaties but a dramatic increase after World War II. Evidencing an increas-ingly dense global legal environment, the number of "significant" multilateral treaties in force rose from 187 in 1950 to almost 800 by 1988.[18]

Even more striking is the increase of litigation in its different forms that, as we noted, is evidence of "agency" at work. Even in a country with an im-pressive history of judicial review, such as the United States, we see a marked upturn in this regard.[19] The increase in the caseload in the Euro-pean Court of Human Rights and the European Court of Justice is widely noted, but there are other notable indicators: references under Article 177 of the EEC Treaty have increased as well.[20] Article 177 allows, and some-times requires, judges in national courts to request an authoritative inter-pretation of the laws within the ambit of the European Community. In 1970, there were roughly forty references of this kind, and by 1990, almost 200 references. (United Kingdom judges refer more cases to the European Court of Justice under Article 177 than any other member-state.[21] This is significant, for reasons discussed below.) This is notable because it illus-trates the growing role of the judiciary in a dual sense—it shows the extent to which national judiciaries are acting, so to speak, "extraterritorially," as well as how the judicial arm of government is strengthened as a conse-quence. Migration is one of the more significant topics to generate refer-ences.[22] The proportion of litigation, at least in the UK, tends to be under-reported because areas where European Union law has been most heavily invoked—immigration, taxes, social security, and labor—are areas in which quasi-judicial entities are dominant, such as immigration adjudica-tors, whose decisions are rarely reported.[23]

The growing web of judicial rights in all kinds of organizational contexts makes agency possible.[24] Agency, involving all kinds of individual actors, generates adjudication of rights, interests, and the like. Thus, agency reinforces the process of judicial rights that made it possible in the first place. The democratic process, on the other hand, is not removed so much as it is contained. The density of the legal process is not only on the public level—domestic or international—but has progressively filtered into private organizations and corporations, where individuals can "litigate" internally, for example, over race discrimination. Thus, the containment of the republican, or democratic, process is taking place not only in the political arena, but in "everyday life," notably in the workplace. Patterns of litigation are growing across Europe (not just in the United States) with reference to the workplace, especially regarding racial and sexual discrimination. Sexual and racial lawsuits filed in Employment Tribunals in the UK rose 76 percent in the year ending in June 2000 compared to the five previous years.[25]

Within the European Union, individual litigation is likely to be encouraged further by Article 13 of the Amsterdam Treaty.[26] Article 13 (formerly Article 6a), originally adopted as part of the Treaty Establishing the European Community[27] and revised through the Amsterdam Treaty, includes stronger wording, which seems to encourage, or allow, positive enforcement by the EU directly against the member-states.[28] It was enacted in response to the recognition that, although the Maastricht Treaty on European Union (TEU) provided a specific competence to adopt general measures in the sphere of human rights and to combat discrimination, there was no positive mechanism through which the Union could take effective measures against racism, xenophobia, and other forms of discrimination.[29]

Such developments have implications for notions of "multicultural" and immigrant populations. The growth of "agency" enables different forms of cultural expression, which the courts facilitate. Conversely, "parliamentary sovereignty" restricts (but does not completely preclude) majoritarian and collective national expression.

The changed nature of political engagement, reflected in the shifting balance between agency, empowered by legal rights and obligations, and more traditional "democratic" consent modes of "voice" or politics, is illustrated in the following examples regarding sexual equality and discrimination. Political demands for greater protection of women in the workforce led to public service experimentation with various quota systems at the state level in Germany. There seemed to be a political consensus throughout Germany, which led to the enactment of sixteen separate statutes at the state level establishing various forms of quota systems.[30] But through Article 177 references to the ECJ, however, certain of these German provisions have been placed famously in doubt.[31] The ECJ determined in *Kalanke* and *Marschall* that EU law, specifically the equal treatment principle embodied in Articles 2(1) and

2(4) of the Equal Treatment Directive, distinguishes between equality of opportunity and that of result, and foreclosed any positive action going beyond that necessary to ensure individual equality of opportunity.[32] The new sex equality provisions in the Amsterdam Treaty, Articles 137 and 141 (ex Articles 118, 119) have strengthened the EU position regarding the underrepresentation of women in the workforce, while setting the guidelines within which the ECJ will determine whether the measures comply with EU law.[33] More recently, the EU has provided for stronger measures to eradicate sexual harassment, which will place additional burdens on member-state employers.[34]

These and other legal provisions and directives at the EU level provide individuals with a forum through which sensitive issues, traditionally worked out through political channels at the national level, can be revisited and redefined in the ECJ. In one important respect, certain employment rights and protections are being severed from national citizenship. For example, in a number of cases, the ECJ determined that sexual orientation is not a protected category under EU law.[35] In forming its decisions, the Court ignored the general political trend among the member-states toward providing protection for sexual orientation discrimination in employment and equal treatment for same-sex couples.[36]

In another work, Ruffer has attempted to characterize the nature of the set of organizationally based rights and protections as a "virtual citizenship," which is, in important respects, independent of national citizenship.[37] Thus, the rights and protections that accrue to an employee on, say, gender discrimination in a corporation, public or private, are not a function of formal citizenship status (though, of course, the presumption is that the employee is at least a legal resident).[38] In this regard, the expansion of rights has diluted national citizenship, at least in its traditional republican sense.

THE NESTING OF ORGANIZATIONS AND AGENCY

Critical questions remain, namely, what are the institutional mechanisms of agency and how do they operate? That is, how is agency regulated, realized, and woven into social and political organizations and patterns of governance? How is agency institutionally "mediated," and what are the key institutions in that regard? *How* is agency mediated through such institutions? This is an issue, which we commence addressing here, that has not been sufficiently addressed in the debates on globalization or, for that matter, on human rights. It is an issue that is all the more crucial to attend to as we are increasingly unable to limit such questions to the traditional, relatively bounded institutions of the nation-state. Furthermore, the salience and role of different institutions *within* the state shift as global, legal, political, and social relations grow more "dense."

Agency, and the associated human rights claims, is not expressed *prima-rily* at the international, regional, or even the national level. Rather, the dense legal webbing enables the "acting out" of human rights (for example, on gender issues) at the lower-order organizational level—such as, prominently, the workplace. In recent decades, in order to generate change at "lower level" organizations, appeals have been made to the "higher level" organizations to change institutional patterns at the original organization. This results in a nesting effect, where people will go to a higher nested organization to appeal, judicially, for recourse, but only so far as they have to go (for example, the province is preferred over the state, or the state over a regional organization).

Once a change is generated, however, internal mechanisms are introduced within the "local" organization to implement the change. "Internal mechanisms" include appeals boards or arbitration committees, such as in universities and corporations, on discrimination or harassment. These mechanisms are set up within the organization in order to bring it into line with legal mandates and judicial rulings. Appeals to "higher level" organizations (be it state or regional judicial bodies) are less likely on issues where such intra-organizational mechanisms are available for redress of grievances; the grievance may be remedied internally and, thus, not necessitate any external appeals. In this way, much of the activity on salient civic and human rights issues are acted upon (in terms of claims and institutional responses) "locally," that is within the organizations in which people actually work and live.

This nesting effect, however, also works in reverse: higher nested organizations—such as the European Court of Human Rights—will have wide-ranging effects. Effectively, they close off certain options for lower organizations. For example, a ruling by the European Court of Human Rights has, for example, "closed off" the gender of a spouse as a criterion in determining immigration status; "gender" in this context ceased to be a category that states could turn to in determining who could or could not enter enter their country.[39] More broadly, court rulings on significant civic or human rights issues create constraints for a broad range of organizations under their respective jurisdictions. Once such rulings have been legally integrated and adopted by states and by private and public organizations, the human rights issue once in question is less likely to be played out at the national or regional level.

This nesting phenomenon is, in a sense, another radically different form of the global-local nexus. Certain issues, such as judicially determined values regarding gender discrimination, filter down to the point where they become so embedded—legally, politically, and in everyday life—that they are normatively presumed, almost outside the discourse on human rights. "Global" norms are expressed most readily in "local" foci—local, here, being from workplaces and other organizations, to cities and counties, to provinces and the like. This just points to the remarkable extent to which human rights has become, in the long term, the armature, the frame, and the skeleton girding the social and political architecture of society. It is like the syntax of language; it is presumed, not thought about. The "present" discourse of human rights shifts then to new frontiers, with different parties trying to broaden their reach to new social categories, such as female genital mutilation in asylum laws. And because new frontiers involve contested issues, and thus frame the issue of "human rights" in the public consciousness, the embedded nature of the larger scaffold of human rights and the degree to which it has closed off options is often overlooked. The institutional mechanisms, in this context, are primarily judicial and administrative.

This nesting process also is legally inscribed, as captured in the concept of subsidiary and layered legal authorities, and is characteristic of both the United States and the European Union (and, for that matter, the European Convention of Human Rights). However, it makes sociological sense as well: Absent internal rules on areas like gender or racial discrimination, endogenous change within an organization is very difficult to effect. So the actor will move to a "higher-level organization" to generate change exogenously, but that actor is unlikely to go to a point beyond that which is necessary to effect the change sought. Judicial and administrative change is also dramatic (and rapid) because often—especially in the United States—the change will then affect a whole class of individuals and organizations, such as in gender and race discrimination. Judicial and administrative decisions can have, and have had, the effect of expanding agency extensively in this way. Once such rulings have filtered down and are institutionalized, "human rights" will be acted on endogenously to the affected organizations.

The case of the United Kingdom is particularly interesting in terms of the "nesting" of organizations and legal authorities. The British political system has been one where the sovereign Parliament was at the pinnacle, and the courts were secondary, possessing very limited powers of judicial review. The UK, though it has long recognized the jurisdiction of Strasbourg, in contrast to most other Council of Europe member-states, only recently incorporated the bulk of the European Convention of Human Rights into domestic law. In this context, it is no surprise that—at least prior to the incorporation of the Convention—the United Kingdom received special scrutiny by Strasbourg and that British judges have made so many references to the European Court of Justice.[40] The notion of the individual as agent was highly constrained in this circumstance of parliamentary sovereignty and thus had to appeal to exogenous legal authorities—notably the European Convention of Human Rights and the European Court of Justice—to effect change. The European Union and the European Court of Human Rights has, in effect, required a fundamental shift in the relationship between the individual and the state. Instead of a majoritarian institution in Parliament representing a republican collective will in which individual rights were derivative, a more liberal vision has been instituted by the European Convention of Human Rights and the European Court of Justice around which individual freedoms are promoted and where "as much space is preserved for autonomous behavior by private individuals as possible."[41] It was because of the European Convention of Human Rights and the European Court of Justice that judicial review became a significant factor in the UK since the 1980s. Clearly, the Human Rights Act, which recently took effect in the UK, will reinforce this process.[42]

The legal developments in the UK also reveal how human rights become embedded institutionally (primarily through the courts), and no more so than in the immigration area. Both immigration and asylum legislation have been significantly affected by the European Court of Human Rights. The very creation of the immigration appeals system was rooted, in significant part, in the European Convention of Human Rights. Through the *Abdulaziz* case, which concerned Articles 6 and 8 of the European Court of Human Rights, sex discrimination was eliminated in United Kingdom laws.[43] The Asylum and Immigration Appeals Act of 1993, facilitating the rights of appeal of asylum seekers with respect to Article 13, was significantly furthered by the *N.K.* (1987) case in Strasbourg. *Chahal* (1996), concerning Article 3, most recently impacted the Special Immigration Appeals Commission Act of 1998. Home office policy guidelines have also had explicit reference to the European Convention of Human Rights.[44] Human rights issues become embedded such that, in the example noted previously, because of the *Abdulaziz* decision, the concept of sex discrimination on immigration becomes inconceivable and not even an issue on the regional or national level. Furthermore, other areas of rights now taken for granted, such as consumer rights, are no longer "debated" internationally but simply become part of the broader social fabric.

Part of what accounts for the variation in the turn from international instruments—comparing the United States to the United Kingdom for example—is the extent to which the growing stress on "agency" can be accommodated internally. If, as described above, actors will move "up" (for legal and sociological reasons) the layers of legal and organizational authority in order to affect change at "lower levels" of organization, then change can be generated before resorting to international instruments or even national instruments. In the context of the U.S. constitutional framework, the dense net of rights and legal rules as well as the historical and ever-growing role of the judiciary (especially in recent decades) provides extensive possibilities to effect agency. Even in the case of the United States, however, four points should be noted: The legal (as well as social and political) discourse concerning "*human* rights" (not just "civil" rights) has expanded dramatically in the last three decades;[45] there is growing reference to international human rights instruments in that period, even in the United States, though modest and not nearly as marked as in Europe; presumptions about global human rights inform cases in the United States even without explicit reference to international instruments (see, for example, *Nebraska v. Al-Hussaini*);[46] furthermore, one must remember that postwar human rights instruments, especially the Universal Declaration of Human Rights, were heavily informed by the United States Constitution, among other sources, indicating a certain affinity.

But the shifting modality of politics to the politics of agency, with its presumption of universal individualism and human rights, is revealed in the remarkable convergence of law on agency, such as in the area of migration. Across the Euro-Atlantic arena and in much of the democratic world, almost across the board, family unification and economic and humanitarian criteria are the touchstones of migration policy (albeit with different definitions in each category cross-nationally).[47] As this law converges, so it trickles down to sub-state jurisdictions and organizations (and the word "trickles" does not, perhaps, reveal the rapidity of this process) and reveals, on the one hand, growing legal density on a global level and, on the other, the "nesting" effect described above. We would suggest that growing transnational activities (or "globalization"), "judicialization," and agency as the modality of politics are interrelated phenomena and, as such, would have this effect of generating isomorphism of legal norms.

Issues such as "gender" and "race" are legally *closed off* as options for discrimination to a remarkable extent across these countries. When we step back and comprehend the extent to which human rights institutions and idiom have closed off such policy options, the remarkable impact of human rights begins to dawn on us.

The nesting process is legally and institutionally inscribed: Legal sources, terminology, and institutional structures have shifted in response to the changing modes of political engagement and demands of agency such that they allow for the nesting process to flow quite naturally. For example, legal principles have been created to provide mechanisms whereby the differing legal systems and laws of member-states in the European Union can successfully integrate with emerging European Union law. In order to coordinate the competing legal competency of the EU and national authorities, Article 5 of the Treaty of the European Union formalized "subsidiarity" and "proportionality" principles.[48] In 1999, the Amsterdam Treaty added Protocol Number 30 on the application of these principles.[49]

The principle of subsidiarity derives from the first paragraph of Article 5, which dictates that the EU can act only when it possesses the legal power to do so, that the EU should act only when an objective can be better achieved at the supranational level, and that the means employed by the EU when it does act, should be proportional to the desired objective. The

TEU further strengthened the notion of subsidiarity by making it a fundamental Community law limitation and stating, in Article 53b, that Community action "shall not go beyond what is necessary to achieve the objectives of this Treaty." National powers, according to subsidiarity, remain the norm, with European Union action the exception. On the other hand, the TEU enlarged the realm of Community competence to include the areas traditionally within the exclusive authority of member-states: industrial policy, health, education, culture, and the particularly sensitive areas of immigration and social policy.

Although in practice subsidiarity remains ambiguous, it does appear to enhance the kind of "nesting" activity discussed in this paper, while at the same time contributing to the evolution of European Union integration. For example, in the area of immigration, although the EU has moved in the direction of greater competence over the question of immigration by moving it to the first pillar and, more recently, forming a special Committee to draft one policy for the EU, the fundamental determination of "nationality" still remains with the member-states. Such divisions of legal competence provide the "cross-border" spaces within which nesting occurs.

The purpose of subsidiarity, from the perspective of a country such as Germany, which had urged its introduction, is to protect areas, such as environmental policy, where national governments might have taken great strides in formulating effective policies. The German fear was that "harmonization" might result in a lowering of national environmental standards. Thus, even harmonization has been interpreted as a regulatory floor, not a ceiling. Since it remains unclear which areas are within the Community's exclusive competence, there is much room for maneuver. The effect of these principles, therefore, is that the ambiguity they introduce opens up a number of "nests" where litigation to enforce and affect policy (for example, environmental policy) can occur.

CONCLUSION

As relations, both regionally and globally, become more multifaceted and the legal frameworks that institutionalize such relations become more extensive, we are likely to see the growing importance of judicial and administrative mechanisms to mediate these legally embedded relations. This will remain the case insofar as executive and legislative bodies are absent, or relatively weak, on the regional or even global level. The globalization and regionalization of law has a certain affinity with judicial and administrative institutions. Thus, the clash between agency and democracy—as in the acute example of the executive orders following the 11 September 2001 terrorist attacks—will be reinforced through the current structure of human rights or European Union law, which promotes the agency of the individual.

NOTES

1. We draw the quoted terms, used in a different context, from James E. Block, *A Nation of Agents: The American Path to a Modern Self and Society* (2001).

2. The use of the term "agency" here is different from the use of the term in the extensive literature on agency in social theory. One could also argue that republicanism is a form of agency, though distinct from the judicialized form of agency we speak of here. One can even trace the different philosophical traditions such that judicially mediated forms of agency has its roots in the writings of Locke, Adam Smith, Bentham, and John Stuart Mill, who in different ways rejected tradition, grounded society in the social contract between individuals, and saw individuals as calculating actors determining their own interests and, in more present-day terms, their own lifestyles. Collective, republican-like "agency" instead views the individual as less driven by material and self-directed interest but rather "realized" through his or her interactions with other humans in legislating a shared morality—more akin to Rousseau. Here we refer to agency in the restricted "judicial" sense, as described above. *See* Mustafa Emirbayer and Anne Mische, *What is Agency?*, 103 AM.J.SOC. 4, 962 (1998). *See also* Hannah Arendt, *On Revolution* (1990).

3. J. H. H. Weiler, *The Constitution of Europe: 'Do the New Clothes Have an Emperor?' and Other Essays on European Integration* (1999).

4. J. H. H. Weiler, *The European Union: Enlargement, Constitutionalism and Democracy* available at <http://www.rewi.hu-berlin.de/WHI/deutsch/>.

5. Ibid.

6. "Direct effect" refers to the European Court of Justice's determination in the case *Van Gend En Loos* (1962) that European Community law constitutes a new legal order directly applicable in the member-states. "Subsidiarity" embodies the principle that the EU can act only in areas where it has explicit power to do so, and that the region, as a whole, should act only when an objective can be better achieved at the supranational level. "Proportionality" is defined within the context of subsidiarity as the qualification that European action must not go beyond what is necessary to achieve the objectives of the Treaty of Rome. "Harmonization" is a phrase used to describe the overall process of coordination and legal integration of the member-states, with particular regard to the internal market.

7. For example, the use of a credit card and the Internet to purchase airline tickets, the freedom of movement between the United States and Canada, freedom of religion and charitable contributions, and the right to privacy were all cited by the American administration as ways the terrorists exploited the democracy. *See* generally Saskia Sassen, "Global Cities and Diasporic Networks: Microsites in Global Civil Society," in *Global Civil Society Yearbook 2002* (Center for the Study of Global Governance ed., 2002), 217.

8. Steven Erlanger, "A Nation Challenged: Berlin; Shocked Germany Weakens Cherished Protections," *New York Times*, 1 Oct. 2002.

9. *Ammur v. France*, 22 Eur. Ct. H.R. 533 (1996). See discussion on Ammur and following ECHR cases in Hugo Storey, *Implications of Incorporation of the European Convention of Human Rights in the Immigration and Asylum Context*, 4 European Human Rights Law Review 452 (1998).

10. *Ammur v. France*, 22 Eur. Ct. H.R. 533 (1996). See discussion on Ammur and following ECHR cases in Hugo Storey, "Implications of Incorporation of the European Convention of Human Rights in the Immigration and Asylum Context," 4 *European Human Rights Law Review* 452 (1998).

11. *D. v. United Kingdom*, 2 Eur. Ct. H.R. 273 (1997).

12. *See Chahal v. United Kingdom*, App. No. 22414/93, 23 Eur. H.R. Rep. 413 (1996); *Soering v. United Kingdom*, App. No. 14038/88, 11 Eur. H.R. Rep 439 (1989).

13. Treaty Establishing the European Community, 10 Nov. 1997, O.J. © 340) 3 (1997) [hereinafter EC Treaty] art. 6a (as in effect 1994) (now art. 13).

14. Treaty of Amsterdam Amending the Treaty on European Union, the Treaties Establishing the European Communities and Certain Related Acts, 2 Oct. 1997, O.J. © 340) arts. 1, 2, 6 (1997) [hereinafter Treaty of Amsterdam].

15. Treaty of Amsterdam Amending the Treaty on European Union, the Treaties Establishing the European Communities and Certain Related Acts, 2 Oct. 1997, O.J. © 340) arts. 1, 2, 6 (1997) [hereinafter Treaty of Amsterdam].

16. The European Union is made up of three pillars. The first pillar represents the European Communities, the second pillar Common Foreign and Security Policy, and the third Co-operation in the Fields of Justice and Home Affairs. Treaty of Amsterdam, *id.* at art. 1.

17. The British Parliament adopted the Human Rights Act of 1998 in November of that year. The Human Rights Act became effective in the UK on 2 October 2000.

18. *See* David Jacobson, "New Border Customs: Migration and the Changing Role of the State," 3 *Journal of International Law and Foreign Affairs* 443, 443 (1998–1999); figures compiled from M. J. Harris and D. J. Harris, *Multilateral Treaties: Index and Current Status* (9th Cum. Supp. 1993). Thanks to David John Frank for making this data available.

19. The increase in the salience of the judiciary and of the idiom of rights since roughly the 1970s and 1980s are illustrated in the following stark figures: The caseloads of the federal courts on all three levels—Supreme Court, Court of Appeals, and U.S. District Court—jumped in most cases dramatically between 1970 and 1995—in the Supreme Court from over 4,000 cases in 1970 to over 7,500 cases in 1995, and in the Circuit Court from over 11,500 in 1970 to almost 50,000 in 1995. In the district courts the picture is a little more complex: "Commenced" civil cases increased massively from 87,000 to 240,000 in that time period but only a small and declining percentage of cases reached trial. The number of criminal cases increased from 1970 to 1995 more modestly—about 15 percent. David Jacobson, *Place and Belonging in America* (2002), 173.

20. *See* Alec Stone Sweet and Thomas L. Brunell, *The European Court and the National Courts: A Statistical Analysis of Preliminary References* (Jean Monnet Program, Working Paper, 1997) available at <http://www.jeanmonnetprogram.org/papers/97/97-14-html> (9 Nov. 2002).

21. *See* Alec Stone Sweet and Thomas L. Brunell, *The European Court and the National Courts: A Statistical Analysis of Preliminary References* (Jean Monnet Program, Working Paper, 1997) available at <http://www.jeanmonnetprogram.org/papers/97/97-14-html> (9 Nov. 2002).

22. *See* Alec Stone Sweet and Thomas L. Brunell, *The European Court and the National Courts: A Statistical Analysis of Preliminary References* (Jean Monnet Program, Working Paper, 1997) available at <http://www.jeanmonnetprogram.org/papers/97/97-14-html> (9 Nov. 2002).

23. Damian Chalmers, The Much Ado about Judicial Politics in the United Kingdom: A Statistical Analysis of Reported Decisions of United Kingdom Courts Invoking EU Law 1973-1998 (Harvard Law School, Working Paper 1/00, 2000).

24. Consider the proliferation of NGOs as "pollinators," so to speak, of this process.

25. *See* Suzanne Kapner, "Britain's Legal Barriers Start to Fall: Discrimination Lawsuits Are Becoming More Commonplace," *New York Times*, 4 Oct. 2000, at W1.

26. The Amsterdam Treaty of 1999 amended and renumbered the Treaty on European Union and the Treaty Establishing the European Community. See art. 6a (as in effect 1994) (now art. 13).

27. The Treaty of Rome that established the European Economic Community in 1957 remains the penultimate source of EU law. In November 1993, the Treaty of Rome was officially renamed the Treaty establishing the European Community. At the same time, the Maastricht Treaty on European Union (TEU) was superimposed over the Treaty of Rome. The resulting document is titled the "Treaty on European Union together with the Treaty establishing the European Community."

28. The Council has authority (although limited in that it must act unanimously on a proposal from the Commission and with consultation of the European Parliament) to "take appropriate action to combat discrimination." Treaty of Amsterdam, *supra* note 14, art 13.

29. *See* Alexander Somek, "A Constitution for Antidiscrimination: Exploring the Vanguard Moment of Community Law," 5 Eur. L. J. 3 (1999).

30. Dagmar Schiek, "Sex Equality Law After *Kalanke* and *Marschall*," 4 *European Law Journal* (1998), 148, 152.

31. Ibid., 152.

32. Ibid. The decisions in *Kalanake* (ECJ 17/10/1995—Case C 450/93, 1995 ECR I-3051); *Marschall* (ECJ 11/10/1997—Case C 409/95 nyr) were both initiated by individual men seeking protection through EC law.

33. Treaty of Amsterdam, *supra* note 14, at 118-19.

34. The European Commission has proposed laws to outlaw sexual harassment in the workplace and other measures to promote equality between the sexes. *See* Barry James, "EU Drafts Measure to Outlaw Sexual Harassment," *Internationall Herald Tribune;* available at <http://www.iht.com/IHT/BJ/00/bj060800.html> (9 Nov. 2002).

35. For example, the ECJ had determined that sexual orientation was not a protected category under EU law. *See* Case C-249/96, *Grant v. Southwest Trains Ltd.*, 3 BHRC 578 (1998). In that decision the Court referred to the new Article 13 that had not yet come into force. Thus, although the Court held that Article 119 (now Article 141 of the Consolidated Version of the Treaty Establishing the European Community) of the EC Treaty did not encompass sexual orientation, it noted that the Community now had the power to take appropriate action to include sexual orientation within its scope. Since that case, the European Parliament has adopted resolutions calling for an end to discrimination based on sexual orientation (*see* Resolution on Equal Rights for Gays and Lesbians in the EC, Minutes of 17/09/1998—Provisional Edition; Minutes of 20/02/1997, based on

Document No. C4-0565/96-Final Edition; and Minutes of 20/02/1997, based on Document No. A4-0046/97-Final) and the Council of Europe has, in a series of opinions, backed equal treatment for all EU citizens irrespective of sexual orientation (Opinion No. 216 [2000]; Report on the Draft Protocol No. 12 to the European Convention on Human Rights Doc. 8614; Opinion of the European Court of Human Rights on Draft Protocol 12 to the European Convention of Human Rights [adopted at the plenary administrative session of the Court on 6 Dec. 1999]); Debate on the Opinion on Draft Protocol No. 12 to the European Convention on Human Rights; *Situation of Gays and Lesbians and Their Partners in Respect to Asylum and Immigration in the Member-States of the Council of Europe*, Doc. 8654, available at <http://stars.coe.fr>. These developments have essentially removed the issue of sexual orientation from member-states' authority and have placed them within the rubric of EC law.

36. *See* Mark Bell, "Shifting Conceptions of Sexual Discrimination at the Court of Justice: From P v. S to Grant v. SWT," 5 *European Law Journal* (1999), 63, 72.

37. Galya Benarieh Ruffer, "Virtual Citizenship: Migrants and the Constitutional Polity" (Ph.D. diss., University of Pennsylvania, 2002).

38. Ibid.

39. The European Court of Human Rights ruling referred to here is that of: *Abdulaziz, Cabales, and Balkandali v. United Kingdom*, 7 *European Human Right Law Review* 471 (1998).

40. Chalmers, *supra* note 23.

41. Chalmers, *supra* note 23.

42. The British Parliament adopted the Human Rights Act of 1998 in November of that year. The Human Rights Act became effective in the UK on 2 October 2000.

43. *See Alam v. United Kingdom*, 10 Y.B. 478 (1967); *Abdulaziz, Cabales and Balkandali v. United Kingdom* 7 (1985). Article 6 of the ECHR concerns the right to a fair trial, and Article 8 the right to respect for private and family life.

44. *N. K. v. United Kingdom*, (App. No. 9856/82) 52 D.R. 38 (1987); *see* Storey, *supra* note 9. Article 13 of the ECHR stipulates that everyone whose rights have been violated under the ECHR shall have an effective remedy. In the Chahal case, the individual of that name had been involved in terrorist acts in India where he had also been tortured. The European Court of Human Rights ruled that he could not be returned to India as there was a "real risk" he would be treated by Indian security services in a way that was incompatible with Article 3 (which prohibits torture). The Court thus overruled British claims that he should be returned as Chahal's presence in the UK threatened national interest. The British Government reformed the asylum appeals process, as codified in the Special Immigration Appeals Commission Act of 1998, to account for the ruling in Strasbourg. *See* Chahal, *supra* note 12; Colin Warbrick, "The Principles of the European Convention on Human Rights and the Response of States to Terrorism," 3 *European Human Rights Law Review* (2002), 287.

45. The growing reference to "human rights" in U.S. federal court cases is evident in the following figures: From 1945 to 1960 the term "human rights" appears in only sixty-eight cases, and from 1961 to 1970 the figure is 159 cases. Then we witness a surge: from 1971 to 1980, 861 cases; from 1981 to 1990, 2,224 cases make reference to human rights; and from 1991 to 2000, over 6,300 human rights cases are noted. Figures are derived from a search of the universe of all federal court cases for the years noted from the *Westlaw* database.

46. *State of Nebraska v. Latif Al-Hussaini*, 579 N.W. 2d 561 (Neb. Ct. App. 1998).

47. *See* Kathleen Newland and Demetrios Papademetriou, "Managing International Migration," 3 UCLA Journal of International L. and Foreign Affairs (1998–1999), 637.

48. Article 5 (ex Article 3b) is part of the Treaty establishing the European Community that, together with the Maastricht Treaty on European Union (TEU), form the "Treaty on European Union together with the Treaty establishing the European Community" of 1993. In this article, we refer to the 1993 treaty jointly as the "TEU."

49. Protocol 30 is part of the Treaty Establishing the European Community (as amended and renumbered by the Amsterdam Treaty of 1999).

This chapter originally appeared as David Jacobson and Galya Benarieh Ruffer, "Courts Across Borders: The Implications of Judicial Agency for Human Rights and Democracy," in *Human Rights Quarterly* 25: 1 (2003): 74–93. It is reprinted here with permission of The Johns Hopkins University Press.

2

The Nation-Centered Perspective

Adrian Favell

THE NATION-CENTERED PERSPECTIVE

Debates about migration policy now sit at the end of more than a decade of intense scholarly work on immigration politics. The contest over nation-centered versus post-national or global perspectives on immigration politics has followed the lead of U.S.-trained comparativists working on almost exclusively European terrain, the main inspirations being the path-breaking work on immigration and the nation-state by Rogers Brubaker (1992) and Yasemin Soysal (1994), and on immigration and the market by James Hollifield (1992), Gary Freeman (1995), and Saskia Sassen (1996). These debates have already produced several exhaustive collections of work. The best of these also include excellent, state-of-the-art summaries of the field, taking the central works above as the conceptual starting point (i.e., Joppke 1998b; Koopmans and Statham 2000b). In revisiting these debates, then, my main goal here is not to go over familiar ground but to offer arguments for the relevance of the issue of the "integration" of immigrants—a subject not dealt with in any depth by any of these authors—to understanding the continuing force of nation-centered arguments to the debate.

A BRIEF REVIEW OF POST-NATIONAL/GLOBAL ARGUMENTS

The nation-centered perspective has almost always taken the form of a corrective to claims made in the name of a new, "post-national" or "globalist" vision of immigration politics. It may be helpful therefore to start by briefly summarizing the main forms that the post-national or global argument has taken, notably the kinds of empirical issues in the European context over which these arguments have been contested.

Post-national and global arguments have taken two main forms, with variations: the first, an economic argument about global markets and the state; the second, a more institutionalist argument about the emergence of new political and/or legal structures, enabling post-national rights claims or forms of mobilization.

The first main form of argument, associated with the work of Saskia Sassen (1991, 1996) and Alejandro Portes (1996), is the observed *de facto* transnationalization of sovereignty over immigration processes, caused by the growing significance of global economic forces and enhanced by transnational capital flows and information networks and the increasing geographical autonomy of global cities. These macro-structural changes have, it is argued, led to an irreversible shift in the relation between markets and (nation-) states, demonstrated, for example, in the growing power of multinational corporations and their influence over international trade negotiations. In its train, the new high-end service industries in global cities have spurred a barely controllable influx of poor migrants to fill the lower-end service positions in a polarized post-industrial economy. In response, there has been a pragmatic adjustment by nation-states to the need for international forms of governance over these global economic processes: new international institutions, such as the EU and WTO, shaping the movement of persons, alongside the liberalized flows of capital, goods, and services.

The second, institutionalist form of the post-national/global is more explicitly linked to contemporary political and legal structures, and derives its story from a historical understanding of the extension and deepening of rights in the postwar period. The most well-known—Yasemin Soysal's (1994) account of immigrant rights in the postwar period in Europe—starts out essentially as a nation-centered description of comparative immigrant rights in Europe. But its explanation is driven by an internationalist argument about the emergence of the category of "personhood," an isomorphic product of the integrating global political system in the postwar world. This in turn has become the crucial legal and political resource—voiced most notably in human rights claims—with which migrants have been able to demand better rights and representation at the national level. In essence, this is an argument about the normative legitimation of political arguments and their embeddedness in evolving modern political forms on a global scale.

This political/legal argument has itself taken a number of variations. In the work of David Jacobson (1997), Soysal's political institutional argument is given stronger legal foundations in an argument about the functioning of the international legal system as autonomous from the political system. For him, post-national isomorphism is expressed in the emergent concept of legal "agency" as the key, an original product of the organizational autonomy and nesting of the international legal system in the postwar world. In this volume, Jacobson illustrates his argument with example of international legal jurisprudence from the United States and elsewhere. Political sociologists, meanwhile, have also made a post-national argument in relation to emergent forms of transnational mobilization, in which new international norms or ideas have provided new opportunities and incentives for migrant organizations to re-frame their incorporation and inclusion arguments in terms of international norms and ideals (Soysal 1993; Kastoryano 1997, 1998; Tarrow 1998).

ENTER THE EU

It is no accident that the European Union has so often become the favorite institutional context for these arguments. The European Union is a largely *sui generis*, and certainly unique, supranational organization that has indeed changed the relationship between national sovereignty and the market in Europe, and led to the extraordinary creation of new transnational political and legal structures in the postwar continent. The institutionalization of freedom of movement—of capital, services, goods, *and* persons—within a borderless internal market does indeed constitute a powerful revision of the territorial integrity of national state power. Yet, despite the fundamental centrality of freedom of movement to the European integration process, immigration in general and the integration of immigrants in particular, has had only the most peripheral place in the EU's agenda until very recently.

Post-national and global scholars, however, have been overly hasty to look to the EU for potential proof of their general argument. For sure, there has been the excitement of new international courts and their jurisprudence: the European Court of Justice, a pillar of the EU's institutional framework, and the European Court of Human Rights (which is not in fact an EU institution). Legal action in these contexts has been argued to challenge unbridled national political jurisdiction over areas of immigration policy constrained normally by national discretion. And, beyond this, amid the wealth of activities of the Commission and its attendant lobbyists and NGOs, the EU has been linked with sources of funding and institutional opportunity structures of the kind theorized by post-national and global commentators. Their arguments may not need European illustrations, as such, but it is a valid *prima facie* presumption that the EU should be one place where post-national and global developments would first become visible. I will thus confine my argument here to these EU-centered debates, although global and transnational proofs might be found in other contexts.

The problem with such EU-based proof is in the empirical pudding. All of the general post-national and global arguments that refer to examples from the EU—such as those suggested above—have been more or less successfully refuted with specific case material from the European context, that pays closer attention to what is actually going on in the European integration process.

First, as Freeman points out (1998), the idea of a transnational economy overrunning state control of policy exaggerates the nation-state's weakness in the face of the new political economy and its ability to adapt and recapture new tendencies. As many leading EU scholars concur, many of the powers and institutions created at the European level can be most plausibly explained historically in terms of the fairly conscious "rescue" of nation-state in Europe, via the carefully legislated pooling of sovereignty over selective issues (Milward 1992, Moravcsik 1998). In the arena of immigration policy, nation-states have learned to use the EU in order to devolve control functions "up, down and out" (Guiraudon and Lahav 2000) to render state functions more effective: up to supranational institutions and law, down to regions and local actors, and out to private companies.

Second, scholars such as Guiraudon (2000b) and Joppke (1998a) have extensively detailed how immigrant rights in the courts have been implemented because of nationally rooted norms of democratic fairness and not because of the ostensible new dimension of supranational law. These arguments link back to the "embedded liberalism" identified in earlier work by Hollifield (1992). In addition, they have found that internal national political dynamics have played a key role in the generally expansionist direction of immigrant rights in Europe, usually via state bureaucracies and courts keeping policy-making out of the public eye (Guiraudon 1998, 2000a). Moreover, any such international law—such as human rights—has to be ratified, interpreted, and implemented by agents of the nation-state. On the claims-making side, meanwhile, Koopmans and Statham (1999) and Giugni and Passy (2000, 2002) have effectively shown that immigrant minorities themselves have understood the priority of the national sphere in their campaigning, dominantly shunning the framing of arguments in post-national legitimations, which are seen to be less effective at a national level.

Third, Favell (2000) and Favell and Geddes (2000) have drawn the consequences of these nationally focused studies for the EU level, by showing that the supposed new transnational immigrant mobilizations within the EU have in fact not been immigrant led but dominated by go-between policy entrepreneurs, who have monopolized the opportunity structures within the new European space. Their Brussels-based study was confirmed at the national level in Italy and Spain in research by Danese (1998), which showed how immigrant organizations failed to seize these opportunities, while they did indeed become fertile ground for the church and trade union organizations operating within the national civil society, who successfully claim to represent migrant interests.

These skeptical political science–inflected responses to the post-national sociological argument build on a more general and pervasive problem with the global and post-national arguments: the slippage of empirical analysis into a familiar combination of normative idealism and functionalist explanation. For the globalists, the motor of progressive change is more often than not a residual normative assumption about how expanding rights or liberties in the world are linked to the progress of modern human rights norms and democracy. When this argument is framed in explanatory terms—that is, in terms of the institutional isomorphism of these norms around the globalizing world (Meyer et al 1997)—all observed changes or developments at the national level end up being explained by functional changes at the world system level, however politically mundane the local proximate causes might appear. But why would self-interested national political actors voluntarily give up control over policy and law to international agencies that strip them of sovereignty—unless they were in some way also served by them? Globalists fall into the Parsonian trap of holistic thinking, projecting a worldwide gestalt change in the global system, when more often than not any changes can probably be better accounted for by more standard interest-driven political dynamics, of the kind marshaled by those more skeptical of the nation-transcending powers of the EU.

My goal here is not to adjudicate definitively on these specific debates, although the balance of empirical evidence on European developments clearly favors the nation-centered perspective on policy. What I will do, rather, is to present a further argument why the nation-centered perspective remains fundamental to nearly all *post*-immigration policies: that is, on questions concerning the integration of immigrants.

INTEGRATION AND THE NATION-CENTERED PERSPECTIVE

Post-national/global arguments on immigration policy are clearly not without some force. Unambiguous national jurisdiction over policies of entry and control, on family reunification, or on deportation is certainly nowadays empirically debatable and in some cases controversial. International migration has certainly upset any unproblematic nation-centered notions of sovereignty and enforcement, even if the resilience of nation-states remains on balance the most convincing line to take. One can also debate endlessly the impact of global flows and mobility, free-moving elites and their money, or the sprawling networks of transnationalism and so forth on the viability of any taken-for-granted notions of a world made up of closed, container-like nation-state societies. International law and norms may indeed have had some impact on the rights of temporary residents and non-nationals.

Yet notwithstanding these various controversies, one area of observable policy definitively remains beyond the reach of the international or post-national. It is an indubitable fact that no nation-state in Europe—whether ostensibly republican or multiculturalist in orientation—has been willing to give ground over policy on questions concerning the social, economic, and political *integration* of immigrants, once they are settled and recognized as new (or about-to-become new) citizens in the host country. On this question, at least, it is universally accepted that nation-states—that is, national government, its agencies, and its institutions—still have the primary responsibility and prerogative to shape and oversee the social processes involving these populations that take place within its territory. This role remains untouched by the external claims of the post-national.

Understanding why this is centers on an appreciation of the deep paradigm of bounded social integration that lies at the heart of the modern notion of the nation-state. Though not immediately apparent—particularly in countries that style themselves as pluralist, diverse, or multicultural in nature—this paradigm can be glimpsed in the kinds of official integration policies all kinds of different countries have fashioned in recent years to deal with the question of post-immigration policy. At the policy level, the notion of integration and its synonyms (inclusion, incorporation, assimilation, etc.) essentially encompass all kinds of mechanisms and structures aimed at reproducing a unifying (national) social cohesion or solidarity in the face of class, ethnic, and foreign differences. As I will argue, its translation to the area of immigration is merely a recent adaptation of longer-standing ideas and mechanisms about social inclusion honed via nation-building processes in the past. Numerous areas of policy thus can be connected to the notion: from education, civic instruction, and culture, to social policy, economic redistribution, political participation, or law and order. Typically, these are areas of policy where nation-states have adamantly refused to see any benefits or necessity in pooling approaches at a supranational level.

Try as it might, the European Union and its institutions, for example, are assiduously kept out of most of policy areas linked with post-immigration integration. This is largely because few of them involve any of the central market-building concerns on which the EU is primarily seen to have legitimacy (the one partial exception to this being regional and urban development policy, which has, in some cases, impacted indirectly on immigrant-related inner-city policies). The tight link between nation-state sovereignty and the notion of state-created integration is no accident. Underlying the policy idea of integration lies the deeper, social theoretical notion of nationalist "social integration"— premised on a culturally shared, territorially bounded, and historically rooted notion of society—that has found its dominant actualized expression in the modern world as the contemporary idea of the nation-state. Nation-states, in other words, universally conceive of their social unity and historical continuity in terms of what might be called an "amateur" public theory or *philosophy* of integration (Favell 1998) that combines a kind of functionalist social theory of what it is that holds nations together, with a normative political philosophy that expresses nationhood in terms of abstract civic values (usually citizenship). Post-immigration policies today translate these dominant assumptions about nationhood into concrete political forms.

How this happened historically has been well documented by various scholars who have shown how the historical taming of migration and mobility coincided with the final coalescing of the modern nation-state. Modern European nation-states were formed out of the construction of insider/outsider conceptions of citizenship, and the institutionalization of social closure linked to the emergence of the pastoral welfare state and large-scale citizen armies at the end of the nineteenth century (Torpey 1999; Brubaker 1992). Hence, the identity of nations was bound up in large part with both the definition of who remained outside, as a foreigner, and conversely who belonged and could be transformed into a full member of the society: a citizen *à part entière*. In some cases, this integration process concerned immigrants—the Polish and Italian workforces in France, for example—but the process was very much central to the integration of *all* peripheral or problematic members of the nation: whether regional minorities, conflictual working classes, or disadvantaged women. This familiar Marshallian story was the blueprint for all later ideas of integration that have been promoted in relation to newer, ever more "foreign" populations (Marshall 1950). Hence, the centrality throughout in ideas of integration of essentially nationalizing policies and practices in areas such as culture, education, language, and so on. Moreover, frameworks for reconciling immigrant foreignness or difference with the nation have remained nationalist in orientation even when flavored with an ideology of multiculturalism.

The dominant expression of the national in these terms can be found across all European nation-states, regardless of superficial distinctions often drawn between so-called ethnocultural, republican, pluralist, or multicultural nations and differences in the details of their immigration policies. Putting aside the marginal voice of "cosmopolitan" academics and activists, the "national" finds itself articulated with staunch reliability by nearly all politicians, national media, and nationally oriented public figures in all such modern nation-states. Even in the most plural nations, such as Switzerland or Belgium, there is still always some notion in public discussion of nationhood ·through social integration lying behind the politically pluralist structures: They would not (still) be nation-states otherwise. These are, in any case, limited cases of the European model of nationhood, much less fragile elsewhere. So-called "multicultural" nations such as Britain, Sweden, or the Netherlands turn out on closer inspection to be highly nationalist in their notion of the limits of the "multiculturalism" they endorse—as something encompassed, bounded, and achieved by the historical nation-state. This reveals them to be much closer in essence to more self-consciously unitary traditions of France or Germany, which see their nationhood in either republican/universalist or (sometimes) ethnocultural terms. Nation-states (in the European model, at least) thus uniformly see themselves in these highly functionalist terms, as aspiring to a shared, bounded, and rooted notion of integration, in which the integration of newcomers fulfills the ideal-type social closure aspired to by all ideologies of nationhood and citizenship. Durkheimian republicanism—usually, of course, identified only in its most overt form in the citizenship ideologies of the French (i.e., Schnapper 1994)—is, in fact, latent in all kinds of modern countries' practices of integration. Even in an age of anti-state suspicion and widespread rolling back of its powers, on the symbolic issue of pulling together the pieces of cultural and ethnic difference introduced by immigration, the nation-state remains supreme—in fact, the only available model of social unity and social order on offer.

European immigration politics in the postwar period should thus be understood as the playing out of well-established nation-building strategies in the post-colonial age (see Favell 1998 on how this works out for both Britain and France; see also Banton 2001). New immigrants from the colonies, or guest-worker systems have over time been seen to be permanent residents who also need to be integrated in some fashion into the mainstream of society. Sometimes this was seen in republican terms, sometimes in terms of a new kind of "multiculturalism-in-one-nation," but in every national case it was presumed that the nation-state would have the capacity to absorb the newcomers and reinvent itself in inclusionary terms in the process. The older processes of integrating peripheral regions and problematic populations thus have been adapted over time to immigrants, with the same tensions and social difficulties arising. Initial periods of racism or anti-immigrant hostility have slowly but surely given way across the continent to a firm commitment to "integration" (albeit spoken of in different terms, ranging from assimilation, through inclusion and incorporation, to multiculturalism and pluralism), in return always for a willingness among migrants to submit to an often coercive re-nationalization. The most problematic immigrants have come to be seen as those who assert different cultures and values to the nation, as opposed to those racially distinct minorities who have become increasingly accepted as long as they were well socialized into dominant national values and perspectives. Immigrants, thus, have played a crucial symbolic part in the self-reaffirmation of nation-states, who might otherwise have been thought to face an inevitable period of national decline in the face of globalization.

In such a way, migrants and new minorities have become a key and fertile battleground for on-going nation-building efforts, played out as struggles between national political elites for control over the notion of a national historical identity. Repositioning integrating immigrants as further proof of the vibrancy of European nation political cultures, more progressive national political actors have been able to underscore their faith in state-centered political action able to control and reshape threatening international social forces: that is, those carried (ironically) by such a typically transnational, market-led phenomena as international migration. The concept of immigrant integration—and the imagined nation-building properties of a society able to respond to international free movement phenomena this way—has allowed states to conform to international rights and responsibilities on the treatment of migrants, while replaying older historical narratives about the integrity, unity, and inclusive strengths of the nation.

Throughout the last few decades, there has of course been a notable challenge to this in the prominent anti-immigrant, right-wing nationalist voices heard in several countries, which have often explicitly centered on ending immigration. But faced with the need for resoldering national unity through proactive integration policies, the anti-immigrant position ends up being seen as in fact undermining nationalism (and national pride) by stressing the ineffectiveness of the state in keeping borders closed, repatriating migrants, or in transforming them into good citizens. It suggests that the national state can do nothing to preserve national values in the classroom, or preserve the continuity of national political culture, when newcomers are for better or worse an unavoidable part of the scene. No true nationalist is likely to be happy with such a negative assessment of state capacity, and thus many mainstream commentators have come round to accepting that the immigrant presence must be recognized in a more positive way and included in the on-going political reconstruction of the nation. Nationalists need the state to be proactive, yet clumsy state-enforced exclusion—such as attempts to install full-scale policies of repatriation in France and Germany in the 1970s—have generally failed. Over time, politicians have turned to more pragmatic ways of including their immigrant populations, now seen as "here for good"—meaning, "here for the good of our nation".

It is for this reason that pro-immigrant, progressive forces do not ever formulate their policies for the state in post-national terms—which would again be tantamount to admitting the ineffectiveness of the nation-state as a society-shaping force—but rather always opt to dress the language of inclusion, integration, even multiculturalism and diversity, in terms of the resoldering of national identity. Generally, their influence along with a mainstream ready to embrace an inclusive form of integration has seen the formulation of more inclusive, usually "universalist," visions of the nation, which will have space for the new, international presence. This was not a great stretch for some European countries with older "universalist" colonial traditions of nationhood—notably Britain, France, the Netherlands—that spanned the globe prior to the postwar shrinking back of territory into the original nation-state borders. Again, these nation-states are much more similar in their orientation to nationhood that their ostensible policy frameworks suggest. Both French "republican assimilation" and British "multiculturalism" find a comfortable spot together within the overarching nation-centered fundamental belief in integration and the unique capacity of the nation-state-society to successfully welcome and absorb immigrant minorities. Alternative, post-national visions of multiculturalism and transnationalism have had much less appeal to national political actors not keen to downgrade their own powers. Instead, these actors have always sought ways of squaring ideas about the rights and recognition of immigrants, with a re-stressing of the need for immigrant cultural and linguistic adaptation to the norms and values of the nation.

British policy-makers in the 1960s and 1970s were the first to formulate "middle way" notions of integration in these terms. After years of very nationally specific discussions about race and multiculturalism, these older ideas have resurfaced again in many recent statements and reflections on integration policy in the face of new asylum seekers. French policy-makers, meanwhile, spent much of the 1980s debating integration in these same terms, reformulating a workable notion of an integrating, culturally diverse nation, unified around familiar historical values; an exclusive conception of national culture was no longer seen as an option for French nation-building, except on the very far right. In the 1990s and early 2000s, this has been followed by similar efforts to define a national "model" of integration by governments and independent commissions in Denmark, Sweden, Germany, the Netherlands, Spain, and Italy that reprise many of the same debates (on these debates and their relation to changing scholarly conceptions, see Favell 2001a, 2003b).

The ordinary language appeal of the paradigm of integration has thus mattered, over and above whether nation-states are actually effective at rebuilding the kind of national coherency their integration policies promote. Whether nation-states today or in the past have ever been able to pull off such a remarkable feat of self-contained self-construction is highly questionable. Social integration—even the notion of "society" itself—might well be a functionalist illusion, papering over conflicts, tensions, and broken borders with a nation-sustaining ideology increasingly archaic in the fragmented contemporary world. The fact behind this rhetoric—of course—is that European nation-states are far less bounded and unified than their most prominent politicians and public intellectuals claim. The world has indeed washed through the nation, and overflows much of what used to be considered the prerogative of national sovereignty. However, for the nation-building reasons documented above, immigration policies—and hence the dominant terms of post-immigration politics—remain firmly anchored in the nation-centered idiom, limiting the space with which transnational or international dimensions of immigrant-host relations can be recognized in policy terms. Politicians, public officials, and public intellectuals talk the national talk, and they continually cement in the public mind—and the minds of immigrants themselves—that the home front is the place where the action over post-immigration politics take place.

And, although my arguments here are limited to European examples, it is by no means clear that new world countries of immigration are ultimately less secure or committed to the functionalist reproduction of nationhood and nation-stateness by politicians, the media and public actors. Indeed, there is no nation-state more "self-contained," more convinced about the bounded, internal nature of its immigration policies, and (above all) the irrelevance of the post-national, than the United States of America—for all its supposed multiculturalism and immigrant diversity.

CONCLUSION

These comments lead to a paradoxical conclusion. Much of our sociological intuition should indeed be alert to the possibility of a growing influence of the global and transnational on social relations in Western societies that surely in some way have declined in their powers to effectively enact sovereignty over their bounded, unified territories and populations. Yet, at the same time, the way that immigration becomes an issue, and the main focus of immigration politics—especially the integration of immigrants—remains dominantly state centered, because of the nation-centered investment of actors in talking up the nation through immigration and integration. I argue that this holds for all European nation-states—regardless of more superficial distinctions between their republican, ethnocultural, pluralist, or multicultural flavoring. Immigrants and ethnic minorities are among the most disadvantaged populations and hence particularly vulnerable to the nation-building prerogative of states, keen to offer inclusion but only when conditional on successful nationalization. It is, of course, significant that the most obvious opportunities for living out a truly post-national lifestyle via international mobility—for achieving personhood or agency beyond the nation-state—are very much stratified according to class and the privilege of Western national origin, in ways which make them largely inaccessible to the more disadvantaged migrants: disempowered refugees or migrants at the bottom of the economic hierarchy (Bauman 1998).

Even on this point, however, I would still caution any premature announcement of nation-state obsolescence. Blithely assuming the frictionless global or post-national nature of international elites itself underestimates the intense struggle going on among elites over the continued preeminence of the national in any definition of social power. There is a great deal of evidence that in many cases the old nation-centered elites are themselves quickly learning to adapt to the challenges of global mobility, to pre-empt any outflanking by post-national cosmopolitans, and ensure the reinforcing of national social closure and the power it bestows. My own research on the "middling" professional migrants attempting to benefit from free movement accords within the EU, suggests that even under such highly attractive legal conditions, the route to successful "normal" lifestyles and careers in foreign "global" cities is far from easy, when compared with the more conventional national paths to social mobility (Favell 2003a).

Neither this empirical caveat nor the absence of immigrant integration issues in the limited areas of competence the EU has asserted over immigration policy has deterred the globalists and post-nationalists. They made a series of over-hasty—and in some cases, false—claims about the internationalization of immigration politics, riding on the fad of globalization promoted by scholars from the mid- to late 1990s. For sure, there is much to be explored empirically on this question, but the evidence for internationalization so far is thin, and a nation-centered perspective on immigration politics would seem essential. The nation-state context is surely the first stop for any researcher looking for explanations of immigration policy development and change—in Europe and elsewhere.

Commentary

The De-nationalizing of the State and the Re-nationalizing of Political Discourse over Immigration

Saskia Sassen

The framing of an argument matters to its outcome. While both papers focus on the institutional insertion of immigration policy in the EU, a context where receiving countries are also members of a supranational entity, they differ radically in the framing of their arguments.

Favell frames his argument against a binary conception of the nation-state versus the EU. He wants to show us that there is little supranational and much national in the current European condition. In a direct frontal argument we would have Jacobson and Ruffer wanting to show us that the EU level is winning over the national level. But they frame their argument differently. Jacobson and Ruffer trace a particular *filiere* that bridges the EU and national levels: They argue that national immigration policy internalizes—willingly or not so willingly—supranational norms. Because this insertion occurs through the judiciary the individual immigrant emerges more forcefully as a rights-bearing subject than she would in the context of national politics where the immigrant as subject is largely subsumed in the immigrant population as a whole and immigration policy generally. Thus Jacobson and Ruffer detect a triangulation—member-states, the EU, and the role of the judiciary in connecting both—where Favell sees a binary.

I agree with many of the empirical observations in each paper. Where it gets trickier is in the interpretive moves in each. In this regard I will conclude this comment with what we might describe as a third interpretive position, one that can accommodate critical empirical elements contained in each of these papers, yet takes it all in another direction.

SEEING LIKE A STATE

Favell's paper is undoubtedly what we might think of as the majority or consensus position among scholars, not only on immigration in the EU but also generally on the relation of the EU and member-states. The author focuses on several conditions critical to the question of immigration and to his argument that states are the authoritative institutions in the EU generally and regarding immigration and post-immigration integration specifically.

Important to the logic of Favell's argument is that he positions this continuing weight of the nation-state as a "contest over nation-centered versus post-national or global perspectives on immigration politics." In his analysis the state wins hands down even after decades of growth in EU institutions. He reviews multiple conditions and trends, mostly familiar ones, to support his argument. Let me single out some of those I consider particularly important as they point to a dynamic interaction which, I would argue (though Favell does not), can accommodate questions of change and unstable meanings, subjects I will return to at the end of my commentary. First, "many of the powers and institutions created at the European level" are the result of "the fairly conscious 'rescue' of the nation-state in Europe, via the carefully legislated pooling of sovereignty over selective issues." Second, in the arena of immigration policy, "nation-states have learnt to use the EU in order to devolve control functions 'up, down and out' to render state functions more effective: up to supra-national institutions and law, down to regions and local actors, and out to private companies." In the arena of immigration policy, nation-states devolve control functions to make states more effective. Third, politicians insist in their speeches and political work that national states control immigration policy. All three of these are indeed present in the EU.

More problematic is Favell's characterization of the view he is contesting—variously referred to as the global, postnational, transnational, and/or European Union perspectives. It is not clear whom he is referring to generally in his assertions. Let me just quote a few of these. "Globalists fall into the Parsonian trap of holistic thinking, projecting a worldwide gestalt change in the global system." "Transnational, global, or post-national explanations" posit that "all observed changes or developments at the national level end up being explained by functional changes at the world system level." "The general post-national and global arguments that refer to examples from the EU . . . have been more or less successfully refuted with specific case material from the European context." "The absence of immigrant integration issues in the limited areas of competence the EU has asserted over immigration policy, has [not] deterred the globalists and post-nationalists. They made a series of over-hasty, and in some cases false, claims about the internationalization of immigration politics" and "the idea of a transnational economy overrunning state control of policy."

I am trying to think who among scholars in the many disciplines now working on these non-nation-centered perspectives is represented by these types of assertions. I cannot think of anyone in political science, or sociology, or economic geography, or anthropology, or political economy. The only ones who come to mind are the business writers such as Ohmae and Wriston, who to some extent engaged in boosterism of the global sort. It is always troubling when a scholar of the quality of Favell, whose book on philosophies of immigration (1996) I admire, creates strawmen to defend an argument. But enough said on this: It is well established by now that the images Favell trots in have long been discredited in the scholarship of most pertinent academic disciplines.

When Favell names specific scholars, there is some misrepresentation. My apologies for repeating what has already been said many times in the scholarship and should not require repeating. All I ask is more precision in the reading of a text. Let's stop circulating the misrepresentations of Soysal's (1994) arguments. She explicitly says that the national state matters. Similarly with Jacobson's (1996) much misrepresented book: his argument is far more complex than the either or that Favell posits.[1] Finally, while the misrepresentations of Soysal and Jacobson can be put partly in the realm of interpretation, in his more "precise" statements Favell turns out to be flatly incorrect: thus he asserts that in my 1996 book I make some sort of globalist argument that the national state is finished. This misrepresents even the title of the chapter on immigration, titled "Immigration Tests the New Order." I examine and use immigration precisely because it is a complex instance where the global makes evident its limits and its embedding in the national, which is, of course, the same analytics I used in developing my global city model. It is very clearly not, as Favell posits, an either-or analysis.

TRACKING EUROPEAN UNION NORMS INSIDE NATIONAL STATES

Jacobson and Ruffer argue that we are seeing a complex shift in the locus of the individual as a result of the ascendance of the judiciary in the Europeanization of rights. They find that this shift and the role of the judiciary take the current condition beyond the common interpretation of tensions between the EU level and its national member-states. In this tracking they inevitably enter the state apparatus and begin to discern differences. They see the struggle between the judiciaries and the executive and legislatures as a struggle between an increasingly individual centered form of the political and the state's republican national project. The authors find that the growing role of the judiciary in this process is predicated in good part on the increasing density of the law, which promotes rights and prerogatives. The judiciary mediates and adjudicates this web of law, at both national and regional

levels, both for domestic and international law. In this shift toward the judiciary the authors see the rise of a form of agency that is individual centered.[2]
Further, Jacobson and Ruffer find much significance in the transfer of the coordination of immigration policy from the third pillar in the EU to the first pillar: "Legal provisions emanating from the third pillar are not part of community law; they are norms regulated by public international law. In contrast,
legal instruments emanating from the first pillar become part of European
Community law and are binding on each member-state." Moreover, given
that "individuals have the legal capacity to invoke first pillar laws and bring
them to bear against member-states, the changes of the Amsterdam Treaty
may give the judiciary, here the European Court of Justice, more control over
immigration policy." Similarly, the now formal commitment of the EU to human rights under the Amsterdam Treaty may enhance the ECJ's authority in
such matters over member-states.

These and several other changes examined by Jacobson and Ruffer, do
give us a different perspective not just on the relation between the EU and
member-states but also about how to construct an object of study that allows
us to go beyond the binary EU–nation-states still common in much of the
scholarship on the EU. I would want to differentiate the authors' tracking of
the changing role of the judiciary from the two interpretive moves in the paper: the strengthening of individual agency and the "dilution" of national citizenship, at least in its traditional republican sense. When it comes to interpreting the implications of the changes they track, one might posit that there
are other ways of doing so.

CONCLUSION

It is not easy to juxtapose these two papers. In this paper at least, Jacobson
and Ruffer are not functioning within the EU–nation-state binary. Their paper is thus less argumentative than Favell's and is, so to speak, protected
from the familiar impulse of strawmaning the opposite argument. They basically track and document in considerable detail and with great care a particular development. In a way these two papers are talking past each other.
Thus when Favell, for instance, asserts that "immigrant rights in the courts
have been implemented because of nationally rooted norms of democratic
fairness and not because of the ostensible new dimension of supranational
law" he is partly wrong in positing that this goes against what authors such
as Jacobson and Ruffer posit because one of their arguments is precisely the
insertion of international norms inside national institutions, where they become part of national law. It is not an either/or. The second problem is the
level of generality in Favell's argumentation compared with the details and
specific focus of the Jacobson and Ruffer paper.

On the role of the judiciary in inserting supranational norms in national law, Jacobson and Ruffer are on solid ground when one examines the legal scholarship on the subject. The filtering of supranational norms into national law can take many forms.[3] For instance, to mention just one of the more recalcitrant EU members, in 2000 the UK incorporated the bulk of the European Convention of Human Rights into domestic law.[4] The fact that national systems are critical for the expansion of rights is not necessarily incompatible with the growing weight of international norms in national courts and in national law. Many of the legal scholars who actually have the technical knowledge and the erudition about these shifts would argue that one of the novel processes is the filtering of non-national norms into national law. Positing matters as an either/or is far less valid today than it was even ten years ago. The last decade has seen very significant changes, not only in the EU but also in a country like the United States, one of the most closed and "nationalist" in the world—as Favell correctly observes. Even the U.S. Supreme Court has in the last few years acknowledged that it needs to consider international and foreign law—two very different types of law—in its interpretations. Specifically, when it comes to human rights norms, the United States has seen sharp growth in the use of these norms in national courts, and it has seen the federalizing of these norms through rather informal processes that make these norms part of customary practice, eventually enabling their federalization—their becoming national law.

While I have confined myself here to the human rights regime given the Jacobson and Ruffer paper, there is a far larger case to be made: Multiple different types of international law are becoming part of the fabric of national law, both through legislative law making and through use in judges' interpretation. In my reading of where we are at, there is a whole new research agenda that is not concerned with the familiar binaries of European (or global) versus national states.[5] What we need is detailed and precise tracking of the sort that Jacobson and Ruffer offer us in their paper, whether or not one agrees with their interpretations.

Even as I can agree with Favell's general notion that the member-states are the most important actors in the EU, I would want to examine to what extent there has been significant institutional transformation within these states. Some of the dynamics described by Favell implicitly acknowledge what we all know: that states have had to adapt to, learn about, and absorb EU norms in order to stay in play. He interprets this as showing the overwhelming power of the nation-state over the level of the EU: the state uses the EU. But this begins to read a bit like state capture not only of the EU but also of Favell's analysis. Should we not raise the question as to how this capacity of the state to use the EU has in fact transformed the state. Here Jacobson and Ruffer offer us an insight that Favell does not. Close examinations of the institutional insertions of the immigration question are precisely what we need in order to understand the complex and often micro shifts that are taking place in the regulation of immigration and in the construction of the immigrant as a rights-bearing subject.[6] Yet I do find in Favell's analyis, though he may disagree with this, the elements for such a more complex third position: Thus when he posits that the state has adapted and learned, he is implicitly acknowledging the possibility of a rather dynamic interaction and a far more ambiguous power relation that the simple notion that if the national is involved in this process of adopting non-national norms, it must mean that it wins. In other words, why not take that vast literature focused on what is the self evident status quo in the EU and subject it to more dynamic interpretations, allowing for the presence of changes even if they are not fully legible?

The point is that the EU is a process in the making, and it has been so for over half a century. Let us also recall that many scholars asserted with great conviction that a monetary union was impossible in the near future, and when the euro was eventually established, they asserted that it was going to fail. I would rather emphasize the work, the institutional innovations, the practices, the discursive domains: given the weight of nation-states, the remarkable condition is the fact of Europeanization, not the ongoing weight of nation-states. These types of changes are partial, highly specialized, or particularized, not all encompassing. The state is too powerful an administrative capacity to do without. But that does not mean that the state does not change, including the possibility of foundational change in its structures.

From my perspective one of the foundational transformations lies in the extent to which a good part of the Europeanization project inhabits and gets structured inside the complex institutional apparatus of the state. It does so often dressed in the language of the national. We need to inquire to what extent the dynamics and policies emphasized by Favell, and so many others, need to be decoded rather than taken at face value: even though formulated as national might they have little to do with the national as historically constructed. Such an analysis is at the heart of how I have researched the global over the last fifteen years, and, I admit, I find it far more useful (2006). For the purposes of some of the critical issues at hand in these two papers, it would seem to me that we need to keep asking what is the analytic terrain within which to examine the question of rights rather than fall into the binary of EU/nation-state. We need to examine the tension between the de-nationalizing of economic space and the re-nationalizing of political discourse in most of the member countries when it comes to immigration. We cannot assume that the re-nationalizing of politics indicates that not much has changed in the position of the state. Immigration provides a crucial nexus in this dynamic in that it often becomes the main and easiest target for this re-nationalizing of politics. But it also brings to the fore the contradictory role of the state in this particular period. The state itself has been transformed by its participation in the implementation of laws and regulations necessary for the denationalizing of economic space. We cannot ignore this and simply focus on re-nationalized political discourses about immigration. Insofar as the state remains the main actor when it comes to immigration, its internal transformation should be part of the analysis.

NOTES

1. Both authors say that the state continues to matter: Jacobson finds the bureaucratic role of the state enhanced by the growing weight of international regimes. Soysal sees nation-states as declining but certainly not disappearing because she argues that the transition to human rights is partial. Soysal, Yasemin Nuhoglu. 1994. *Limits of Citizenship: Migrants and Post-National Membership in Europe.* Chicago, IL: University of Chicago Press. Jacobson, David. 1998/9. "New Border Customs: Migration and the Changing Role of the State." UCLA Jnl of Intl. Law and Foreign Affairs, Vol 3: 443–463.

2. The authors note that the Treaty of Amsterdam formalized measures to extend the rights of citizens and sought to improve accountability and participation in the institutions of the EU. Further, in a significant departure from the past, the Treaty called for enforcement of non-discrimination principles within member-states, and opened the channels of communication not just to address issues such as gender inequality, discrimination, public health, and consumer protection but to enforce these rights through the European Court of Justice.

3. This includes established scholars, such as Harold Koh, Undersecretary for Human Rights in the Clinton Administration and now the Dean of the Yale Law School, one of the leading experts in the world on human rights (Koh, Harold Hongju. 1997. "How Is International Human Rights Law Enforced?" *Indiana Law Journal* 74: 1379). It is not possible to develop this critical issue in such a short comment, but I have an extensive analysis in Sassen, *Territory, Authority, Rights: From Medieval to Global Assemblages* (Princeton, NJ: Princeton University Press, 2006: chapters 5 and 6). In another domain—international law concerning the global economy—my model of the global city does that for all kinds of financial and economic requirements.

4. The British Parliament adopted the Human Rights Act of 1998 in November of 1998; it became effective in the UK in October 2000.

5. Examples of research I find path-breaking in this domain are Knop, Karen. 2002. *Diversity and Self-Determination in International Law.* Cambridge, United Kingdom: Cambridge University Press; Rajagopal, Balakrishnan. 2003. *International Law from Below.* Cambridge: Cambridge University Press; and Ong, Aihwa. 1999. *Flexible Citizenship: The Cultural Logics of Transnationality.* Durham, NC: Duke University Press.

6. There are a number of research efforts that seek to capture how what we think of as national may well be a far more complex and ambiguous condition. For instance, the question of the localizing of citizenship, which also can function as a qualification on the national/global or national European duality (e.g., Rogers, Alisdair and Jean Tillie, eds. *Multicultural Policies and Modes of Citizenship in European Cities.* Aldershot: Ashgate, 2001). On the other end of the spectrum is the effort to track the extension of the national state beyond its confines: for instance, an emphasis on various transnational processes and dynamics that arise with colonialism, a process in which states are involved, thereby overriding the duality of global versus transnational (e.g., Doomernik, Jeroen and David Kyle, eds., 2004. "Special Issue: Organized Migrant Smuggling and State Control: Conceptual and Policy Changes." *Journal of International Migration and Integration.* Vol. 5, no. 3 (Summer)).

II

DETERMINANTS:
ECONOMY OR POLITICS?

3

Economy versus the People? Swiss Immigration Policy between Economic Demand, Xenophobia, and International Constraint

Etienne Piguet[1]

INTRODUCTION: CONFLICTING EQUILIBRIUMS

The first article of the fundamental legal Swiss text on immigration[2] mentions two "equilibriums" which the law should target: an "equilibrium" between the size of the population of Swiss nationality and that of the foreigners and an "equilibrium" between demand and supply on the labor market. Although the meaning and levels of these equilibriums are not clearly stated, these potentially contradictory aims point to a fundamental question of migration studies: What are the driving forces behind immigration policies?

The following paper will try to bring elements of answer to this controversial question through an analysis of fifty years of immigration to Switzerland. Our central thesis is that governments trying to formulate an immigration policy are usually caught between economic demands on one side and the fear of popular xenophobia on the other. For reasons which will be detailed further on, we consider the case of Switzerland as exemplary for showing in which direction these two factors have exercised their influence, which of them has been decisive, and to what extent other factors have contributed to the determination of the policy. Among those other factors, we shall consider changes in the balance of power of internal politics, international relations, social climate, the subjective representations of the different actors of immigration policy, etc. Our second thesis is that the factors we have just mentioned have evolved a lot during the period, for instance the economical interests, to which we shall give a specific attention, have fragmented from a simple claim for open door policy to more contradictory and sectorial demands. Interests that were contradictory in the past might thus converge towards new alliances, which explain turns in immigration policies.

Methods, Theory, and Limits of the Study

The present discussion will be focused on immigration policy in a narrow sense of "admission policy" putting aside "integration policies" or "immigrant policies" (Hammar 1985).[3] A further restriction is that we shall focus mainly on "non-humanitarian" immigration: Asylum policies and the admission of contingent refugees (Wimmer 1996) will be mentioned as contextual, but without further analysis.

On a theoretical level, the aim of this article is to contribute to a general model of migration policy formulation. More generally, we shall contribute to two on-going debates: Do immigration countries constitute specific ethno-national models of immigration or variations of a common liberal democratic immigration regime (Freeman 1995)? To what extent can a country afford a certain margin of autonomy concerning immigration policy and to what extent is it committed to follow international trends (Jacobson 1997; Joppke 1998a; Soysal 1994)?

On the methodological side, our contribution follows the lines of Actor Centred Institutionalism (Scharpf 1997) as we consider immigration policy as the product of both the institutional frame and the play of different actors. Considering the kind of data at our disposal, we cannot offer a systematic test of our hypotheses about the explaining weight of different factors, but our historical survey allows us to get an insight of the general process of policy formulation.

Our first section will explain why Switzerland constitutes an interesting laboratory for studying immigration policies and immigration in general. In the following sections, we shall make a chronological description of Swiss immigration policy since 1948 with an attempt to isolate the main changes and their explaining factors.

SWITZERLAND, A CASE FOR MIGRATION RESEARCH

With one-fifth of the population foreign-born—a figure twice as high as classical countries of immigration such as the United States or Canada—Switzerland constitutes an interesting case of diversity and conflict around immigration. From an emigration country during the eighteenth century, it turned to an immigration country at the end of the nineteenth. After World War Two, Switzerland relied massively on foreign workers and implemented a "guest-worker" system. Although many of these workers ultimately returned to their country of origin a significant part of them settled down: Without immigration at all since 1950, the population of the country would be five million instead of seven (Piguet 2005).[4]

The Swiss case is interesting for our aim to evaluate the driving forces behind immigration policies while, in spite of the absence or moderation of most of the problems other European immigration countries were confronted with—such as high unemployment rates of migrants, ethnic segregation, and social unrest (Mahnig 1999)—the immigration issue has almost constantly occupied Switzerland's political agenda for fifty years. At the same time, the system of "large coalition" government has imprinted an important continuity and "readability" to Switzerland's immigration policy, without sudden changes due to new majorities in parliament.

At the same time, many experiments and "trial and error" attempts have been made. This gives us a kind of *sample of policy measures* that can be seen as our "dependant variable" and then linked with the evolution of the main forces hypothetically shaping the policy.

Additionally, we argue that some of the "independent variables" explaining the policy are also somewhat easier to analyze in Switzerland. This is particularly the case concerning the effect of democracy and the public opinion: In contrast to other important immigration countries such as Germany, the United Kingdom, the United States, Canada, Australia, etc., direct democracy gives the Swiss citizens the opportunity to express their opinion on every change made to the immigration policy and even to impose changes unintended by the central government. The analysis of these popular consultations allows us to appreciate the people's impact on the policies.

The recent history of Swiss immigration policy can be divided into five periods. After a first period of open-door policy following the war (1948–1963), growing popular xenophobia forced the Swiss government to try and curb the immigration of manpower (1963–1973). The oil crisis of 1973–1974 opened a third period and created a sudden and dismal consensus between anti-immigration movements and the economy as tens of thousands of immigrants lost their jobs and had to leave the country. In a fourth period (approximately 1980–1992), the economy recovered its role as the main driving force of an important new wave of immigration, but a general complexification of the context of immigration led to a fifth period of incertitude, conflicts, and attempts at a complete re-foundation of immigration policy, which is still going on.

FIRST PERIOD: THE "FREE ENTRY" POLICY

At the end of World War Two, Switzerland faces an acute lack of manpower: Its production infrastructure has not suffered from the war and can respond

to an important domestic and international demand on goods. In 1948, the
Swiss government signs an agreement with Italy concerning the recruitment
of manpower. This agreement marks the beginning of a period of intense immigration. The postwar economic boom being expected to last only temporarily, the immigration policy aims at a "rotation" (turning) to prevent immigrants from staying permanently (Hoffmann-Nowotny 1985): About one
half of the workers entering Switzerland every year are seasonal workers allowed to stay during a nine-month period without their family.

From 271,000 persons in 1950 (5.8 percent of the total population), the
number of foreigners living in the country climbs to 476,000 in 1960 (9.1 percent) (see figure 3.1). During this period most of the foreign population in
Switzerland is of Italian origin (59 percent in 1960). A first important feature
of the policy is the hypothesis, by the Swiss government, that immigration is
not due to last a long time and that immigrant are and should stay temporary
sojourners. After having earned a certain amount of money, they will leave
the country or should be encouraged to do so. The Federal Council acts then
with the official motto that "there is no objection to an inflow of foreigners at
the condition that they don't intend to settle in the country."[5] The agreement
of 1948 with Italy is a direct expression of this conception as it imposes a
threshold of ten years of work before Italian workers can get a permanent residence permit (Cerutti 1994).

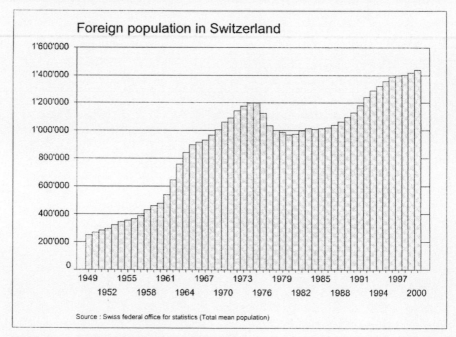

Figure 3.1.   Foreign Population in Switzerland

Considering the high level of unemployment in Italy, the Swiss economy can expand with virtually unlimited access to foreign workers. In industry, the inflow of workers allows Swiss manpower to migrate to more rewarding activities in the tertiary sector: Between 1950 and 1960 the number of Swiss industrial workers diminishes by 117,000 while the number of foreigners increases by 118,000. Foreign workers are also welcome in large numbers in the building sector (80,228 in 1960).

During this first period, it is clear that the needs of the economy have been the most important criterion for the elaboration of the immigration policy.

SECOND PERIOD: GROWING XENOPHOBIA

At the beginning of the sixties, the liberal admission policy of "workers rotation" is subject to growing criticism. First, the rising rate of inflation is seen as a consequence of the additional demand by foreign workers for goods and services (Jöhr and Huber 1968). Second, the level of xenophobia is growing among the public opinion; third, the Italian government is increasingly critical against the poor condition of settlement offered to its 400,000 nationals and tries to obtain a better agreement for family reunification, length of stay, medical insurance, and unemployment benefits. This leads to a general pressure on the government, which tries for the first time to limit immigration.

The "Simple Ceiling"

From 1963 onward, Swiss immigration authorities attempt to implement a restrictive policy whereby residence permits are issued to foreign workers only if their employer refrains from recruiting too many workers: The total number of Swiss and foreign employees of a company has to remain stable or experience a maximum 2 percent annual growth. The idea is that immigration must compensate only for the foreigners who have left the country. This policy aims at limiting immigration while, at the same time, halting uncontrolled economic growth and inflation.

Employers react with hostility toward this measure, which is seen as a barrier to economic development: Instead of using immigration to promote an increase in employment supply, which could lower salaries and prices, the government is trying to reduce the supply in order to reduce growth.

The results of the simple ceiling are disappointing: five months later, 50,000 new foreign workers are recorded, a 7 percent increase. In reaction, the government prescribes, in February 1964, a 3 percent reduction in the total number of employees as a prerequisite for any new authorization to employ immigrants. But once again, these measures do not have the desired effect and the number of foreigners increases of 30,000 (4.5 percent) by August 1964. The inefficiency of that policy is due to the significant number of Swiss workers who changed employers during this period, shifting from the secondary to the tertiary sector. Secondary-sector companies then replaced them with foreigners without increasing the total number of their employees. A second reason why this policy was ineffective stems from the federal organization of the country, which gives the cantons the choice to grant exceptions and to relax control in enforcing the immigration legislation.

This situation does nothing to lessen the xenophobic tendencies of a part of the population. These are further strengthened when Italy, by means of an agreement (10 August 1964), is granted improved conditions for its residents in Switzerland. Italian workers who have resided for at least five years are granted the right to change jobs and to establish indefinitely. Seasonal workers who have worked in Switzerland for five consecutive years are entitled to an annual residence permit, and the waiting period for family reunification is reduced from thirty-six to eighteen months. These improvements go against the ongoing attempts to limit foreign labor but are justified from an economic point of view, maintaining the capacity of the Swiss economy to compete on the international market by keeping it attractive for immigration (Cerutti 2005).

These changes however create turmoil in the Swiss public opinion and trigger a mediatic battle. In the eyes of a large section of public opinion, the Federal Council is simply a puppet depending on the will of the Italian government. The agreement signed is seen as a decision increasing the threat of "overforeignization" (Misteli and Gisler 1999). To dissipate these fears, the Federal Council firmly states that the immigration limit has now been reached and that it shall make sure that no more new growth of the foreign workers population shall occur.

The situation is further complicated by the emergence of a xenophobic movement on the political scene. On June 30, 1965, the first people's initiative "against foreign penetration," supported by 60,000 signatures, is submitted.[6] This initiative calls for changes in the constitution so that the number of foreigners would be reduced to 10 percent of the resident population (at this time, 15 percent of the resident population in Switzerland are foreigners).

The Federal Council agrees with the action committee, that "the significant increase in the number of foreigners over the last few years" constitutes "a serious danger of foreign penetration" (Feuille fédérale 1967, 109). At the same time, however, it considers that the requested measures—the number of foreigners should be reduced by about 260,000, among which 200,000 workers—could not be borne by the national economy. The Federal Council sees the initiative as excessive and advises the voters to reject it. It announces once again that it will take the necessary steps to reduce the number of foreigners. Swiss authorities are therefore committed to find new ways to curb immigration.

The "Double Ceiling"

Seeking to find an efficient means to reduce the foreign population, the Federal Council decides, in February 1965, to create a double ceiling of immigration: Employers have to reduce their stock of foreign workers to 95 percent and are not allowed to increase the total number of their employees. In addition, the ways to circumvent these rules by way of exceptions are strictly reduced. A second new measure makes compulsory for every foreigner to hold a permit of abode before starting to work in Switzerland. This is an important measure, which goes against the wishes of the economy. Before that date, it was tolerated that foreign workers could enter Switzerland to find a job and regularize their situation only after a few months of work (Feuille fédérale 1965).

However, the double ceiling produces unintended outcomes: It limits the *total* number of workers and therefore breaks the development of the most dynamic companies. Geographic mobility being reduced for foreign workers, flourishing companies don't even have the opportunity to try and recruit foreign workers from neighboring cantons. Peripheral and less dynamic companies are thus artificially protected against competition. The Swiss government is quite aware of the phenomenon, but no other solution seems at hand. Being the only country in Europe that tries to curb immigration at this

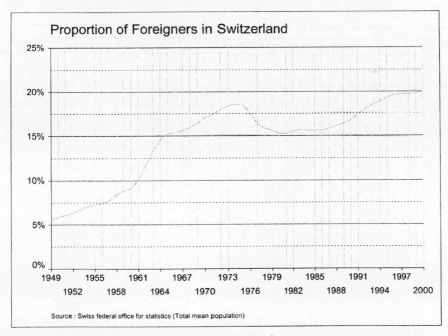

Figure 3.2. Proportion of Foreigners in Switzerland

time, Switzerland cannot use the experience of its neighbors and finds itself in a situation of policy innovation in a kind of *trial and error* (Niederberger 1982, 60). The attempts at a ceiling for the number of workers at the enterprise level are therefore prorogated in 1966, 1967, and 1968 without great success. The proportion of foreigners in the population continues to grow (see figure 3.2).

The "Global Ceiling"

The ongoing growth of the foreign population is perceived by a large part of the population as a failure of the Federal Council and gives rise to a growing crisis of confidence. In May 1969, a second popular initiative against "overforeignization" is launched with 70,000 signatures. This initiative, named after its instigator, James Schwarzenbach, is even more restrictive than the first one and adopts an overtly xenophobic turn: In no single canton shall the share of foreigners trespass the 10 percent mark (a single exception being Geneva where the limit is set to 25 percent to protect its status as an international city). Additionally, no Swiss citizen shall be fired from his job as long as foreign workers occupy similar jobs in the company (Feuille fédérale 1969, 1051), and family reunification shall be severely reduced. The Federal Council opposes the initiative by arguing that it would violate international agreements and that it is in contradiction with the European Declaration of Human Rights. Additionally, it considers that the adoption of the initiative would have a very negative impact on the economy and even force several enterprises to close their doors (Feuille fédérale 1969, 1072).

The Federal Council is nevertheless under pressure from public opinion to make a further move to decrease the foreign population. For this reason, three months before the vote on the initiative, it imposes a new annual quota system for immigration: the global ceiling. This model is based not on the foreign workers' share in the economy but on the total foreign population of the country. In a public announcement, the government seeks to assure the population that this new system is the guarantee of a future and efficient limitation of the foreign population. Preceding the aims of a popular initiative is exceptional in the Swiss political history (Niederberger 1982).

The vote of June 7, 1970, is considered one of the most important in recent Swiss history: 74 percent of the electorate participate, which is a record, and the media coverage compares to the largest sport events. The result is very tight: The Schwarzenbach proposal is rejected by 54 percent of the voters; it is accepted in seven of twenty-three cantons. The Federal Council has won but is now bound by its promise to reduce immigration.

With the Schwarzenbach initiative, Switzerland has passed close to a major political crisis. Even if the initiative had been rejected, it marks a turn in immigration policy with the adoption of annual admission quotas for foreign workers.[7]

Although, the xenophobic initiative has been refused, the majority of the population, afraid of excess immigration, is clearly the winning party of the last match over immigration policy. At the same time, many authors see the government and especially the administration as having instrumentalized the initiative in order to impose on the economy a quota solution, which they considered for a long time as the only realistic one (Niederberger 1982, 87; Mahnig and Piguet 2003). The economy and especially the activities that are heavily dependent on foreign workers are clearly the losers of the new compromise between the actors of immigration policy. Following Hoffmann-Nowotny (1985): "It is quite correct to say that the introduction of the global ceiling . . . was not dictated by economic interests at all. It was instead the result of grassroots pressure based mainly on the issue of overforeignization."

By imposing quotas, the government contradicts strongly the free-market policy, which had dominated the fifties and the sixties. The new system gives birth to a negotiation procedure involving the local administrations, the economy, and the trade unions.[8] It aims at a fair repartition of immigration among regions and activities. This procedure has been qualified as neo-corporatist (Cattacin 1987), because it confronts divergent interests concerning immigration and gives a large place to informal contacts and lobbying. To calm the anger of the most heavily hit economic activities, those of peripheral regions and those which rely heavily on foreign workers, the Federal Council maintains the limitation of internal migration against foreign workers: They have to stay at the same employer for one year after their arrival, and for three years they are not allowed to changer their canton of work or their profession (Niederberger 1982).

Did the Swiss government manage to impose the new system and finally curb immigration? The first years of the quota policy give a nuanced balance sheet: On the one hand, the annual immigration of workers drops from 70,000 in 1970 to approximately 50,000 in 1971, 1972, and 1973. On the other hand, during the same period, the number of seasonal workers, though limited to 152,000, overruns to 200,000 because of a lack of federal control on the cantons. Federalism remains an important obstacle for a restrictive national policy.

Another factor is problematic for the new immigration policy: the international context and, more precisely, the action of the Italian government. The agreement signed in 1964, which entitles the seasonal workers a permit of abode after five years of continuous work, is at the heart of the problem. Because of that mechanism, an inflow of seasonal workers is soon transformed into an inflow of immigrants and contradicts the aims of the new policy. When the Swiss government had attempted to postpone these automatic transformations, the Italian government had reacted quite roughly, threatening to suspend the recent free-trade agreement with the EEC. Switzerland is therefore for the first time bound by its international agreement not to push too far its quota policy. For this reason, but also because of family reunification and a high rate of birth, the foreign population living in Switzerland continues to rise, from 1,059,000 (17 percent of the mean residing population) in 1970 to 1,175,000 (18.4 percent) in 1973.

The pressure on the government remains quite high. The anti-foreigners movements, which are not included in the annual negotiation process over the immigration quotas, circumvent the disadvantage by using again the threat of direct democracy. In November 1972, a third initiative "against foreigner domination and Switzerland overpopulation" is launched. It aims at reducing the foreign population to 500,000 before the end of 1977. To counter that initiative, the government follows the same strategy as it did four years before: It tries to convince the population that the current policy has no alternatives and that the initiative would have catastrophic economic and diplomatic consequences. On October 20, 1974, voter participation is again very high at 70 percent, but the initiative is clearly rejected.

After that new victory, would the Swiss government have been able to keep the promises of the campaign? History does not tell. After years of fighting, the first oil shock will lead to a sudden consensus of nearly all the actors of the immigration policy.

THIRD PERIOD: THE UNEXPECTED CONVERGENCE

At the beginning of 1975, the consequences of the first oil shock hit Switzerland with full force. Although the recession starts later than in other countries, the share of lost jobs is the highest of all the Organization for Economic Cooperation and Development (OECD). Between 1974 and 1977, 15.8 percent of jobs are suppressed in the industry and about 10 percent in the national economy as a whole. Many foreign workers, especially Italians, move back to their country of origin. The number of foreign workers with B or C permits regresses by more than 100,000, the number of seasonal workers by a similar amount. The absolute number of foreigners in the country decreases for the first time since World War Two and the share of foreigners in the total population drops from 18 to 16 percent. The explanation for this is quite simple: At this time, a large part of the foreigners living in Switzerland were entitled only an annual work permit and had no right to unemployment benefits (Schmidt 1985). Through the non-renewal of the permits of unemployed foreigners, the administration gave the economy the opportunity to reduce its work force without increasing domestic unemployment. Considering a total job loss of 340,000 during the period, 228,000 (67 percent) concerned foreign workers.

Switzerland managed therefore to use foreigners as a "conjuncture buffer" for the economy while simultaneously reaching the old goal of reducing the foreign population.[9] At this moment, Switzerland constitutes a unique case of a strict guest-worker system in the sense outlined by Freeman (1986, 59).

At the end of the seventies, the aim of stabilizing the foreign population in Switzerland has been reached thanks to the international recession and without any of the political actors being disadvantaged against the others. The drop in the absolute numbers satisfies the anti-immigration lobby and the majority of the population, while the economy appreciates the opportunity for reducing manpower in a time of recession.

The consequences of the oil crisis shall maintain the stability of the foreign population up to the beginning of the eighties. The old conflict about immigration is nevertheless not over and will become more and more complicated.

FOURTH PERIOD: THE OLD TRACK AGAIN

At the beginning of the eighties, a new actor steps into the immigration policy formation: the pro-immigrants movements. Left-wing politicians and trade unionists form a large share of this movement. They acknowledge the general aim of limiting the foreign population but ask for more solidarity with the immigrants once they are in the country.[10] They use the same weapon as the anti-immigration lobby to influence the immigration policy: direct democracy. A popular initiative is then launched to promote a complete equality between settled foreigners and Swiss citizens. The length of stay will not be limited anymore and the seasonal status—considered as inhumane because of the impossibility of family unification—will be abolished.

The initiative gives birth to an important new conflict between the actors of the immigration policy. The employers who rely heavily on seasonal workers, such as the building, catering, and agricultural sectors, hold the initiative as a dangerous threat and are strongly opposed to it. The Swiss government holds a similar line considering that an unlimited right to family reunification would threaten the global ceiling policy. More generally, unlimited work permits for foreigners are seen as a danger for the native workforce, who should remain privileged against foreign workers.

The vote on the initiative takes place in April 1981. The initiative is massively rejected by 84 percent of Swiss voters. The solidarity movements obviously have not managed to convince the population. This result, however, is not a sign of the return to glory of the anti-immigrant groups. The oil shock episode and the reduction of the foreign population has in fact largely demobilized the advocates of a closed-door policy and anti-immigrant groups support by the population has heavily declined: Two anti-immigration initiatives have thus been clearly rejected in 1977 (see table 3.1).

Table 3.1. Anti-immigrants Popular Initiative in Switzerland

4 October 1968	Initiative "Against foreign penetration"	(abandoned)
7 June 1970	Initiative "Against foreign emprise (Schwarzenbach)"	refused (54%)
20 October 1974	Initiative "Against foreign emprise and Switzerland overpopulation"	refused (65.8%)
13 March 1977	Initiative "To protect Switzerland"	refused (70.5%)
13 March 1977	Initiative "To limit the number of naturalization"	refused (66.2%)
4 December 1988	Initiative "Against overforeignization"	refused (67.3%)
24 September 2000	Initiative "For a regulation of immigration"	refused (63.8%)

The failure of the solidarity movement as well as the marginalization of the anti-immigration groups give rise to a new balance of power in the immigration policy arena, which is very favorable to the economy. At this time, considering the economic recovery of the beginning of the eighties, the needs of this party are clear: abundant immigration to maintain cheap salaries, but fragile permits to retain flexibility in case of a new crisis. Even if the global ceiling is officially maintained, the administration gives a comprehensive ear to the claims of the economy: During the eighties and nineties, 40,000 new working permits a year will be given. Facing a drain of traditional immigration source countries such as Italy and Spain, Switzerland will rely more and more heavily on Yugoslavia and Portugal. Just like in past periods, the new immigrants are dispatched on the basis of negotiations between the different regions of the country and between different economic branches. This situation will continue over numerous years.

Clearly, this period can be interpreted as a return to power of traditional economic local and sectorial criterion for the formulation of immigration policy, the federalist system allowing the local economy to find benevolent ears for their demand among local politicians and civil servants. Progressively, though, many evolutions will undermine this policy.

FIFTH PERIOD: SAND IN THE MACHINE

Three developments will progressively impose a deep re-discussion of the Swiss immigration policy. The first is the growth of the constraints of the international context. The second is the transformation of immigration motives. The third are the integration difficulties encountered by the foreign population in the Swiss society.

The Changing International Context

In the course of the eighties, the traditional emigration countries of Southern Europe experienced a marked economic growth, which reduced the number of their emigrants. In a good position to negotiate with competing immigration countries, they managed to substantially improve the situation of their nationals abroad. In 1989, under pressure from the Spanish government, the minimum length of stay necessary to obtain a long-term residence permit in Switzerland is reduced from ten to five years for Spanish workers. One year later the same is done for the Portuguese, who are now treated the same way as Italians since the agreement of 1964. This situation accelerates a phenomenon of stabilization of the foreign population, which had started already at the end of the seventies. In 1970, the share of permits limited to one year was 70 percent in the active resident foreign population with 30 percent of permits being long-term. In 1990, long-term permits reach 75 percent. Additionally, as the whole foreign population is now granted unemployment benefits, the margin of the government to adjust foreign population to the economic conjuncture by not renewing annual permits disappears. These changes rigidify considerably the whole immigration system.[11] The function of "conjuncture buffer" of the foreign manpower is no more than a souvenir. The economic interest of strong immigration in a period of growth thus decreases heavily because of the risk of a surge in unemployment in case of a downturn.

A second change linked to the international context is the growing isolation of Switzerland in regard to the European integration process. This situation starts to be perceived as a major stake in the Swiss political arena. According to pro-European circles, Switzerland should strengthen its links with Europe and concludes a free-circulation agreement. Such an agreement would put an end to the guest- and seasonal workers system still supported by a large share of the economy. Anti-immigration circles fear that such an agreement would lead to a massive inflow of foreign workers due to the extremely low level of Swiss unemployment. Many experts reject this last hypothesis (Straubhaar 1984; Dhima 1991b), but it influences heavily the political and popular debates and gives a new strength to xenophobic and nationalist movements. The relationship with the EU thus becomes one of the most polarizing questions of Swiss national politics during the nineties. Immigration is central in a debate that does not follow the traditional cleavages of the past. For the first time the economy appears strongly divided between those who favor more openness toward Europe and those who prefer to keep the flexibility offered by the guest-worker system (Mahnig 1996).

A third change has to do with the influence of international law on the margin of action of the Swiss government regarding migration. This factor had played only a minor role in the past. However, it takes more and more importance as shown by three examples:

- Free movement inside the country: The Fourth Protocol to the European Convention of Human Rights allows every legal immigrant to choose freely his place of residence in his immigration country.[12] Such a liberty is not granted by Switzerland to seasonal and annual workers, which puts the country in the difficult situation of being one of the few countries not able to sign the protocol.
- National preference: The U.N. International Convention on the Elimination of All Forms of Racial Discrimination, ratified by Switzerland in 1994, gives more strength to claims concerning the selectivity of Swiss immigration policy.
- Asylum: International norms concerning asylum[13] and especially the "Non-refoulement" provision embodied in many declarations ratified by Switzerland compel the country to accept a new form of immigration whose economic advantages appears weak,[14] the asylum seekers (Gibney 2001).

Because of the evolving international context, Swiss immigration policy loses a lot of the flexibility it had in the past. It also loses specificity and has to adapt its choices to common international norms.

Diversification of Immigration Motives

A second evolution has to do with immigration motives. It has to be remembered that annual quotas of immigration refer only to workers and have no direct influence on other forms of immigration. At the beginning of the seventies, a large majority of the immigrants were indeed workers, but the proportion of non-occupied persons (renters and people coming through family reunification) grows progressively since then: In 1991, the share of non-occupied immigrants entering Switzerland each year passes 50 percent. This evolution undermines the effectiveness of the quota policy. It also dissociates the volume of the flows from the needs of the economy because these new forms of immigration continue during economic downturns.[15] From a migration mainly determined by manpower demand (pull migration), Switzerland evolves then gradually toward a migration determined by supply (push migration) and disconnected from the needs of the economy (Zimmermann 1996).

A new category of immigrants, not submitted to the quota system, takes additionally more and more weight: the asylum seekers. From a few thousand a year at the beginning of the eighties, the number of asylum requests climbs to more than 35,000 in 1990 and 41,000 in 1991. The government faces important difficulties in dealing with this rapid growth. It denounces the existence of "false refugees," while at the same time does not manage to speed up the processing of asylum requests and the execution of the decisions. This situation leads to a loss of credibility of the asylum policy and of all the immigration policy in the public opinion, offering the xenophobic movements a new battleground. Although many reforms of the asylum policy intend in the following years to restrict access to the asylum procedure, this question becomes the center of all the debate on immigration policy (Parini 1997).

Diversification of Origins and Integration Difficulties

The third evolution, which tends to alter the context of elaboration of the immigration policy, is the growing impression of an "integration problem" among the foreign population. This perception does not stand on very solid empirical grounds and is mainly diffused by popular medias and opportunistic political movements. One of the few empirically documented aspects of the phenomenon is the growing difficulty faced by several foreigners' groups on the labor market. The foreigners' unemployment rate grows rapidly during the economic downturn of the middle nineties: In December 1996, the unemployment rate of Swiss citizens is 3.7 percent while it hits 10.8 percent for foreigners. It varies from 1.6 percent for Northern European citizens to 7.8 percent for Italians, 11 percent for Portuguese, 17.3 percent for Turks, and 21.3 percent for people originating from the former Yugoslavia.[16] This situation reinforces a growing sentiment of dissatisfaction toward immigration policy.

A Policy in Crisis

The three evolutions we have just traced impose a severe turmoil on Swiss immigration policy: The annual quota set every year seems unable to offer any more suitable compromise between the aim of containing the foreign population and giving enough flexibility to the economy. The interests of the economy, clearly oriented in the past toward an open-door policy, are getting more complex. Several branches still ask for an immigration of low-qualified and low-paid foreign workers, but these workers meet growing difficulties on the labor market as soon as they try to change their activities or region of work. The growing share of the foreign population entitled to a long-term residence permit has the consequence of increasing the welfare and unemployment cost of immigration for the whole economy. Numerous enterprises would therefore prefer to target a highly qualified immigration. Several scientific studies go in the same direction and criticize strongly past immigration policies. According to these studies, the inflow of low-qualified foreign workers imposes a burden to the economy and, on the long run, constitutes a bad choice for the national economic interest as a whole. According to economics professor Thomas Straubhaar (Straubhaar and Fisher, 1994), "All in all, the economic benefits of the Swiss labor-market immigration policy remained insignificant." The arrival of new actors, the immigration experts, in the political arena is quite new in Switzerland and will have an influence on the balance of power by increasing the weight of the national economy as a whole against sectoral and regional interests.

Trying to answer to these new stakes, the Swiss government will explore three directions of reform, two of which will be experimented with and then partially abandoned, and a third being chosen for the future immigration policy.

THE QUEST FOR A NEW MODEL

The Proposal of a Global Migration Balance

Since the middle of the nineties, in reaction to the growing flow of asylum requests, several actors have made the proposal to merge the traditionally distinct asylum and immigration policies. In January 1989, a governmental working group had already made that proposal, under the title "Strategy toward a refugee and asylum policy for the nineties" (Interdepartementale Strategiegruppe 1989). Their central argument is that the reasons for migration are nowadays too complex to distinguish between economic and political migration motives. Predicting that migration toward Europe is bound to increase in the future, they propose to set once and for all the total number of foreigners who should live in Switzerland. On that basis, a migration balance would be calculated every two years. In case of an inflow of refugees or an upsurge in family reunification, the number of workers admitted would be decreased and vice versa.

This proposal can be seen as an attempt to generalize the old model of a global ceiling by applying it not only to foreign workers but to the whole foreign population. It gives more weight to the objective of fighting "overforeignization" against economic aims.

This proposal will fail to be implemented for two reasons: First, it cannot guarantee to satisfy the needs of the economy, even concerning highly qualified manpower (for example, in the case of an inflow of refugees). Second, this policy imposes a quota on refugees and family reunification that might contradict many international commitments of Switzerland. The failure of this proposal illustrates the growing importance of the international context, this time with the alliance of economic interests.

Cultural Distance as an Admission Criteria

Swiss authorities quickly realize that the implementation of a global migration balance is impossible. In another report, published in 1991 (OFDE 1991), representatives of the federal administration attempt once more to conciliate two contradictory aims: liberalizing migration within the EU while at the same time paying attention to the fear of "overforeignization" expressed by a large share of the population. Their proposal will be called the "three circles model." A first geographical circle includes the EU and European Free Trade Association countries and should benefit from free circulation with Switzerland. A median circle includes the United States, Canada, and Eastern European countries. These countries are considered "culturally close" and should benefit from immigration opportunities according to the needs of the economy. Finally, the citizens of an "external circle" grouping all other states should not be able to migrate to Switzerland except in very specific cases. This proposal is based on the idea that the number of immigrants alone does not lead to a xenophobic sentiment among the national population but that the "cultural distance" between immigrants and natives does.[17] It is therefore possible to admit more EU nationals provided that the number of people coming from more distant regions is strictly limited.[18] This proposal is reminiscent of the old ethnic selection policies practised by the United States and Australia but will be accepted by a large proportion of the Swiss political forces and implemented immediately at the beginning of the nineties. It can be considered a new compromise between the demands of the economy, the pressure of anti-foreigners groups, and a new international context.

Very soon, the three circles model has a direct impact on immigration patterns: In September 1991, the Federal Council relegates Yugoslavia—a traditional immigration country of the eighties—to the third circle. The citizens of Yugoslavia are thus not allowed to immigrate to Switzerland anymore, although 50,000 of them still work as seasonal workers at this time. These workers have to leave at the end of the year and will not be allowed to come again. This decision meets a strong but unsuccessful opposition from trade unions—by solidarity with Yugoslav workers—and from the hotel and catering industry where most of them are employed. The fact that this last group is not able to influence the decision is a symptom of the loss of power of this economic actor. In contrast with the sixties, activities with low levels of added value and capital intensity are no longer considered representative of the interests of the Swiss economy as a whole.

The three circles model will operate for several years but will quickly be under attack from two new fronts. A first critic shall come from the multinational corporations, industry, and the high-tech branch of the economy. These very internationalized activities wish to recruit their highly qualified manpower worldwide, without circles of geographical limitations. A second critic comes in 1996 from the Federal Commission against Racism created after the ratification by Switzerland of the U.N. Convention on the Elimination of Racial Discrimination in 1994. On the basis of a juridical expertise, the Commission considers the selection of a third circle as discriminatory (Auer

1996). Although it refutes the argument, the government is bound to form a new expert commission to elaborate proposals for an immigration policy. Once again, the international context and part of the economy have undermined the attempts at limiting migration.

The "Australo-Canadian" Model Based on Levels of Qualification

The report of the new commission is published in August 1997 (Commission d'experts en migration 1997). Its main proposal is to suppress the three circles model and to replace it with two systems: free circulation within the EU and an admission model based on a "point system" for the rest of the world. The point system, which is inspired by Australia and Canada's systems, should select the most qualified immigrants on the basis of their school achievement, professional experience, language competencies, etc. (Wimmer 1997).

In 1998, the Swiss government follows its experts and officially abandons the three circles model. It nevertheless refrains from adopting a formal point system and simply affirms that the level of qualification will be the main criterion for granting immigration permits to people from outside the EU. The situation therefore is that of a two circles model, as a bilateral free circulation agreement with the EU is applied progressively since June 2002. The asylum policy remains clearly distinct from general immigration policy. Fast-track procedures and an alignment of asylum procedures on the neighboring countries are hoped to be sufficient to keep the number of asylum seekers under control and avoid the asylum question that inflames the whole immigration debate.

With the setup of a two circles model based on qualification, the old dilemma of Swiss immigration policy—to limit xenophobia while responding to the needs of the economy—is resolved with a new solution: The needs of the whole economy will not be limited anymore by way of quotas but will be restricted to the European supply of manpower. Enterprises needing highly qualified manpower will be able to prospect worldwide. The implicit hypothesis of the new system is that these new forms of immigration will remain of modest size and will not generate hostile reactions in the public opinion.[19]

CONCLUSION

Our review of fifty years of Swiss immigration policy brings numerous interesting elements to the debate on the foundations of such policies in Western countries. The diachronic approach allows us to weight the influence of different actors and throws light on a clear evolution of the factors affecting the policy.

The Needs of the Economy: A Necessary But No More Sufficient Condition

The needs of the economy constitute a preponderant driving force of the Swiss policy. Even if other factors such as xenophobia have played a central role, too, it stems from our analysis that the economic situation has always been the determinant of the concrete practices of opening or closing the immigration door. Although numerous attempts have been made to limit the foreign population during the sixties, the high conjuncture has always prevented the government from reaching that goal. It is only when the economic situation experienced a severe downturn following the oil shock in the middle of the seventies that the previously non-economic aim of reducing the number of foreigners has been reached. During the following years, the periods of economic boom of the eighties and nineties have lead each time to important growth in the foreign population.

It must be admitted at the same time that the link between economic conjuncture and migration has progressively lost its strength.

First, the Swiss immigration system has been less and less able to respond with enough flexibility to economic demands. During the seventies, it had been possible to send back home tens of thousands of foreign unemployed. More recently, the stabilization of residence titles imposed by international context has not allowed such flexibility, and immigration has taken a character of irreversibility. The economic interest of immigration, especially for low-qualified jobs, has therefore decreased.

Second, the economy cannot be considered a homogeneous actor in the immigration debate. Recent developments have given more and more weight to those economic actors who benefit from high levels of productivity and international competitiveness. On the contrary, the needs of local enterprises of the tourist sector, construction, or agriculture have lost a large part of the influence they had thirty years ago. For the government, the definition of the "national economic interest" has clearly shifted from the aim of satisfying equitably the manpower demands of all economic sectors and regions to the aim of privileging the more competitive activities.

Xenophobia: A Constant But Always Mastered Background

The fear of foreign "overpopulation" is a constant of the Swiss immigration policy and constitutes probably its most specific feature. Direct democracy gives it a concrete impact as populist parties have at all times the opportunity of trying to block the government action by putting to the vote a maximum ceiling of foreign population or any other policy measure. Such attempts have been made seven times during the period. It is therefore clear that grassroots movements and xenophobia had a major influence on the formulation of the Swiss political discourse in general and that immigration would have been stronger if the government had not constantly monitored the level of xenophobia and had simply followed the open-door policy suggested by the economy.

At the same time, the Swiss government always managed—mainly by invoking publicly the interests of the economy and by taking strong commitments to curb immigration in the future—to prevent xenophobic attempts to fully reach their goals. During the past fifty years, the Swiss electorate has acknowledged no single anti-immigrant popular consultation although the share of foreigners in the Swiss population rose nearly continuously. Symmetrically, attempts by pro-immigrants groups at improving the situation of foreigners in Switzerland also failed when it came to the popular vote.

In conclusion, the Swiss political system gives immigration policy a very strong importance in the public debate and constantly puts the government under pressure. It is, however, not obvious that it has had a major concrete impact on the levels of immigration of the past fifty years. The *vox populi— vox dei* system does not make Switzerland such a different case from the other liberal democratic immigration countries.[20] Economic demand as well as, with more and more strength, the international context remains a far more important explanation.

The International Context: A Growing Constraint

The international context has had numerous impacts on the Swiss immigration policy. In 1964, Italy managed to obtain substantial improvements for its citizens in negotiations between Switzerland and the EU. On a multilateral basis, Switzerland has been implied in numerous international conventions and agreements having to do more or less directly with immigration.[21] The study of the last fifty years shows, however, that, until a recent past, this external influence on the immigration policy itself has been limited in comparison to the effect of internal policy consideration.

Recently, however, the international context has imposed itself on Switzerland in at least three very concrete ways: First, Switzerland has had to grant much more long-lasting immigration permits to keep its immigrant attraction in a context of drying traditional sources of migration. This had as a consequence an important loss of flexibility. Second, the will to get closer to the EU led to the suppression of the seasonal worker status and to a free circulation agreement. This true revolution regarding the past immigration policy implied a loss of control and flexibility. Third, the extension of international norms of right has progressively narrowed the margin of freedom concerning the control and management of immigration especially in the humanitarian and asylum realm.

The New Alliance

The constellation of factors, which characterizes the Swiss immigration policy at the beginning of the twenty-first century, is quite different from the past century. From a clear opposition between the interests of the economy as a whole and the popular fear of "overforeignization," the situation has shifted toward a new alliance. The dominant fraction of the economy as well as a majority of the population that is hostile to massive immigration have agreed to a new policy of free circulation in Europe but to a strict selection of highly qualified immigration from the rest of the world. This compromise should allow supplying most of the economic needs while protecting against uncontrolled flows from non-European immigrants (Mahnig 1996). Several sectors of the economy and the extreme wing of anti-immigration groups are neglected in that compromise, but they lack the strength to counteract.

It is on the international scene that antagonistic forces can now be found that could put the new policy in danger. The evolution of the international law imposes to a growing extent policies which neither the national economy nor a majority of the population would have chosen. Anti-immigration groups have been quick to realize that new threat: More than immigration policies per se, it is nowadays the Swiss participation in the international system that is their target.[22]

At the end of our analysis, our central thesis that governments trying to formulate an immigration policy are caught between economic demands and the fear of popular xenophobia is confirmed by the Swiss case. The evolving economic interests remain dominant, although somewhat losing strength during the period. The old antagonism between these two dimensions has been narrowing constantly and a new important determinant of Swiss policy is now the international context. It imposes on the country a margin of autonomy that, although still substantial, is getting smaller. Our hypothesis is that these main features and trends are common to many other immigration countries. In that sense, Switzerland, contrary to its frequent auto-definition, is not a *Sonderfall*[23] anymore.

This research has benefited from a grant of the Swiss National Science Fund (National Research Program 39).

NOTES

1. This article wouldn't have been possible without the research conducted with Hans Mahnig (1966–2001) on Swiss immigrant and immigration policies. We are very much indebted to him.

2. "Ordonnance limitant le nombre des étrangers" (OLE) from 6 October 1986. *Stricto sensu*, the fundamental legal text concerning immigration is the Federal Law of Abode and Settlement of Foreigners (*Loi fédérale sur le séjour et l'établissement des étranges* (LSEE)) of 1931, but it's the OLE which gives the policy it's directions and aims. Switzerland know three main categories of permits for foreigners: the Permit of Abode valid for one year (B), the Permit of Residence (C), and the Seasonal Permit valid for nine months. These permits serves as both work and residence permits.

3. An analysis of Swiss integration policy (or absence thereof) has been conducted by Mahnig and Wimmer (Mahnig and Wimmer 2003). Their central thesis is that four factors explain to a large extend the specificity of Switzerland to this regard: federalism, municipal autonomy, consociational direct democracy, and the specific character of Swiss national identity. In other research, Mahnig has argued that it is only when they are viewed as a threat for social cohesion that immigrants' integration appeared on the public agenda (Mahnig 1999).

4. It is therefore very surprising that Switzerland remained until recently what Hoffmann-Nowotny called a "non-immigration immigration country" (1995), persisting to see immigration as a temporary epiphenomenon and failing to encourage the participation of immigrants to the society.

5. As stated by Mahnig and Wimmer (2003): "The Swiss immigration regulation goes back to the prewar period: In 1931 the Federal Law of Abode and Settlement of Foreigners (*Bundesgesetz über Aufenthalt und Niederlassung der Ausländer*— ANAG) was enacted. It can be regarded as a "police law" aimed at border control and the defence of the national territory, profoundly inspired by the international political context of the time, the economic crisis, and widespread xenophobia. Xenophobia during this period was directed against what was called "overforeignization" (*Überfremdung*), meaning a situation where society had become "strange" to its own members because of immigration and establishing a causal link between the number of foreigners and the threat of Swiss identity.

6. The Swiss political system makes it possible for citizens to submit a request for a change to be made in the constitution, accompanied by a sufficient number of signatures. "Initiatives" of this kind must be put to the vote of the whole population. This system allows the population to become directly involved in government decisions. It is an important weapon for populist groups (Kriesi 1982).

7. An indication of how seriously the government intends to exercise that control is the creation of the "Central register of foreigners." It represents at this time the most onerous statistical database used by the administration (Haug 1980, 127).

8. The parliament remains on the contrary quite absent in the discussion on migration policy (Dhima 1991a, 153–196).

9. During the same period, the unemployment rate in Switzerland rose by only 0.7 percent. On that basis, numerous authors have advocated the these of an "unemployment export." For Kuhn (1978, 218), it is clear that the good performance of Switzerland regarding unemployment during the crisis is due to the flexibility of its immigration policy. The same argument can be found by Haug (1980, 9), Bruno and Sachs (1985, 221), Masi and Henry (1996) as well as Schmidt (1985, 62). The causal link between the emigration of the foreign workers and the amplitude of the recession is nevertheless contested by Kohli (1979) and Lambelet (1994) who argue, in a

Keynesian way, that the departure of foreigners induced a severe diminution in demand for goods and services which worsened the recession.

10. For a general discussion, see (Giugni and Passy 2004).

11. An empirical confirmation of that diminution of flexibility can be found by observing the evolution of the correlation between unemployment rates and the variation of the foreign population. During the period 1971–1980, the coefficient was strongly negative, indicating that a growth in unemployment had for consequence numerous foreigners leaving the country whereas during the period 1981–1997, this correlation disappears (Piguet and Mahnig 2000, 37).

12. Protocol No. 4 to the Convention for the Protection of Human Rights and Fundamental Freedoms of September 16, 1963, article 2: "Everyone lawfully within the territory of a State shall, within that territory, have the right to liberty of movement and freedom to choose his residence."

13. Among others, the Universal Declaration of Human Rights (Art. 3, 5, 14) and the 1967 Protocol to the Refugee Convention.

14. Asylum seekers contribute to enlarge the supply of manpower especially in low-qualification sectors, but their occupational rate remains low and many are supported by welfare benefits (Piguet and Ravel 2002).

15. This is, for example, briefly the case during the middle of the nineties.

16. Sources: Secrétariat d'Etat à l'Economie

17. The emergence of "cultural distance" as a central concept of Swiss immigration policy coincides with its diffusion in the Swiss scientific discourse on migration. The concept is used in a normative way by one of the most renowned researcher on immigration, the sociologist Hans-Joachim Hoffmann-Nowotny (1992). The adoption of that concept has, at this time, met no explicit opposition from other Swiss academics, the only theoretical critique coming from an Australian scholar (Castles 1994).

18. The presence of ethno-cultural stereotypes in the formation of the Swiss immigration policy is not new, and Swiss authorities have always preferred geographically close countries (Rohner 1991, 3–5). But the three circle model is the first that states explicitly the link between "overforeignization" and cultural distance.

19. On September 24, 2000, the Swiss population rejected clearly (63.8 percent) a new popular initiative intending to lower the share of foreigners in the population to 18 percent. This result comforted the government in the chosen way. A detailed description of the new policy and of the opinions of the different political forces and representatives of the civil society can be found in an extensive report (Département fédéral de justice et police 2001). For a scientific commentary, see Wimmer (2001).

20. It seems that a similar statement can't be generalized to *immigrant* policy (Mahnig and Wimmer 2003).

21. For an inventory, see (Fibbi and Cattacin 2000).

22. The recent adhesion of Switzerland to the U.N., ratified by a popular consultation, shows however that—just as it was the case for immigration—managing to put a theme on the national debate agenda is not sufficient to influence concrete choices.

23. German term frequently used in Swiss political discourse to design a supposed irreducible specificity of the country.

4

Immigrants, Markets, and the American State: The Political Economy of U.S. Immigration

James Hollifield, Valerie F. Hunt, and Daniel J. Tichenor

INTRODUCTION

Politics and national states are assigned at best a marginal role in most theoretical scholarship on immigration flows (Hollifield 2000; Portes 1997). According to the economic logic of push-pull, changing economic conditions (demand-pull and supply-push) in sending and receiving countries by and large dictate levels of immigration in countries like the United States (Martin and Midgley 1994). Likewise the sociological literature on immigration stresses the growth of transnational, informational, and kinship networks, which facilitate cross-border movements (Massey, Alarcon, Durand, and Gonzalez 1987; Sassen 1996; Portes 1996).

Since there has been a virtually unlimited supply of migrants ready to cross international borders during the past century (a more or less constant supply-push), most adherents to the economic model contend that shifting economic demand for immigrant laborers in receiving countries primarily determines immigration flows (a variable economic pull). Major shifts in the volume of immigration are thereby driven by the labor market demands and the business cycles in receiving countries. At the same time, the economic model assumes that government actions designed to control immigration are of little or no explanatory importance. Either policy interventions by national states merely rubber-stamp labor market demands and the business cycle, or they have no effect because they defy these determining economic forces (Simon 1989).

Sociological theories of immigration to some extent replicate the basic microeconomic logic of push-pull but with the major innovation that

international migration is heavily dependent on the development of informational and kinship networks between the sending and receiving communities (Massey, Alarcon, Durand, and Gonzalez 1987; Portes 1996;
Massey, Durand and Malone 2002; Sassen 1988, 1996). Neither economic
nor sociological arguments leave much room for the state or public policy
as major factors affecting immigration flows.

Our research on immigration to the United States demonstrates the independent effects of policy change on immigration flows. Employing a time-
series model that enables us to separate economic and political effects on
immigration to the United States from 1891 to 2003, we find that *both* government policy interventions and changing U.S. economic conditions have a
significant impact on immigration flows. In particular, our model suggests
that shifts in unemployment and gross domestic product (GDP) had a sizeable and significant effect on levels of immigration until 1945. During the
postwar years of 1946–2003, however, the effects of unemployment and
GDP on immigration flows weaken over time while the impact of government interventions significantly increase.

These findings, we argue, are supported by considerable evidence that
federal policies, which significantly influenced immigration flows after World
War Two, won important support from national political officials whose
goals reached well beyond the demands of the labor market or business cycle. Against the backdrop of Cold War competition, executive and congressional officials after 1945 came to view immigration control as an important
instrument for advancing American foreign policy objectives (Tichenor
2002). Anti-communism animated contending immigration policy camps in
the late 1940s and 1950s. Congressional isolationists successfully defended
biased national origins quotas and established new ideological exclusions in
the early 1950s, despite economic conditions that were conducive to large-
scale immigration. By contrast, internationalists in the White House and Congress expanded refugee admissions and ended Asian exclusion in order to
enhance American power and prestige abroad.

By the 1960s, New Frontier and Great Society reformers dismantled restrictive national origins quotas in the name of advancing racial justice and
equal rights. Immigration reform in 1965 expanded alien admissions to re-
unify families, to provide haven for refugees fleeing communist regimes, and
to offer new immigration opportunities for ethnic and racial groups long dis-
criminated against in American immigration law. During the 1980s, new reforms more dramatically expanded immigration. They were propelled by an
unlikely coalition of liberal lawmakers, who embraced human rights and
ethnic fairness in national immigration policy, and free-market conservatives
in Congress and the executive branch, who saw immigration restriction as
antithetical to "regulatory relief" and open markets. Finally, the federal courts
became increasingly active after the 1960s in protecting the due process

rights of aliens in admissions, asylum, and deportation proceedings (Schuck 1998). The development of American immigration policy in the postwar era, then, captures changing U.S. economic conditions as often less consequential than policy interventions by various actors of the national state. Indeed, as we shall see below, national officials at times have promoted immigration policies that run counter to economic trends in the United States.

The strong impact of changing U.S. economic conditions on immigration flows before 1945 and the larger significance of state actions in subsequent years underscore the need for greater theoretical balance in the scholarly literature on immigration. In the pages that follow, we first will examine U.S. immigration trends from the late nineteenth century up to 2003 in light of labor market dynamics and the business cycle. This discussion highlights the inadequacy of economic and sociological factors alone in explaining U.S. immigration over the past century, especially during the postwar era. We then consider efforts by the American national state to regulate immigration and speculate on their possible independent influence on American immigration.

Glaringly absent from the immigration literature, we argue, is a model of immigration flows to the United States that incorporates the effects of both economic change and policy interventions. The next section presents the findings of a time-series model we have constructed to separate economic and political effects on U.S. immigration. Finally, we argue that our model improves on the prevailing economic and sociological models in three respects: (1) it incorporates economic *and political/policy* effects in a manner that distinguishes their relative influence and provides a stronger overall account of immigration flows; (2) it is more useful for understanding the restrictionist turn in American politics in recent years and its potential to substantially curtail immigration in the future; and (3) it is far more promising in accounting for not only the volume of immigration but its composition as well. We conclude by suggesting avenues for future research.

IMMIGRATION TRENDS, LABOR MARKETS, AND THE BUSINESS CYCLE

Most immigration analysts simply presume or assert that immigration flows to advanced industrial democracies have long been a function of market forces, as defined by the economic supply-push of sending countries and the economic demand-pull of receiving countries (Martin and Midgley 1994:21; Simon 1989). While supply-push factors in sending countries undoubtedly influence immigration flows, an unflagging supply of migrants have been ready to cross national borders when opportunities have presented themselves in receiving countries throughout the past century. As a result, changing economic conditions in receiving countries are assumed to have the greatest effect on immigration. Martin and Midgley, for instance, neatly capture these theoretical predilections and findings in much immigration research. Their work aims to show that the number of immigrants who have come to the United States over time has fluctuated largely with economic conditions. Such assumptions are not reserved to academic circles; they abound in popular discourse and in the media. Popular magazines and newspapers like *The Economist* and *The Wall Street Journal* have observed that immigration to the United States is best understood as a function of changing economic conditions.

But what specifically has been the relationship between immigration, labor markets, and the business cycle in the United States? Do the actions and policies of the American state have any independent influence on immigration? In particular, have interventions by the state had a significant effect on immigration flows, if we control for changing economic conditions? A good starting point for addressing these questions is to review immigration trends and economic demand-pull factors in American history from 1890 to 2003.

Figures 4.1 through 4.4 depict trends in legal immigration to the United States, percentage change in real GDP, and fluctuations in the unemployment rate. Immigration decreased from about 600,000 per annum in 1892 to 250,000 by the end of the decade. This decline coincided with the 1893–1897 recession, affirming the responsiveness of immigration flows to economic conditions.

Immigration rebounded strongly at the turn of the century, as did the economy, reflected in positive growth trends and shorter and shallower economic cycles (excepting 1908). Meanwhile in the labor market, unemployment rates were historically well below the average. In short, demand-pull factors were especially conducive, and immigration flows reached record levels. Indeed the foreign-born population of the United States climbed to 15 percent, an all-time high. No major immigration legislation was passed during this period, except for literacy tests imposed by Congress in 1917, restrictions that were rendered moot by the effects of World War One, which parenthetically abruptly ended the so-called third wave of American immigration.

In the interwar years, immigration revived but fluctuated markedly— perhaps in reaction to the volatile economic conditions of the "Roaring Twenties." The 1924 Immigration and Naturalization Act (also known as the Johnson-Reed Act) brought the nation's first permanent and sweeping numerical limits on immigration. These restrictive measures codified the national origins quota system, writing racial bias (in favor of Northern and Western Europeans) into law (King 2000). The new measures also introduced skill-based, human capital criteria into immigration policy for the first time. Nevertheless, countervailing economic forces, for example, low unemployment, apparently dampened the effects of the 1924 act. The migration mix began to shift away from Europe and toward the Western Hemisphere, with Canadians and Mexicans making up the largest number of newcomers.

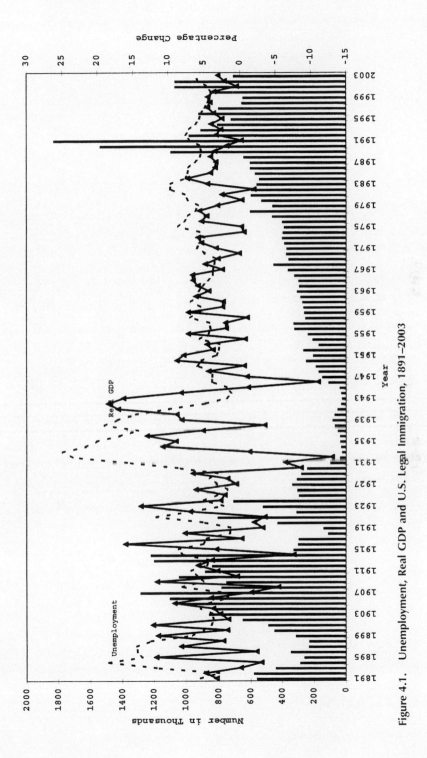

Figure 4.1. Unemployment, Real GDP and U.S. Legal Immigration, 1891–2003

The onset of the Great Depression in 1929–1930 demonstrates quite clearly the powerful effect of business cycles on immigration flows in the pre-1945 period. Demand-pull forces ceased virtually overnight, as the economy shrank and unemployment soared (see figure 4.1). Annual immigration remained markedly low during the economic hard times of the 1930s.

The recovery of the American economy during World War Two led to a rapid decline in unemployment rates and a surge in GDP, but no real increase in legal immigration. Adherents of the push-pull model can account for these outcomes by emphasizing the anomalous and exceptional effects of global warfare that cut off the United States from traditional sources of immigrant labor. Tellingly, various U.S. employers turned to Mexican and Central American guest-workers to address growing labor market demands—a trend that was codified in the 1942 Bracero program that continued until 1963 (Calavita 1992).

As a way of further illustrating the relationship between immigration and the business cycle during the period from 1890 to 1945 bivariate correlations were calculated. These reveal no significant association between percentage change in real GDP and immigration flows; however, there is a correlation ($r = -0.425$; significant at 0.01 level) with changes in the unemployment rate. This suggests that immigration was sensitive to demand-pull forces, even though the overall performance of the American economy (in terms of national income) had less effect in this regard.

During the postwar years of 1945 to 2003, we see in figure 4.2 that immigration has slowly trended upward for virtually the entire era, producing the so-called fourth wave in the 1970s and 1980s. The United States is now well into the fourth great wave of immigration in its history. Strikingly, immigration flows did not expand markedly in the early 1950s (1950 and 1952 witnessed declining immigration numbers) despite significant increases in GDP and new lows in unemployment—economic conditions deemed conducive by the economic push-pull model to increased immigration. Just as intriguing is the gradual increase in immigration during the 1970s and early 1980s, a time when unemployment levels were rising in connection with the two oil shocks and the steep recession that followed. U.S. immigration, however, began to soar in the late 1980s amid declining unemployment and fluctuating GDP, whereas sharply rising immigration continued unabated in the 1990s despite increased unemployment and substantial drops in GDP.

If we look at simple bivariate correlations for the postwar period (1946–2003), we again find no significant relationship between percentage change in GDP and flows. Although there seems to be a significant relationship between labor market performance (as measured by the unemployment rate) and immigration flows, the correlation (0.27, significant at the 0.01 level) is the opposite of what we would expect. How can we account for U.S. immigration trends over the past century that defy or elude the predictions of the economic push-pull model?

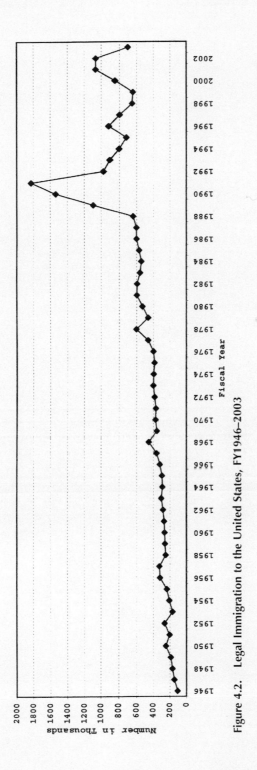

Figure 4.2. Legal Immigration to the United States, FY1946–2003

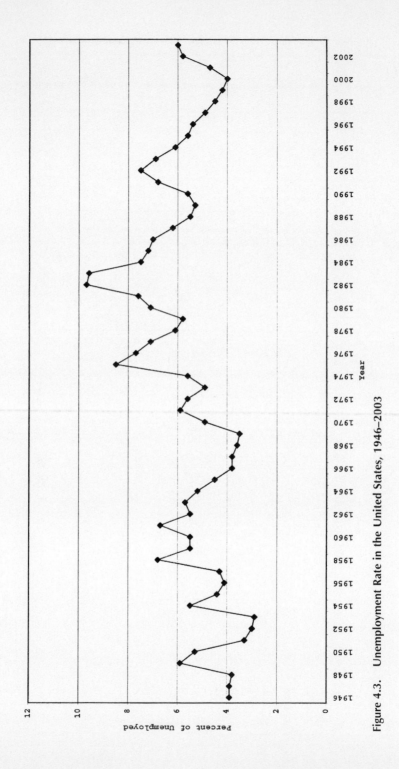

Figure 4.3.   Unemployment Rate in the United States, 1946–2003

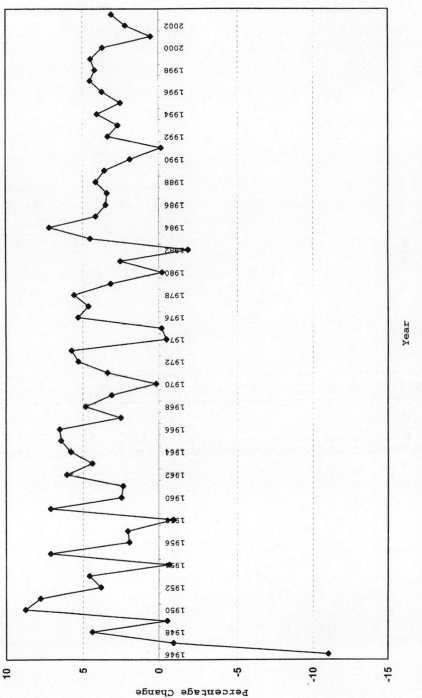

Figure 4.4.   Annual Growth Rate of U.S. National Economy (Percentage Change of Real GDP), 1946–2003

The influence of policy interventions by the American government on immigration, a subject to which we now turn may help us fill in some of these theoretical gaps.

IMMIGRATION AND THE AMERICAN STATE

From the 1890s through the Second World War, levels of immigration to the United States correspond closely with the performance of the American economy. Indeed, the time-series model we present in this section suggests that shifts in levels of unemployment and real GDP were among the most significant influences on annual immigration totals before 1945. Yet even as the traditional push-pull model goes far in helping us to explain U.S. immigration trends before mid-century, the unprecedented activism of the national state in these decades had a marked effect on the nature of immigration flows. The dramatic decline of immigration during American involvement in the World Wars One and Two highlights the extent to which the U.S. government's pursuit of foreign policy objectives may profoundly transform migration trends. Moreover, if changes in the American labor market and business cycle before mid-century go far in helping us to explain *how many* immigrants were admitted in these years (immigration volume), they do not help us understand significant shifts in *who* was granted entry during these decades (immigration composition).

For most of the nineteenth century, the U.S. federal government maintained an essentially laissez-faire immigration policy, with most regulatory authority devolving to states and localities (Hutchinson 1981; Schuck 1998; Hatton and Williamson 1998). When the national state first developed the legal and administrative means to regulate immigration in the late nineteenth century, its efforts to control immigration often were motivated as much by a devotion to ethnic and racial hierarchy as by a concern for the country's economic and national security interests (Smith 1997; King 2000). Against the backdrop of intense electoral competition during the post-Reconstruction period, congressional and executive officials of both parties clamored to curry favor with Sinophobic voters of the Far West by enacting the first Chinese exclusion laws in the 1880s (Sandmeyer 1973; Mink 1986; Daniels 1990; King 2000). During the interwar years, the economic impact of immigration figured prominently in the minds of national officials, and they wasted no time in slowing immigration to all but a trickle during the 1920s and 1930s. But the centerpiece of this period's restrictive immigration policies, a so-called national origins quota system, was deeply informed by a new scientific theory—eugenics—that reinvigorated old distinctions between desirable and unworthy immigrants on the basis of race, ethnicity, and religion (Higham 1985; Fuchs 1990a; Smith 1997; King 2000).

The new quota system was explicitly planned to favor Northern and Western European immigrants, and to exclude Asians, Africans, as well as Southern and Eastern Europeans. At the same time, Mexican migrants were viewed by most officials as a returnable labor force—due to a contiguous border—which could meet the nation's shifting demands for low-skill labor without making any permanent claims for membership in U.S. society (Reisler 1976; Calavita 1992). Until the 1960s, U.S. immigration essentially reflected these policy goals; Northern and Western Europeans made up most overseas immigration to the country, while Mexican and other Latin American newcomers were typically admitted as guest-workers subject to removal whenever their labor was not in demand (Garcia 1980; Ngai 2004). The American state's influence on immigration flows before 1945, then, captures not only its responsiveness to changing economic conditions but also its pursuit of foreign policy interests and ascriptive and hierarchic visions of racial order, which cannot be explained simply in economic terms.

Whereas shifts in the U.S. business cycle comport well with immigration trends before World War Two, they have diverged sharply on several occasions during the past sixty years. Despite an impressive postwar economic recovery, underscored by low unemployment rates and surges in GDP during the 1950s, the modest levels of U.S. immigration remained relatively stable. Immigration flows not only failed to keep pace with the postwar economic expansion as predicted by the push-pull model but in fact declined in the early 1950s. To understand declining immigration amid economic growth requires knowledge of how government policies shaped immigrant admissions independently of postwar economic developments. Although both the Truman and Eisenhower administrations called for more expansive immigration policies, their efforts were derailed by restrictionist committee chairs in Congress who vigilantly defended national origins quotas. During the early 1950s, anticommunist isolationists in Congress secured legislation that reaffirmed national origins quotas while constructing new immigration barriers intended to tighten national security (Tichenor 1994, 2002). In short, McCarthyism overshadowed economic growth in the immigration realm. Later in the 1950s, the Eisenhower administration took autonomous executive action to grant admissions above the existing quota ceiling not in response to changing economic conditions but to offer refuge to Hungarians and others fleeing communism.

The demise of the national origins quota system finally came with the enactment of the Hart-Celler Act of 1965, an event that was undoubtedly fortified by national prosperity. But reformers in the executive and legislative branches had far more than the economic utility of immigration in mind when they embraced a new visa preference system. In making immigration reform an important feature of the Great Society juggernaut, the White House and its congressional allies argued that discriminatory national origins quotas—like

domestic racial barriers—undermined American global prestige and influence amid urgent Cold War competition. Civil rights and foreign policy interests loomed large in immigration policy-making of the 1960s. The 1965 law
replaced national origin quotas with a new emphasis on uniting families, providing an unlimited number of immigrant visas to immediate family members
of U.S. citizens and most numerically limited visas to other close relatives of
citizens and the immediate family of permanent resident aliens. Remaining
visa slots were allocated to refugees and skilled workers. Policy-makers were
careful to stipulate that the 1965 immigration reform was strictly designed to
remove ethnic, racial, and religious biases from the immigration code—*not* to
expand the volume of annual legal admissions (Reimers 1992).

Although expected by its architects primarily to benefit European migrants,
the family-based system established in 1965 would spur unprecedented
Third World immigration to the United States as a result of unanticipated
chain migration during the next quarter-century. Whereas the Hart-Celler Act
contributed to a dramatic shift in the composition of U.S. immigration, it did
not substantially expand legal immigration; annual admissions increased
only incrementally during the decade following its passage (see figure 4.2).

Against the backdrop of economic stagnation in the 1970s, characterized
by high levels of inflation and unemployment, mass opinion strongly supported significant decreases in legal immigration (Fetzer 2000). Illegal immigration also drew attention as a prominent public policy problem. New calls
for immigration restriction and stronger border control were perfectly consistent with the economic logic of the push-pull model. Economic stagnation
and decline in receiving countries builds pressure for lower levels of immigration. Yet the push-pull model could not anticipate formidable political resistance from a number of strategically situated lawmakers and special interests, like the growers in California and the Southwest, who supported
large-scale immigration and who postponed policy action during economic
hard times by brokering support for a bipartisan commission to study immigration (Cose 1992; Freeman 1995; Joppke 1997; Tichenor 2002).

After several years of political stalemate, Congress finally enacted the Immigration Reform and Control Act (IRCA) in 1986 to address illegal immigration. Initially designed to discourage unlawful entries by severely penalizing
U.S. employers who knowingly hired undocumented aliens, the law's final
employer sanctions provision lacked sufficient teeth to meet its purposes.
IRCA's most significant legacy was an amnesty program that granted legal
status to record numbers of undocumented aliens residing in the country.
Troubled by the civil liberties violations and discriminatory effect of past deportation campaigns, national officials embraced amnesty as a more palat-
able policy solution (Tichenor 1994).

Even as illegal immigration continued unchecked and unemployment levels swelled in 1990, national policy-makers passed a measure, the Immigra-

tion Act of 1990, that expanded immigration admissions. Increasing annual visas for immigrants with family ties to U.S. citizens and permanent resident aliens, those with needed job skills, and those from countries disadvantaged under the 1965 preference system, policy-makers defied the push-pull model in 1990 by substantially expanding legal immigration opportunities despite an important economic downturn (Schuck 1992). Increased public concern regarding both legal and illegal immigration did prompt national policy-makers to consider restrictive immigration measures. In 1996, Congress came close to passing a bill that would have significantly scaled back annual legal immigration against the backdrop of robust economic growth and scant unemployment. In the end, however, the 1996 Illegal Immigration Reform and Immigrant Responsibility Act (IIRAIRA) targeted immigrants (both legal and illegal) through the mechanism of welfare reform. Thanks to the intense lobbying efforts of high-tech industries, such as Intel and Microsoft, legal immigration levels were left unchanged, while new measures were adopted to curtail illegal immigration. Apart from increased border controls and a small pilot program to force employers to check the legal status of workers before hiring them, the main impact of the IIRAIRA was to cut Aid to Families with Dependent Children (AFDC) and Supplementary Security Income (SSI) for legal immigrant residents—cutbacks that were, at the insistence of the Clinton administration, eventually restored for certain groups of resident aliens.

The consequential interests and actions of the American state concerning immigration more than occasionally have transcended the economic predictors of the push-pull model, as well as straight interest-based explanations à la Freeman (1995). Reducing U.S. immigration levels to a basic economic causality or to a strict interest group dynamic is inadequate in both explanatory and predictive terms. We gain little, however, by denying the powerful influence of changing domestic economic conditions over immigration. Rather, it is far more promising to consider the relative importance of economic and political forces. To understand and distinguish the influence of economic forces and government actions on U.S. immigration requires us to develop a preliminary (multivariate) model that incorporates the two.

A NEW IMMIGRATION MODEL

Toward this end we constructed a time-series model that enables us to separate economic and political effects. The results of the analyses are presented in tables 4.1 through 4.3. We used the log of immigration flows (the dependent variable) in our models in order to meet the model requirements of linearity and stationarity. We then calculate an impact range from the coefficients of each predictor variable by multiplying the coefficient by the highest and lowest value of that variable. This impact range allows for a greater ease of interpretation and discussion of the model results. Both the coefficients and the impact range are reported in the tables.

The first thing to note is that, conforming to the conventional wisdom, economic conditions in the receiving country, in this case the United States, have an impact on legal immigration flows. Specifically *demand-pull* forces, as measured by unemployment rates have a modest impact on flows in the United States for the period 1891–2003. The coefficients, which assess the influence of a unit change (here, 1 percent) in unemployment on immigration flows (logged annual legal immigration), is −0.03 and significant at the 0.05 level. In the model, we control for a variety of policy interventions (specified as the five most important immigration acts passed during this time-span), as well as the effect of World War One and World War Two. Note that labor market conditions have almost twice the impact of changes in real GDP, which again conforms to the economic literature.

Recalling our argument developed in the first sections of this chapter, we predicted a weakening of economic effects over time, as immigration policies changed to reflect the rise of rights-based politics, a new legal culture, and more expansive definitions of citizenship and membership (Cornelius,

Table 4.1. Labor Market and Policy Effects on Immigration, 1891–2003

	Impact	T	Impact Range (low-high)	
Labor Market	−.03	−4.8**	−.40	−8.22
(% Unemployed)	(.01)			
Real GDP	−.01	−1.5	.12	−.17
(% change)	(.01)			
WWI	−.56	−3.8**	0.0	−.56
	(.15)			
WWII	−.40	−2.6**	0.0	−.50
	(.15)			
1924 Johnson-Reed Act	−.39	−3.4**	0.0	−.4
	(.12)			
1952 McCarran-Walter Act	.10	.9	0.0	.11
	(.12)			
1965 Hart-Celler Act	−.07	-.8	0.0	−.07
	(.09)			
1986 IRCA/ 1990 Imm. Act	.15	1.4	0.0	.15
	(.10)			
Lagged Logged Immigration	.69	12.7**	6.93	9.95
	(.05)			

N=113 r²=.90 D−W=1.8 F=125.7 Sig.=.00
Dependent Variable=logged annual legal immigration

*Significant at the .05 level, one directional test (standard errors in parentheses)
**Significant at the .10 level

Table 4.2. Labor Market and Policy Effects on Immigration, 1891–1945

	Impact	T	Impact Range (low-high)	
Labor Market	−.03	−2.8*	−.04	−.75
(% Unemployed)	(.01)			
Real GDP	−.01	−.76	.09	−.13
(% change)	(.00)			
WWI	−.56	−2.9*	0.0	−.56
	(.18)			
WWII	−.32	−1.5	0.0	−.32
	(.21)			
1924 Johnson-Reed Act	−.46	−2.5*	0.0	−.46
	(.17)			
Lagged Logged Immigration	.71	8.8*	7.1	9.93
	(.08)			

N=55 r^2=.90 D−W=1.8 F=82.4 Sig=.00
Dependent Variable: logged annual immigration

*Significant at the .05 level, one directional test (standard errors in parentheses)
**Significant at the .10 level

Martin, and Hollifield 2004; Schuck 1998), especially during the 1950s and 1960s. Accordingly, we segmented the data into two (pre- and postwar) periods. Table 4.2 reports the effects of political and economic change on flows from 1891–1945. Once again, we find a highly significant labor market effect while real GDP registers no statistically significant effect. Percent change in unemployment has a strong, inverse relationship with legal immigration flows, (omega co-efficient = −0.03, significant at the 0.05 level). The corresponding impact range tells us that for every one percent change in unemployment there is a decrease in the logged values of immigration ranging from −0.04 to −0.75 of a one-point change. When we refer back to the actual annual immigration levels, this corresponds to the level range of a low of 23,068 immigrants in this period to a high of 1,285,349 immigrants. In the pre-war period, percentage change in real GDP has no statistical significance.

We also controlled for the effects of World War One and World War Two and the 1924 National Origins Act (the Johnson-Reed Act), which wrote into law the principle of racial/ethnic exclusivity. World War One had an obvious and highly significant effect on immigration flows, as did the 1924 policy intervention. We measure policy interventions as dummy variables (0,1) so that the calculation of the minimum value will always be zero. The ranges for both the war and for the 1924 Johnson-Reed Act reflect our expectations. World War One curtailed flows during this period (as evidenced by the negative sign); the 1924 Act also reduced immigration dramatically (with a coefficient of −0.46), showing the power of the state to restrict immigration flows during this period, marked by isolationism (in foreign policy), protectionism (in trade policy), and restriction of immigration. World War Two, however, does not have a statistically significant impact on flows. This meets our expectations that as policies and World War Two curtailed immigration flows, these interventions decreased the capacity of prior immigration streams to draw more immigrants into the country. Mean immigration for the entire period averaged 4.3 percent per annum. Thus, even when controlling for policy interventions and both World Wars, labor market conditions had a sizeable and significant impact on immigration flows in the prewar period.

Table 4.3 reports the results for the period 1946–2003. Several interesting and counterintuitive findings stand out. Tellingly, economic *demand-pull* effects in the United States continue to weaken over time, despite a more highly integrated global labor market, associated improvements in transportation and communication, and more efficient migration networks much in evidence (Massey, Alarcon, Durand, and Gonzalez 1987; Massey, Durand, and Malone 2002; Sassen 1996). Indeed, the coefficients for unemployment and real GDP change show no significant effect for the postwar period. The McCarran-Walter Act of 1952 is not statistically significant. The contours of the act corroborate the statistical evidence. The McCarran-Walter Act resulted in only marginal changes to key restrictionist quota provisions of the 1924 National Origins Quota Act.

A number of policy interventions, by contrast, are significant. Surprisingly the Immigration and Nationality Act of 1965, which often is cited as the most important immigration reform since the 1924 Act (Reimers 1985), has less of an empirical effect than the other acts on immigration flows. The caveat, of course, is that the 1965 Act led to a gradual change in the composition of

Table 4.3.   Labor Market and Policy Effects on Immigration, 1946–2003

	Impact	T	Impact Range (low-high)	
Labor Market	.02	.9	.06	.18
(% Unemployed)	(.02)			
Real GDP	−.01	−.7	.08	−.06
(% change)	(.01)			
1952 McCarran-Walter Act	.00	.0	0.0	.00
	(.09)			
1965 Hart-Celler Act	.24	2.2*	0.0	.24
	(.11)			
1986 IRCA/1990 Imm. Act	.30	3.1*	0.0	.3
	(.10)			
Lagged Logged Immigration	.55	5.8*	5.73	7.86
	(.09)			

N=58 r²=.90 D−W=1.78 F=93.56 Sig=.00
Dependent variable: logged annual legal immigration

*Significant at the .05 level, one directional test (standard errors in parentheses)
**Significant at the .10 level

these flows, by stimulating family unification (which was after all the purpose of the act) and encouraging larger flows from non-European sources (which was an unintended consequence of the act). Two major immigration reforms of the late twentieth century, the Immigration Reform and Control Act of 1986 (IRCA) and the 1990 Immigration Act, however, combined to have an influence on immigration that simply dwarfed all others modeled here. In sum, our model shows the significant influence of economic factors on immigration until 1946 and the growing impact of government actions on flows in the postwar period. Our time-series analysis fundamentally challenges presumptions of much of the economic and sociological literature on immigration, that policy interventions of the American state have had at best a marginal effect on immigration levels. It underscores the influence of both changing economic conditions and government actions on U.S. immigration during the past century.

TOWARD A MORE POWERFUL IMMIGRATION MODEL

The emphasis our model places on markets and states improves on the prevailing economic and sociological theories of immigration in three significant ways. First, it incorporates economic and *political/policy* effects in a manner that distinguishes their relative influence and provides a stronger overall account of immigration flows. Economic forces alone clearly are insufficient for this task. Second, bringing the state and public policy into immigration analysis offers greater promise for understanding the restrictionist turn in American politics in recent years and its potential to curtail immigration despite economic prosperity. Electoral and national security interests of government officials figure prominently in today's restrictive politics, while low levels of unemployment and increases in real GDP offer few clues. Finally, an immigration model that integrates both markets and states is far more promising than push-pull or transnational models alone in accounting for the volume and composition of immigration flows. These findings are consistent with other studies of the political economy of immigration in Europe (Hollifield 1992a). While they do not contradict the emerging literature in political economy that focuses on interest-based explanations for changes in immigration policy (Freeman 1995), they do offer us an alternative, rights-based, and institutional explanation for the rapid rise in immigration among industrial democracies in the late twentieth century (Brettell and Hollifield 2000). The liberal state has played and will continue to play a vital role in regulating levels of immigration.

Commentary

Does Politics Trump the Market in Contemporary Immigration?

Gary P. Freeman

Despite differing methodologies and significant disparities between their cases, the authors of these two chapters arrive at a single broad and provocative conclusion: Immigration flows to both the United States and Switzerland are increasingly disconnected from domestic labor market conditions. Hollifield, Hunt, and Tichenor see this as evidence of the growing significance of state regulations, albeit expansive regulations, in the late twentieth century; for Piguet, it represents less a triumph of policy than the transformation of migration for work to migration for reasons that are less responsive to labor market considerations. These conclusions and interpretations have major implications for understanding the contemporary political economy of migration. If state regulations of migration are becoming more extensive or more effective, this could open up new opportunities for states, individually or collectively, to shape migration for national, regional, or global purposes. On the other hand, if new migration flows have simply slipped the leash of former market constraints, then a different scenario may be in view, one that is less sanguine about the prospects for political control of immigration.

The hypothesis that Hollifield, Hunt, and Tichenor seek to test is whether migration flows into the United States over a century (1891–2003) can be accounted for by fluctuations in the American domestic economy, or, alternatively, if these flows are decisively affected by direct policy interventions by the state. Is the magnitude of immigrant entries primarily a response to autonomous market forces or is there evidence that the state matters? The authors develop a time-series model to explain immigration flows and to isolate the effects of economic conditions and immigration policy decisions.

They find that (1) there is a statistically significant connection between economic conditions and immigration flows to the United States over the whole period from 1891–2003; (2) labor market conditions are more strongly related to flows than changes in GNP; (3) in the period from 1891–1945, and controlling for policy interventions and WWI, labor market conditions are significantly related to flows; and (4) for the period from 1945–2003 neither labor market effects nor GNP is significantly related to flows, whereas several but not all of the policy interventions they consider are. Generally, they argue that market factors are becoming less important over time whereas policy interventions are becoming more important. Lest we jump to the conclusion that they mean to say that policy is becoming more effective in controlling migration flows, their results indicate that although the 1952 McCarran-Walter Act reduced migration flows and the 1965 Hart-Cellar Act had no significant impact, both the 1986 Immigration Reform and Control Act and the 1990 Immigration Act had very powerful positive effects on flows. In other words, immigration legislation in the last forty years has had either neutral or highly stimulative effects on migration flows. The authors take their findings to constitute a major challenge to the bulk of the economic and sociological literature on migration that has either ignored or denied the impact of state regulation over migration flows.

Etienne Piguet investigates the evolution of Swiss immigration policy over the half-century since 1948 through non-quantitative, discursive case-study methods. For Piguet, the key to Swiss developments is that the authorities are caught between the often conflicting needs of the economy and the constraints of popular xenophobia. Their management of these tensions is, in turn, conditioned by the necessity of taking into account partisan configurations in government and exogenous events that are only partially predictable. Indeed, one of his principal findings is that Swiss policy has changed repeatedly in response to alterations in the migratory, economic, and political context. He divides Swiss events into five periods and argues, for example, that over time a general demand for immigrant labor has been transformed into specific sectoral demand and that interests that were contradictory in the past now converge. The only constant in his story is Swiss xenophobia, which may be more or less manifest but is always in the background. Three trends affect the viability of Swiss policies: a changing and increasingly pertinent international context, a shift in the predominant motives of migrants from work to settlement, and growing preoccupation with integration problems that were previously ignored by the government.

Many migration theories, as Hollifield, Hunt, and Tichenor point out, assume a world without migration controls, an assumption that has not been empirically justified since at least the last quarter of the nineteenth century. Leading statements on migration theory continue, implausibly, to leave aside what is among the central variables affecting migration flows today.[1] Moreover, most empirical studies of international political economy, as Hollifield (2000) has noted, fail to take account of manpower flows. In addition to disciplinary blinders, methodological and data problems may explain a good deal of this myopia; the availability and quality of data on migration flows is greatly inferior to those for finance, goods, and services. To fully incorporate the state into migration models, therefore, we must develop measures not only of migration flows but also of state actions or public policies that are equivalent in quality to the available economic variables. The authors take on this formidable task and, to their credit, make considerable headway.[2]

Their dependent variable captures only legal immigration for permanent settlement, leaving out temporary and illegal migration. They underestimate, therefore, the actual scale of immigration flows while excluding forms of migration, temporary entry for work, for example, that might be more sensitive to labor market conditions than that for permanent settlement. A related problem is that about half of visas for "admission" for permanent settlement in recent years have gone to persons already living, legally or illegally, in the United States, often for many years. They cannot be considered immigrants in the year their permanent residence status was recognized and, therefore, any presumptions relating to how the domestic labor market may have affected their decision to migrate would be problematic.[3]

The authors' dependent variable reflects "admissions" worldwide without providing information on the source countries from which migrants originate. This is regrettable because economic conditions in sending countries should affect emigration decisions of their nationals, thus incorporating supply-push factors into the analysis. Hatton and Williamson (2002) develop measures of immigration to the United States from eighty-one countries for the period 1971–1998. Their dependent variable is the log of the ratio of immigrants admitted by country of birth per thousand of source country population. They find that immigration rates to the United States vary considerably from sending country to sending country and over time; moreover, their conclusions as to the consequences of policy interventions differ in some respects from those of the current paper. Hollifield and his associates may be operating with too gross an indicator of flows to capture the relationship between entries and employment opportunities.

Continuous measures of policy would have been preferable to the dichotomous variables employed. It is true that U.S. immigration policy is broadly demarcated by major legislative acts, but the manner in which policy is implemented may change substantially between legislative reforms (examples include Operation Wetback in the fifties, Operations Hold the Line and Gatekeeper in the nineties, and the end to the easy distribution of visas to Saudis after September 11). Immigrant admissions from particular countries or regions are affected by the placement and staffing of consular offices around the world. These are administrative decisions that do not require Congressional approval. Spending on enforcement, statistics on deportations, and other indicators of administrative policy are in principle available. Their introduction into the analysis would add significantly to the refinement of the independent variables.

The authors' finding that the correlation between migration flows and economic conditions declines gradually after 1945 and more rapidly after 1965 poses a number of interpretive issues. Their argument that U.S. policy after 1965 is so expansive that it weakens the traditional link between employment opportunities and migration flows is tantalizing but hardly what most people mean to imply about immigration policy when they insist that the "state matters" (see, for example, Zolberg 1999). What would be the scale of immigration to the United States in the absence of any immigration policy? Clearly, it would be much greater than at present, hence, even if recent policy changes have increased immigration over that of earlier eras the existing legal framework undeniably has a limiting effect.

A problem that dogs anyone working on these matters is that immigration policy is endogenous and presumably influenced by the same forces that propel migration. Whatever leads to increased migration flows will also stimulate policy responses, making it almost impossible to sort out which is causing which. The authors recognize this and take steps to deal with it. Hatton and Williamson (2002) suggest that one way to get around the endogeneity problem is "to compare the experience in the age of 'free' migration [to the United States] before 1914 with 'constrained' migration of more recent times." Hollifield, Hunt, and Tichenor, because they develop a long time-series, could have spoken to this issue. It may prove useful for them to carry out a separate analysis comparing the period from 1891 to 1914 to that from 1914 to 2003.

Although Piguet's analysis of the Swiss case is less formal and eschews statistical tests, it is even more susceptible to endogeneity problems. For Piguet, economic and political motives and pressures are inextricably connected. His goal is not to figure out which is more important but to show how the interconnections between the two change over time. This he does very well. Leading characteristics of the Swiss experience of immigration make it especially challenging to isolate market from policy causes in any case. Switzerland exhibits none of the enthusiasm for immigration for its own sake that gives to some American flows, such as the family reunion category, a dynamic that is not fundamentally about economics. Swiss policy has been consciously (if not always successfully) orchestrated to match the number and type of entries to specific market needs. In such circumstances, a strong correlation between labor market conditions and migration flows cannot tell us whether markets or policies are the chief causal agents. On the other hand, when the correlation is weaker, as in the most recent period, we cannot tell if it is the result of a failing policy, a resurgence of populist restrictionism leading to political constraints on admissions, or, as Piguet suggests, the emergence of different types of migrants whose motives for migrating have less to do with the labor market.

Piguet's study deals exclusively with immigrant admissions policy, leaving out asylum seekers and programs addressing the integration of immigrants. This tilts his discussion toward a preoccupation with labor market conditions. His independent variables are drawn from Scharpf's actor-centered institutionalism, thereby construing immigration policy as the product of both the institutional frame and the play of different actors. He pitches his analysis at the ground level and is attentive to the actions and motives of the political authorities and interest groups. Most of these operate in the domestic arena, but he also considers international actors, especially the government of Italy, the chief sending country to Switzerland in much of the epoch he covers, and the European Union, a growing factor in Swiss calculations despite their non-membership. Piguet doesn't test hypotheses in any systematic way, trying instead to demonstrate the plausibility of his argument through a chronological narrative. One of the strengths of Piguet's study is his attention to the manner in which the Swiss economy has evolved since 1948. By dividing Swiss developments into distinct periods and following not only the twists and turns of policy but the transformation of Swiss economic life, he is able to provide context to his discussion of the relative roles of market and state. He shows that it has been easier to fit migration to economic needs in some periods than others.

The juxtaposition of case studies of Switzerland and the United States affords an opportunity to explore a few of the variations in the political economy of immigration in two highly divergent states. Switzerland is a leading example of the guest-worker mode of temporary labor recruitment. Permanent settlement and acquisition of citizenship is deliberately difficult. The United States, on the other hand, is the most important traditional country of immigration. A large annual quota of permanent settlers is admitted each year and naturalization to citizenship is relatively easy.

Public opinion is much more critical to the Swiss case due both to the high salience of immigration in national politics and the extreme forms of direct democracy, especially the extraordinary role of popular referenda, that give voice to the public in immigration policy-making. In the United States, in contrast, national election campaigns rarely pay much attention to immigration. There is more disparity on immigration preferences within the two major parties than there is between them, making it difficult to raise the issue in partisan campaigns. The opportunities for populist mobilization around immigration issues are limited. What is remarkable about the American system is the access organized interests have to the parties and to the national government. Groups with a stake in maintaining or expanding immigration are better positioned to get their way than are the less well-organized but widely dispersed opponents of immigration policy. This is consistent with the finding of Hollifield and his associates that policy has been broadly expansive for nearly a half-century. The major legislative innovations of the last forty years were taken in the absence of any noticeable public participation (especially in 1965 and 1990). The political climate that led to new immigration legislation in 1996 was unusually intense, but even then many of the most restrictive proposals were either watered down or, if passed, rescinded by subsequent legislation or judicial nullification (Freeman 2001). The combination of the weak role of popular opinion (which polls show to be moderately to strongly restrictionist) and liberal access of pro-immigration lobbyists to decision-makers leads to expansive policies but not necessarily to policies closely calibrated to the requirements of the labor market.

If Switzerland is more open to populist pressure than the United States, its political decision-making is nevertheless more centralized. One of the striking aspects of Piguet's account is the dominant role of the Federal Council in managing policy. Swiss politics is normally elitist, but elites are seriously hemmed in by the possibility of outbreaks of populist anxiety, hence, the balancing act performed by the authorities. Economic interest groups are strongly committed to immigration to address labor market requirements, but these groups display evolving interests in immigration over time, depending on their assessment of the nature of those requirements. The interests of business and populists are not, however, always in conflict, as Piguet notes. A coalition between the two groups founded on limiting "foreignization" while at the same time recruiting skilled workers has emerged in recent years. It is indicative of the strong competitive pressures in the international economy today that Switzerland, the European country with the institutional framework most favorable to populist expression and with an electorate displaying strong xenophobic tendencies, nonetheless can build at least provisional consensus around the importation of skilled foreign workers.

There are procedural differences in the way annual admissions are established in the two countries that have important consequences for the linkages between migration and labor markets. In the United States the annual ceiling for visas for permanent settlement is periodically fixed in law by Congress although many legal immigrants come in outside the quota—for example, spouses and minor children of U.S. citizens. It would be possible for the government to issue fewer immigrant visas in periods of high unemployment, thus not reaching the ceiling, but the long waiting lists in many countries as well as pressures from the family reunion lobbies make this unlikely. In fact, the ceiling is always met. Changing the annual ceiling requires an act of Congress. Major legislation modifying the ceiling was adopted on average about every two decades in the twentieth century. This peculiarity of American law makes it less likely that entries will mirror labor market conditions as a result of policy interventions since the government cannot move swiftly enough to alter policy.

Swiss policy is a good deal more flexible in theory. Work permits can be expanded or restricted by administrative fiat. Piguet's analysis indicates that Swiss policy was modified frequently as the government sought to link flows more tightly to market conditions. The chief constraints on managing Swiss policy are, according to Piguet, populist agitation, the necessity of satisfying the demands of sending countries, and, increasingly, adapting to the dictates of international law. The first constraint is the most salient and various sorts of ceilings have been imposed in an effort to head off more radical alternatives.

An interesting point of comparison between Switzerland and the United States is the oil shock of 1973–1974. As unemployment rose, all the European states, including Switzerland, announced a general halt to the recruitment of immigrants. In the United States, on the other hand, immigrant admissions remained steady and even increased between 1973 and 1986. Is this evidence that the market is a less powerful constraint on immigration in the United States than in Europe? It is not that simple, as Hollifield and his co-authors point out. Restrictive proposals that sought to respond to high levels of unemployment nationally were blocked by entrenched regional agricultural interests in California and the Southwest, an example of the localism that permeates U.S. immigration politics and vitiates a coherent national policy.

How do markets and politics shape immigration? Do political pressures override labor market needs? Is there evidence of a long-term trend toward political control of immigration? These stimulating papers suggest several conclusions and point the way to new research agendas.

(1) Although intellectually provocative, it is surely a mistake to juxtapose markets versus states in the stark terms I used in the title to this essay. Instead of the global question, does politics trump markets, it is more plausible, as Hollifield, Hunt, and Tichenor suggest, to ask what is the mix of political and market pressures in particular countries, times, and conditions. These studies suggest that the United States (and perhaps Canada and Australia) constitute something of an anomaly among the advanced democracies. Immigration for permanent settlement to these societies is so well institutionalized and of such magnitude that it is to a remarkable degree self-generating and, to that extent, detached from underlying market pressures (on Canada, see Veugelers and Klassen 1994; on Australia, Betts 1999). We may be witnessing the beginnings of such developments in Switzerland and elsewhere in Europe. Pro-immigration movements emerged in Switzerland only in the 1980s; they have been active in the United States since the nineteenth century. In this connection, we should resist our normal inclination to see "politics" as being mainly directed at immigration restriction; some of the most important political effects on migration these days are expansive.

(2) We need to focus on the changing character of migration flows over time, disaggregate migration into its various types, and explore the particular modes of politics and policy that develop around them. The two most

significant recent developments in this regard are the rise of asylum-seeking and the growing interest among governments in skilled migration. These two types of migration have little in common and it would be surprising if they did not evoke distinct forms of political conflict and policy. Whatever the truth in the debate over whether asylum seekers are "really" economic migrants and not genuine refugees, it is obvious that they are not being actively recruited, may not possess skills that have been designated as desirable by the government, and are less easily perceived as contributors to national prosperity than as uninvited beneficiaries of welfare state largesse. Highly skilled migrants, on the other hand, are the object of enthusiastic recruitment efforts by governments and generate relatively little popular unease. Looking only at the asylum drama one might conclude that politics is overtaking economics as restrictive measures are taken against individuals that usually are eager to enter the labor market and take up poorly paid and unpleasant jobs at the bottom of the employment hierarchy. Often, however, the same governments that enact tough measures to deter asylum seekers are busily developing programs to encourage the migration of the highly skilled. In sum, there are multiple political economies of migration.

(3) Finally, as is more readily apparent in the Swiss than in the American study, the contemporary political economy of migration is very much a regional, if not a global, phenomenon. National policies must be seen as taking shape in the context of macro-changes in the world and regional economies and in emerging multinational institutions that regulate or at least constrain autarchic responses to labor market needs and migration pressures. The elimination of borders against the free movement of goods, services, capital, and labor in the European Union has outpaced the realization of common political authority to make policy, especially with regard to immigration. The open logic of integrated markets may, consequently, override the closed logic of still sovereign national political systems in responding to migration flows that are viewed as conducive to growth and competitiveness (Favell and Hansen 2002). A comparative political economy of migration policy cannot neglect the national peculiarities of the cases—peculiarities that these two studies richly illustrate—but it must take account of the extent to which national policies are forged within larger regional and global economic and political frameworks.

NOTES

1. A particularly egregious example is the absence of a political scientist or any serious discussion of state regulation in the highly touted survey of migration theory by a team headed by Douglas Massey for the International Union for the Scientific Study of Population (Massey et al., 1998). On why this is a mistake, see the recent com-

ments of two economists: "[I]t is important to recognize that the ex post migration streams that we have analyzed are largely conditioned by immigration policies that serve as a filter between the desire to migrate and the migration that actually takes place. The fact that economic and demographic variables strongly influence world migration does not diminish the importance of policy. Future trends are likely to be determined largely by policy choices" (Hatton and Williamson 2002).

2. For similar attempts to exploit quantitative data and multi-variate analysis to account for immigration flows, see Money (1999), Kessler (1999), and Hatton and Williamson (2002).

3. I am grateful to Alan Kessler for pointing out the implications of this for the paper in question. Between FY 1996–2001 adjustments of status constituted on average 50.5 percent of all legal immigrants, ranging from 37.9 to 61.4 percent (U.S. Department of Justice, 2002).

III

DETERMINANTS: ETHNICITY OR POLITICAL CHANNELING?

5

The Nature of Ethnicity in the Project of Migration

John Rex

THE FEAR OF ETHNICITY

Ethnicity today is in ill repute. With the collapse of the bipolar world system after 1989, the various groups, nations, and communities that had been held together by the quasi-imperial systems of the superpowers were left to fight for themselves and among themselves. In the name of ethnicity, nationalism, or ethnic nationalism they fought brutally for territory, and the Serbian notion of "ethnic cleansing" came to provoke something of the horror felt toward the Nazi Holocaust fifty years earlier. Meanwhile, even though they were not engaged in nationalist projects, migrant ethnic minorities became the focus of suspicion and hostility in their countries of settlement.

In these circumstances it has not been easy to argue for the political ideal of multiculturalism in Western European societies. It is an ideal which is regarded with grave suspicion in the media, among politicians and social scientists and in public opinion generally, as well as among educated members of the migrant communities themselves who fear that their labeling as "ethnic" necessarily involves their assignment to inferiority.

Although the unitary nature of Western European nations and their cultures can be exaggerated, since, historically they themselves have been ethnically diverse and divided in terms of class and status, it is nonetheless true that, allowing for this diversity, the range of permissible cultural and political variation has been limited and the culture of new immigrant groups, coming often from long distances and having distinct languages, religions, and customs, is seen as "alien."

121

Those members of migrant communities who have been successful in adapting to the demands of their host societies understandably fear that if they represent themselves as culturally different, they will be treated as inferior and denied equal rights, and they are often supported by democrats who see the setting up of separate multicultural arrangements as something which will undermine established and familiar democratic political procedures.

There are a number of ways in which this democratic and universalistic response of democrats affects the thinking of social scientists. From a simple Marxist point of view, ethnic consciousness is seen as false consciousness and a diversion from the class struggle and class politics that are taken to be normal. Liberals and republicans also see any deviation from the notion of universal and equal citizenship as politically dangerous, while social democrats, with their notion of the reconciliation of conflicting class interests under the welfare state compromise, find it difficult to accept the setting up of special and separate institutions for dealing with minorities. More widely, those who see existing societies as based upon a delicate balance between the cultures of status groups, rather than simply on a class compromise, are inclined to see the coming of more distant and alien cultures as upsetting this balance (Rex and Drury 1994).

These fears are understandable, and it is to be expected that European social scientists and politicians will wish to defend institutions that have been slowly and painfully established via political struggles of the past two centuries. Nonetheless, such attitudes are literally prejudiced in that they prejudge the nature of ethnic minority cultures and the goals that ethnic minority communities set themselves. What is necessary for a serious sociology of multicultural societies is an empirical as well as a theoretical study of the nature of migrant ethnic minority groups, based not on the way in which these groups are categorized and classified by the state but on the way in which they see themselves. This is the object of this [essay]. What I shall do is, first to look at the nature of ethnicity in general; second, to look at the way in which the two major projects of ethnicity and nationalism branch from this general ethnic stem; and third, to look in more detail at the actual structure of migrant ethnic minority communities and their relationship to modern nation-states.

THE SIMPLEST FORM OF ETHNICITY

In the literature on ethnicity and nationalism the first major division is that between "primordial" and "situational," or "instrumental," theory. According to the former, ethnic bonds are quite unlike all others; they are recurrent and largely inexplicable and have an overpowering emotional and non-rational quality (Geertz 1963). According to the latter, they are, if not wholly invented by political leaders and intellectually for purposes of social manipulation, at least related to specific social and political projects (Barth 1959, 1969; Roosens 1989).

It is important to understand why the primordialist view can be maintained at all, even if ultimately we reject it as an adequate account of ethnicity and nationalism. What we need to do is to consider the difference between two types of group affiliation, namely that which involves a strong sense of emotional belonging, and even of sacredness, and another in which such affiliation is related in some way to ulterior and rationally formulable purposes. To do this we must consider, first, the very simplest form of ethnicity into which children are born, and second, the formation of more extensive groups, now commonly referred to as *ethnies*.

Our human condition is necessarily a social one. Apart from the so-called feral children brought up by animals, any human infant finds himself or herself caught up at birth in what I have called "the infantile ethnic trap" (Rex 1995): It is brought up within a kin network in which named and categorized individuals play specific roles, and in relation to whom it has clearly defined rights and duties. He or she will also belong to a neighborhood group that may coincide with the kin group, but often simply intersects with it. Such groups as these will also share a language as well as religious beliefs and customs.

On a social psychological level these simple groups will be seen as generating positive warm emotions and as possessing some supernatural qualities. The dead as well as the living are thought of as belonging to the group, and its origins and history are explained in terms of some kind of myth or narrative that is taught to the young as truth.

It should be noted here that language and religion present special problems in that they are often shared with a wider range of people who are not members of the group. Nonetheless, within these larger linguistic and religious communities, smaller groups are differentiated in terms of kin, neighborhood, customs, and history. Language may be modified by dialect, and religious beliefs may be reinterpreted and appropriated to reflect the more specific beliefs of the smaller group.

From this initial base members go on to enter a wider world in two ways. First, through the socialization process (as described in different ways by Freud, Mead, Durkheim, and others) the external role players "enter the head" of the individual whose very personal identity is then a social creation so that he or she acts not simply as a Hobbesian individual but as an ethnic individual. Such an individual may then go on to enter into relations with other individuals of different ethnicity just as his or her ethnic group enters into relations with other groups. Second, however, it is possible that the individual will find that there are larger groups than his or her original one, which can give him or her some of the same feeling of belonging and sacredness. It is these larger groups that we refer to as *ethnies*.

The *ethnie* is differentiated from the simpler type of kin- and neighborhood-based group by the fact that there is no precise definition of the roles of one member vis-à-vis another. Rather the group is constituted, as Smith has suggested (Smith 1986), by the fact that it has a name, shared symbols, and a myth of origin. These elements, however, do mean that the *ethnie* claims something of the strong sense of emotional belonging and sacredness that is to be found in the smaller group.

This is not to say, however, that the *ethnie* does not have its own structure of social relations. Usually there is some sort of status and economic differentiation and complementarity among its members, and there will be some type of role differentiation of those who exercise authority of a political and religious sort. What differentiates the *ethnie* from a modern political nation, however, is that these economic and political structures are subordinated to the community structure. Characteristically, a priesthood exercises more authority than it would in the nation-state.

Smith also tells us that the *ethnie* normally has some sort of attachment to a territory, even though it does not set up the administrative structures to be found in the modern state that claim authority throughout that territory.

Ethnies will, of course, vary in their size and complexity and the term should probably be extended to cover a range of possibilities, including, at one extreme, a group that has little more than a name, a myth of origin, and a shared culture, and, at the other, one that has some of the features of the nation-state.

The *ethnie*'s own self-definition may not be the same as that used in referring to it by other *ethnies*. Generally its self-definition involves the notion of moral worthiness, while other groups might describe it in quite derogatory terms. On the other hand it should not be thought that *ethnies* are of their very nature forced into conflict with one another. This may be the case, if control of a territory or other resources is disputed, but it is perfectly possible for different *ethnies* to live at peace with each other.

The primordialist view of the *ethnie* would be that it exists largely for its own sake. The alternative "situationist" view deriving from the work of Barth would suggest that the boundaries of such an *ethnie* depend upon the situation or on the project in which the group is engaged. There is truth in both these positions, particularly when control of a territory is involved. In this case we should say that the boundaries of the group are at least partly determined by a political project, even though it may call on the solidarity of the pre-existing *ethnie* as a resource. Immediately we will deal with the case in which the project is the creation of a nation. In the latter part of the paper we will deal with groups whose project is almost the opposite of laying claim to a territory in the business of migration.

THE NATION-STATE, NATIONALISM, AND ETHNIC NATIONALISM

The sort of discourse with which we have been concerned above derives largely from social anthropology, social psychology, and history. A quite different discourse, however, has dominated thinking about nationalism and the nation-state. In this discourse the nation-state is thought of as coming into being almost *ab initio* as part of a modernizing project.

Gellner's account (Gellner 1983) of this modernizing project, of nationalism and the nation-state, is probably too narrow. According to him, the nation depends upon a political and intellectual elite imposing a shared culture on the whole population in a territory, particularly through a national education system, which ensures that all members of the nation have a minimum of competence and a degree of flexibility so that they can fulfill a variety of roles. Such a culture and such an education system is, in Gellner's view, essential to the operation of an industrial society.

There is, however, more to be said about modernization than this. Most important is the fact that the polity and the economy are released from their subordination to the communal institutions and the culture of the *ethnie*. Instead they come to dominate it or to erode the very basis of its existence.

In fact, however, in this conception of the nation, it is the polity that is dominant. It rules and administers the whole of a given territory and, in so doing, faces a problem in that the economy, language, and religion have to be brought under its control. The natural tendency of the modern nation-state so far as the economy is concerned is toward economic autarchy. On the linguistic front, it has to ensure that, however much minority languages are tolerated for communal purposes, there is a shared official national language. Finally, so far as religion is concerned, the priesthood must in some way come to terms with the state and cannot be allowed to encourage loyalty to some wider community of co-religionists.

Such a nation-state is also bound to encounter resistance from *ethnies* within its borders. It may deal with this either by destroying the *ethnies* and their culture or by granting them a degree of subordinate autonomy. If it fails to do either of these the *ethnies* themselves may develop in the direction of ethnic nationalism, seeking to establish their own states, whether of a modernizing or traditional sort. Thus the nation-state is likely to foster other nationalisms apart from its own.

The modern nation also rarely rests content with the bonding of its own members simply as individual citizens. It needs to create a national sentiment and a sense of belonging to the nation. To some extent it can do this by converting its population to the ideology of nationalism, but this will probably be possible only among an elite. It also therefore has to create its own symbols, mythology, and sense of sacredness and belonging. In doing this it will be using many of the techniques used by pre-modern *ethnies*.

This is what is happening when the national leaders speak of the mother country or the fatherland.

What the theory of nationalism has to do, therefore, is to describe a complex process of interaction between modernizing nation-states, *ethnies*, and ethnic nationalism. The business of creating the modern nation-state is therefore always incomplete, and what is loosely called nationalism covers a variety of interacting types.

Finally, we have to consider under the heading of nationalism the fact of imperialism and the creation of multinational states. Nations conquer nations and when they do new imperial structures extending beyond the boundaries of the conquering nation come into being. An imperial bureaucracy is created, metropolitan entrepreneurs gain access to the productive system and the markets of subordinate nations, and settlers from the conquering metropolis go to live and work in the subordinated territories.

Just as the creation of the individual nation provokes resistance from *ethnies* and ethnic nationalism, however, so imperial conquest provokes resistance from subordinate nations. If then the metropolitan power becomes weaker for any reason, or if its rule is overthrown, old nationalisms will be released and will flourish in the formerly subordinate territories. In fact they will be stronger than ever in national sentiment as they add to their myths the story of their resistance and their successful national revolutions. At the same time they may still have their own internal problems of dealing with the resistance of their own *ethnies* and ethnic nationalisms. All of these problems are evident in the wake of the break-up of the Soviet Empire and the USSR.

THE SECOND PROJECT OF ETHNICITY: MIGRATION

Although much of the theoretical writing about ethnicity has been concerned with the attachment of an ethnic group to a territory, in fact ethnic communities are often concerned precisely with their *detachment* from a territory, that is to say with the business of international migration.

In attempting to relate such groups to the theory of nationalism, a commonly used notion is that of diaspora. A diaspora is said to exist when an *ethnie* or nation suffers some kind of traumatic event that leads to the dispersal of its members, who, nonetheless, continue to aspire to return to the homeland. Diasporic nationalism is thus seen as one kind of nationalism. It is exemplified by Jews seeking a return to Zion, black Americans seeking to return to Africa, and Armenians seeking a return to Armenia.

The term *diaspora* has also been loosely used, however, to refer to any national or ethnic group dispersed across several countries, and this may be misleading, since many such groups have not suffered a clear traumatic experience and are not primarily concerned with a return to some kind of Zion.

They are not in fact nationalist at all, even though they have some kind of transnational community as a point of reference. There are three cases to be distinguished.

First, there are groups of migrants from economically backward to economically successful countries. Individuals from the former migrate to the latter in order to seek work. Some may have no strong desire to return to their country of origin and simply seek assimilation in the country of settlement. Quite commonly, however, they may send remittances home and plan to return there, and even those who are destined *de facto* to remain in the country of settlement and bring up their children there, may retain some kind of myth of return.

Second, there are those who are part of more extensive migration movements, who migrate to a number of countries and who intend to go on living abroad and exploiting whatever opportunities are available within the several countries. For them there is an international community distinct both from the community of the homeland and that of the nations in whose territories they are temporarily or permanently settled. Often such communities consist of secondary colonialists for whom opportunities open up within another country's former empire. Such is the position of Indians from the Punjab settled in countries ranging from Southeast Asia, through Europe, to North America.

Third, there are communities or refugees whose situations vary enormously. They may constitute diasporas of a kind, seeing their immediate situation as temporary and envisaging a return to the homeland when political circumstances change; given that they are often fleeing from their fellow nationals, they are not necessarily nationalistic in outlook. There will, moreover, be many who cannot envisage such a change in political circumstances at home and are committed to finding a new life in the countries of refuge.

Separately from these cases is a case that is more closely related to nationalism, namely that which occurs following the break-up of empires: In this case there are often settlers in the colonized territories who now look for protection to the former metropolis, while in that metropolis there will be those who feel the need to protect or gather in the former settlers. What occurs in this case is best described as irredentist nationalism, hence the case of the white settlers from the former European empires in Africa and Asia or, more recently, of the Russians living in the former territories of the USSR. It is misleading in these cases to speak of diasporas.

In understanding the second project of nationalism, the most important case is the second of those mentioned above. In order to understand its structure, it may be helpful to consider the case of Punjabi migration and, particularly, the Punjabi Sikh migration by way of illustration.

Looking first at the country of origin, we have to note that the territory of the Punjab, within which the principle language is Punjabi, is divided between

India and Pakistan. Huge population transfers occurred there at the time of the partition of the subcontinent, and it is, therefore, possible to distinguish Pakistani and Indian Punjabi migrants, primarily in terms of their religion. Even if we concentrate on the Indian Punjab, however, the population is divided in religious terms between Sikhs and Hindus and there are separate migrant networks deriving from the two communities. Punjabi Sikhs also support a nationalist movement, the most extreme version of which seeks to establish a separate state of Khalistan. This movement has led to violence and terrorism both in Indian itself and abroad.

There are further divisions among the Punjabi Sikhs based upon caste and class. The most important of the caste divisions, at least among migrants, is that between the Jats, who hold (or seek to hold) land, and the Ramgarias, who were originally carpenters. So far as class is concerned, there is a division between those for whom the nationalist movement is most important and those who support either one of the Indian Communist parties or the Indian Congress Party.

Clearly, even if one confines one's attention to Punjabi Sikhs, it is clear that Punjabi Sikhism is not a unitary phenomenon. Nonetheless there is a shared culture based on religion that is a point of reference for all Punjabi Sikhs, even including the Marxists.

The political position of the Punjabi Sikhs was profoundly affected by the fact that they did not support the mutiny within British India in 1857. They therefore enjoyed a somewhat privileged position within India and also had the necessary skills to enable them to play a role within the wider British Empire, particularly in the development of East Africa, and later in Britain itself. From these bases they were able to seek still further opportunities in other parts of the Empire and in other countries in North America and Europe. It is against this background that the ethnic community of Punjabi Sikhs can be understood.

The basic unit within the international Punjabi Sikh community is probably the extended family. The latter often tries to increase its family estate, a fact that may involve remittances and saving with a view to obtaining land or starting a business in the Punjab itself. This, however, is only one possibility; a Punjabi family in Britain might well envisage further migration to North America, and it might have relatives there as well as in the Punjab.

Beyond the family there are, however, other social and cultural links. Even those who are not particularly religious may participate in the life of the temples, or *gurdwara*, at least with regard to significant life events like birth, marriage, and death. In addition, many men still display the five symbols of Sikhism and wear turbans. Thus Sikhism remains an important point of reference within the transnational community. Such wider cultural links help to produce a degree of solidarity even among families who would otherwise be simply competitors; consequently, in planning their affairs, the separate extended families are able to rely on the networks that these cultural links provide.

Notwithstanding this, the Sikh community has still to develop relationships with the various modernizing nation-states within which its members settle. It has, however, the experience and skills to do this. The development of class-based industrial and political organizations is not something new to the Sikhs, who are thus quite capable of exploiting the opportunities available to them within the politics of the nation-state of settlement. Part of the total political culture of the community is concerned precisely with ensuring that its members have maximum rights in their country of settlement. We are not dealing with a simple traditional *ehtnie* facing a modernizing nation. Rather what we have is a community with a changing and developing political culture, characterized by a strong modernizing element.

One may argue that the Punjabi Sikhs represent a special case. In fact most transnational migrant communities are specific in one sense or another. Yet there are always some generalizable elements. In the case of the Punjabi Sikhs, these would be, first, that despite the internal complexity of the community, even prior to migration, the community has still some basic reference points, particularly those based on religion, which give it an overall unity; second, this community is now located across the world and intends to go on living across the world and exploiting whatever economic opportunities the world provides; third, the existence of this community does not mean that there is no scope for individual family enterprise; fourth, insofar as it is incorporated into the political culture of a modern nation-state, it produces its own ways of dealing with this while, at the same time, maintaining contact with the homeland (taking the economic form of remittances and investment in the homeland and the political form of support for the various nationalist and class-based factions and parties in the homeland into account).

Of course the business of dealing with various nation-states and their social and political institutions involves some cost to the community. Success in the land of settlement may well mean that some of those who succeed within this system may leave the community altogether, and there is strong evidence in the case of Punjabi Sikhs in Britain that some of their successful young members are doing just this. Having achieved educational, business, or professional success they find that they can hold their own in British society and become, to all intents and purposes, British. But, even though this may be the case, this very success depends at the outset on the maintenance of communal solidarity, and that same communal solidarity projected across the world also provides wider opportunities. There may still be advantages, even for an acculturated British Sikh, in using his or her networks to participate in a wider transnational system. Thus, for example, many professionals and businessmen in Britain may still use their ethnic networks to improve their position still further in North America. It is quite possible in fact to take advantage of membership in two societies and communities, one that of the nation in the country of settlement, the other that of the transnational ethnic community.

Looking more widely at the other minorities in Britain and Western Europe, one can, of course, see that there are a number of possible variations from the type suggested for the Punjabi Sikhs, although most of the Asian minorities in Britain reproduce the structural and cultural features mentioned (e.g., Punjabi Hindus, Gujaratis, Kashmiris, Pakistanis, and Bangladeshis). In the case of migrants to the Caribbean there is a diasporic element or at least a diasporic myth of return to Africa, although for many the possibilities presented by migration to Britain, Canada, or the United States are more important than any such return, and the homeland to which they refer is more likely to be a West Indian island than Africa. In the case of the Turks in Germany, mobility to other countries as well as citizenship in Germany is restricted by guest-worker status and the main points of reference are simply Turkey and Germany. Algerians find themselves in a dependent post-colonial relationship with France. The Moroccan situation is more like that of the Punjabis, though the migrants are more likely to be in poorer occupations. Finally, there are the Southern Europeans, who on the one hand can fairly readily assimilate culturally to their countries of settlement, yet are close enough to their sending societies to maintain social and cultural links with them. In all cases much will depend upon the range of occupations that are open to migrants and the skills which they have to exploit them.

Despite all this variation it is clear that in all cases we are dealing with transnational communities that are not primarily nationalist in their orientation (except in relation to surviving homeland issues) and in which an element of diasporic yearning for return is not the overwhelming uniting political factor.

THE RESPONSE OF NATION-STATES
TO IMMIGRANT ETHNIC MINORITIES

The other party to the relationship in which these immigrant communities are involved is, of course, the nation-state, and it is to its reaction to immigrant settlement that we must now turn. It is here that we have to deal with the problems of nationalism, particularly nationalism of the modernizing sort.

There are two aspects to the nationalism of European states. On the one hand, they define their own national identity in relation to each other and to their empires and colonial territories, such notions of identity having been reinforced by wars, economic competition, and resistance to colonial liberation. On the other, they have created a national cultural and political consensus out of conflicting class and status cultures. In Britain Marshall (1950) suggested that with the acquisition of social rights in addition to legal and political rights, British workers now had reason to identify more strongly with their national citizenship than with social class, as Marx had predicted. Williams also suggested interestingly in his book *The Long Revolution* (1961) that these workers were now also beginning to win their cultural rights.

The notions of legal and social citizenship are central to the modern nation-state. In the French Republican tradition it is the legal equality of citizenship that is crucial. Two hundred years after the French Revolution, however, social rights have become more central and most European societies see themselves as having achieved some kind of political compromise between contending classes through the establishment of the welfare state. In any case the central theme of the political culture of these societies involves the recognition of equality of opportunities and, up to a minimum level, equality of outcome. There are, of course, those in most countries who would prefer to define the national culture and identity in terms of upper-class culture, but it is the notion of equality that is the central ideological element in the modernizing nation-state.

Given an ideological consensus of this kind these societies also tend to recognize the possibility of separate cultures, thought of as private matters in which the state does not interfere. Religious tolerance is therefore the norm. This is achieved in France through the secularization of politics and education, while in the Netherlands the policy of "pillarization" recognized the right of the separate faiths to control considerable institutional areas. It is less completely achieved in Britain and in Northern European countries where there is an established church with special duties and privileges.

The social structure of the nation-state is not, however, determined simply by the creation of social equality. There has to be a national language for the conduct of official business; there is a national economy over which the government seeks to retain control, even in the face of international markets and multinational business corporations; there is a civil and a criminal legal system to which all are required to conform, even if, through the political process and through the courts themselves, laws which are thought to be unjust can be changed; there is a national educational system concerned with developing the skills of the population as well as imparting shared national values; and finally, there is also a developing national literary and aesthetic culture.

The question with which we are concerned is that of how a nation that defines itself in these terms reacts to the presence of immigrant communities and their cultures and how these communities themselves fit into the national system.

Two reactions that are to be expected in the receiving society are those of xenophobia and racism on the one hand and of assimilationism on the other. The terms *xenophobia* and *racism* are most frequently too loosely used; as used here they refer to reactions to immigrant communities which involve demands for their expulsion, physical attacks, racial and cultural abuse, and racial and ethnic discrimination which gives the immigrants fewer rights than those of full citizens. All of these elements have been involved in the political reactions of European societies to postwar immigrants. Sometimes they occur simply in the propaganda and activities of anti-democratic parties, but they have also influenced the policies of governments. Of particular importance here is that in the German-speaking countries, while measures may be taken to ensure the legal and social rights of immigrants, they are not accorded political rights.

The assimilationist alternative has been more prominent in France. There is a widespread belief that minority cultures and minority identities threaten French national culture and identity and that while minority members should have equal rights as citizens they should be discouraged from maintaining their own cultures. Politically they should be expected to work through the mainstream parties and there should be no intrusion of minority culture and values into the secular national schools.

The third possible route for the policies of racial and ethnic exclusion on the one hand and assimilationism on the other is multiculturalism. Multiculturalism, professed in Britain, the Netherlands, and Sweden, even if imperfectly practiced, involves both the attempt to ensure the full rights of citizens to minorities and the recognition of their right to maintain their separate cultures.

Our next question is that of how migrant ethnic minorities are likely to react to these various regimes. Obviously, so far as the first is concerned, they will organize to fight against "racism" in all its forms, but in doing this they are likely to have the support of many indigenous democrats. So far as the second is concerned there will be some who are prepared to accept the hard bargain which is offered if it brings sufficient rewards to individual minority members, but generally the attempt simply to destroy minority culture is likely to provoke resistance, both because of the psychological cost in terms of the threat to the identity of minority members and because of the destruction of helpful community networks.

Clearly it is the third possibility, namely that of multiculturalism, which provides most scope for the immigrant minority to attain its own goals. The question is whether it can do this without threatening the society as a whole.

Usually multiculturalism recognizes that there is a private and communal sphere in which there is no need for the government to interfere. This is thought to include the speaking of minority languages within the community, the practice of minority religions, and the maintenance of minority customs in matters relating to the family and marriage. There are, however, problems even about this restrictive definition of the private and communal sphere. Whatever minority customs there may be in relation to family matters there are no cases in which such customs are backed by the law, despite an occasionally expressed demand by Muslims that their family affairs are regulated by the *sharia* law. Often these customs are criticized by human rights activists and feminists who believe that they should be a matter of public concern. There is also often an unwillingness to admit that the propagation of minority cultures should have any place within the educational systems or even be subsidized by the state independently. Minority religions might also be denied facilities through such means as planning regulations.

Usually, however, ethnic minority cultures and social organization can be preserved in these circumstances, though minority organizations will usually have to work to maximize their area of independence. They will do this in order to maintain their community structure nationally and internationally, but if they enjoy a reasonable measure of tolerance, it is likely that their main concern will be to fight against racism and racial discrimination and for social equality.

Ethnic minorities will, however, also have to accept more than this as part of the implied contract into which they enter with the host nation. They will have to accept that there is an official language and that they will have to use it in their dealings with the public authorities; they will have to recognize the criminal and civil law; they will have to recognize that existing national values will be taught within the educational system; and, they may have to accept that there is an established religion which has special privileges.

Most ethnic minority members do accept some sort of contract of this kind. They see it as part of the cost of living in a particular society of settlement that has to be set against the real gains that migration brings. What is likely, however, is that there will be some members of their communities who are more committed to their cultures than this. They cannot be called nationalists. What they are concerned with is achieving what they think of as adequate recognition and respect for their cultures. They may organize public demonstrations against any perceived insult to their culture and religion, as in the case of the Rushdie affair, and they may ask either for separate schools or for adequate recognition of their religion and customs in the state schools. They may also seek to present their own literary and aesthetic culture in the public sphere. Thus what one may expect is the emergence of minority cultural movements pursued with varying degrees of aggression and militancy.

The existence of movements such as these hardly threatens the national society. They can easily be tolerated. They become problematic only if they lead to overt political disloyalty. Such disloyalty or the suggestion of a prior loyalty to some other state has been advocated by a few extreme Muslim organizations in Britain. It is also the case that there are groups that advocate violence and terrorism in their homeland and are prepared to use the migrant community as a base for organizations. It is bound to be the case that national governments will do whatever they can to repress such activities.

What we are concerned with in this paper is the nature of ethnicity in the project of migration. What we have seen is that such ethnicity is not primarily concerned with the project of nationalism. It is concerned with the maintenance of a transnational community in which economic advantages can be pursued. It also has to come to terms with modernizing national societies and is usually easily able to do so. Mainly what one may expect in any particular country of settlement is the emergence of cultural movements trying to strengthen adherence to the culture and enlarge its area of operation. The existence of such movements can easily be negotiated with as part and parcel of the working of a democratic society. The most important problems arise in connection with those movements that deliberately foster political disloyalty or engage in violent and terrorist politics on an international scale. It is to be expected that any such movements and activities will be suppressed in a nation-state. On the other hand it would be wrong to assume that they are typical of ethnic minority communities and their political culture.

We should remember here, however, that immigrant ethnic minority groups do not normally simply have to face the problem of fitting into a society committed to multiculturalism. Even in the societies in which such a policy is professed there will be many individuals and, often, political movements who are hostile to or suspicious of ethnic minority communities and their cultures. Where this is the case, ethnic minority movements will not simply be concerned with the preservation of their culture and networks but will pursue active policies against racism and racial discrimination. Not surprisingly in Britain there is a dispute between those in the ethnic minority communities who fight primarily for multiculturalism and those in more radical movements who see their main task as fighting racism.

It has been assumed in this paper that ethnic minority communities may have a more or less permanent existence on an international basis. This may well be true in some cases. In other cases, however, ethnic minority organizations and movements may be of a more transitional kind. They may exist for a few generations while there is still a need to fight for equality and for cultural respect. But after that what may remain, given religious tolerance, is a purely symbolic ethnicity involving such things as festivals and special occasions as well as some attempt at preservation of the minority language. Such purely symbolic ethnicity is something that troubles nobody and is usually regarded by an indigenous population merely as an exotic enrichment of their own culture.

Going beyond such purely symbolic ethnicity, however, neither the maintenance of the transnational migrant community nor the development of defensive community organizations are really incompatible with the maintenance of the institutions of a modernizing national state. It is very important, therefore, that what has been called here the second project of ethnicity should not be confused with nationalist projects. What has been happening in the former Yugoslavia holds no lessons relevant to the way in which blacks and Asians in Britain or Turks and Maghrebians in various parts of Europe have to be treated by their host societies. The real focus of the problematic of nationalism in these cases has to be in the majority nationalism of the host societies.

This chapter originally appeared as John Rex, "The Nature of Ethnicity in the Project of Migration," in *The Ethnicity Reader: Nationalism, Multiculturalism, and Migration*, edited by Montserrat Guibernau and John Rex (Cambridge: Polity Press, 1997). It is reprinted here with permission of Polity Press.

6

Institutions, Political Opportunity Structures, and the Shaping of Migration Policies in Western Europe

Patrick Ireland

Whether or not they like to admit it, Europeans today live in multiethnic societies. Former immigrant and colonial laborers have become permanent residents. Host societies have responded differently to the challenges associated with them. I argue in this paper that political opportunity structures—including recruitment policies, integration policies, citizenship laws, and the actions of institutional gatekeepers—have played the most important role in determining that variegated response. They have shaped the ethnic and racial makeup of immigrant-origin populations, the nature and management of ethnic relations, the influence of homeland governments and organizations, the integration processes affecting immigrant-origin minorities and their participation, the public role of Islam, and the political impact of anti-immigrant movements.

Concerned primarily about meeting their industries' demands for cheap labor, European authorities implemented few coherent policies for coping with the social and political effects of the mass postwar influx of immigrants, "guest-workers," refugees, and asylum-seekers. They treated people from Europe, North Africa, Turkey, and Asia differentially, depending on whether they came from a European Community partner or potential member, an overseas possession, a former colony, a country with which a bilateral treaty had been signed, or elsewhere. By the time oil shocks had precipitated a rapid economic deterioration in the labor-importing countries in the 1970s, it was clear that most of "guests" were not leaving. The task in all host societies became to integrate the multiethnic immigrant-origin communities that postwar migration and policy choices had created.[1]

CULTURES OR INSTITUTIONS?

In their attempts to explain the evolution of immigration (or admission) and immigrant (or integration) policies, some academic analyses have advanced the thesis that cultural diversity and immigrant communities' "ethnic capital" (Borjas 1999) have driven policy and ethnic relations. The assumption here is that immigrants' ethnic identity is of fundamental importance and will propel policy for the foreseeable future. At least three generations were necessary, according to the celebrated Chicago School of Sociology, for immigrants to become fully assimilated Americans (Schmitter Heisler 2000; see Foner 1997). In some studies a multiethnic racial identity (Banton 1985; Moulin 1985) or a common religious identity (Balibar and Wallerstein 1988; Étienne 1989) plays a comparably independent, durable source of identity and mobilization. Islam, with its allegedly "bloody borders," has been seen as an insuperable barrier to immigrant integration and harmonious social relations in Western liberal democracies (Huntington 1996).

There are clear affinities between this view and the identity politics fad. It rests on the conviction that increasingly fragmented Western societies create new needs for identity, which can perhaps be fulfilled through ties based not only on class but also on race, ethnicity, gender, and lifestyle (Young 1990; Phillips 1991). People are mobilized not because of what they do but in terms of who and what they are. Ethnic or religious mobilization, like other varieties, becomes the "expression of a way of life, divorced from economic and political conflicts" (Rex 1996). The collapse of the Soviet bloc, Germany's arduous unification, and European integration have all produced a fixation with ethnic and other collective identities and an interest in drawing internal frontiers and new sources of differentiation (Krell, Nicklas, and Ostermann 1996).

In such an optic, immigrants organize and articulate their political interests along ethnic, racial, or religious lines. Each group's perspective, as well as policy-makers' reactions to it, emerges from group socialization processes and in response to discrimination and interaction with other groups. The starting point is the "homeland hangover," the legacy of attitudes and social capital that immigrants acquired before leaving their country of origin (compare Ireland 1994). Some scholars see residential ethnic concentrations as havens that offer resources, contacts, business opportunities, a sense of belonging, and access to institutional knowledge and public-sector support helpful to immigrants in adjusting to their new environment (Portes and Bach 1985; Webber 1992).

Other immigration researchers question any focus on the composition of immigrant flows or a "cultural distance" calculus when seeking the sources of policy. They argue that enclaves can degenerate from way stations into ghettoes, circumscribed by discriminatory housing and employment practices

(Cross 1992; Weiner 1995). A cohort of social scientists has joined themselves in making a connection between public policies and other institutional changes and the nature of ethnic relations (Jakubowicz, Morrissey, and Palser 1984; Fuchs 1990a; Rath, Penninx, Groenendijk, and Meijer 1996; Bousetta 2000). Immigrant behavior undergoes structuring by political opportunity structures, legal and political institutions that mold and constrain participatory choice. They include political parties, trade unions, and religious and humanitarian non-profit associations that can weaken or strengthen the effects of differential resource endowments, acting as gatekeepers that control access to the avenues of political participation available to immigrants (Ireland 1994). Ethnic identities, in other words, are malleable, at least to a certain extent.

European societies underwent a bloody, centuries-long struggle to tie nation to state. Their political development created myths of ethnic homogeneity that disavowed their own national minorities and rendered them painfully slow to own up to their recent immigration-generated diversity. As the association between disadvantage and minority status has hardened, however, multiculturalism has gained a committed following in Green and new left Socialist circles and even in pockets on the Christian Democratic center-right. Scandinavians and, at times, the Dutch have embraced it.

Still, many Europeans have little stomach for American-style affirmative action approaches that they feel threaten to freeze minority cultures in place (TWCM 1995). Canadian and Australian multicultural policies have encountered similar criticism for reifying minority cultures and nourishing their most regressive aspects. Such strategies "minoritize" groups and mark them for unequal treatment, Jan Rath tells us (1991).

They also dissociate immigration-related problems from those linked to conflicts of social class interest (Radtke 1990). A staple of European debates has been the socialist critique of multiculturalism. In traditional Marxist analyses ethnicity and race become the modalities in which immigrants experience class relations, representing a false consciousness that hinders working-class cohesiveness. Social democrats have preferred to see immigrant workers in terms of the producer groups to which they belong and between which conflicts are resolved through bargaining and compromise—a process that trains all workers to realize and act on their common class interests. Special multicultural arrangements threaten this learning curve (Rex 1996).

Even as they have made consensual policy-making processes and social democracy possible, highly developed European social welfare states have served as powerful agents of social control. They have connected people to the state in particular ways, strengthening and weakening ethnic and other identities in various places and at various times. In recent years, social welfare restructuring has altered the ways in which the welfare state acts as a source of ethnic differentiation. Welfare policies have not only been privatized; they have also been decentralized everywhere. This evolution has enhanced the importance of local institutions, widening their room for maneuver if not boosting their financial resources. Local officials and immigrant-origin populations have not had the luxury of sitting back and philosophizing about what the ideal society might look like. To understand the *modi vivendi* that they have devised, we need more nuanced treatment than broad "models of incorporation" can provide (Brubaker 1992; Soysal 1994).

COMPARING EUROPEAN CASES

In order to demonstrate the power of institutions in shaping immigration and immigrant policies, I will compare the experiences of the Netherlands, Belgium, and Germany—countries at Europe's heart in which policy-makers are trying to integrate large, diverse immigrant-origin populations. In 1996, the Netherlands' foreign resident population accounted for around 4.5 percent of all inhabitants,[2] over 8.9 percent in Germany, and 9 percent in Belgium (SOPEMI 1998). These three countries have become home to different clusters of immigrant-origin groups, artifacts of history and policy. Their concentration, the problems (both real and imagined) that they generate, and the policies developed to address them have differed across regions, cities, and time as much as across national boundaries. Even at the national level, however, fruitful comparison is possible. Immigrants occupy similar class positions in the three host societies, which have several national/ethnic communities in common—Italians, Spaniards, Turks, and Moroccans. Taking advantage of opportunities to hold certain social class, ethnic, and institutional variables constant in turn, one can gain meaningful insights into the degree to which each factor explains the observed policy patterns. It becomes apparent that institutional forces, more than any intrinsically ethnic particularities, have steered immigration politics.

DETERMINING ETHNIC AND RACIAL COMPOSITION

It makes sense to start with the most obvious way in which institutions have cast the immigration die: by determining who came to Western Europe in the first place. Economic rebuilding and demographic losses led the Netherlands, Belgium, and Germany to accept the mass importation of an ever more diverse range of national groups after World War Two. Thanks in no small measure to institutional factors, their makeup and their legal statuses varied with each host society, as did the timing and volume of the inflows.

Thus the Dutch have little heavy industry and were relatively late getting into the labor-importing game. By the time they looked abroad for workers, there were only a few Southern Europeans available. People came to the Netherlands mostly from former Dutch colonies (Surinamese, Moluccans/

Indonesians, West Indians, and Arubans). Eventually, in the 1960s, Dutch governments signed bilateral treaties with Turkey and Morocco and opened recruitment centers there. The consequence has been fewer immigrants overall but more non-Europeans than many places in Europe (Vermeulen 1997).

In Belgium, Francophone Wallonia recovered first, and its mines and factories drew in Italian and Spanish workers. Later, the Walloon economy and then that in Dutch-speaking Flanders required more labor. The Belgians sought out Greeks and Portuguese and then signed bilateral accords with Morocco and Turkey in 1964. Like their Dutch counterparts, Belgian governments opened recruiting offices. The country's immigration history has made for a larger but more evenly distributed immigrant presence in Wallonia than in Flanders. Brussels has also had a long tradition of relatively high immigration. There are more Turks in Flanders, more Moroccans in the Brussels region, and more Southern Europeans in Wallonia and Brussels (Morelli 1994).

After 1945, finally, refugees from what had once been part of the *Reich* met most of the labor demands in Germany. "Guest-workers" also came up from Southern Europe. They tended to stay in the south, the closer and more advanced German region. Faced with the Berlin Wall in 1961, German employers and public officials looked more intently to the Mediterranean basin to replace the lost inflow of eastern workers. Turkey stood as the main untapped source. By then, northern Germany was in the direst labor drought. Hence, Turks came to constitute a higher-than-average percentage of the immigrant population in federal (city-) states like Bremen, Berlin, and North-Rhine-Westphalia and a lower-than-average percentage in Baden-Württemberg and Bavaria. As elsewhere in Europe, immigrant-origin populations have been bunched in and around large cities, adjacent to industrial employers.

After European host societies banned new immigration in the mid-1970s, family reunification and the influx of the undocumented, refugees, and asylum-seekers continued to add to the foreign-origin populations. Their backgrounds have grown more wide-ranging, as has their socioeconomic status. None of these processes has been identical in the three case countries, and each has been modulated by policies, laws, and the undertakings of institutional actors.

INSTITUTIONS AND IMMIGRANT SETTLEMENT

Immigrants' experiences after their arrival in the Netherlands, Belgium, and Germany have likewise owed more to institutions than to any intrinsic, cultural characteristics. The integration policies put in place, together with other social policies and institutional practices indirectly targeting those of immigrant origin, have governed the nature of ethnic relations in the host societies. Their effects have influenced the next set of policy responses.

The Netherlands

Faced with diversity concentrated in its four-city Randstad region, the Dutch have proved consistently inclusive and have at times espoused a multicultural model. The result has been significant ethnic-based and homeland-oriented mobilization, although not always of the type that Dutch policymakers intended. Sensitive to the risks of fragmentation that cultural pluralism can bring, they have adapted policies to local conditions and have not hesitated to jettison them when they produce unwanted effects.

The Multicultural Experiment

Even before they clearly defined a bundle of policies toward "ethnic minorities," Dutch officials were responding to the givens of postwar migration. In the early 1960s, Southern European workers were first in the care of Catholic non-profit groups that received increasing levels of public support. When large numbers of non-Christians began to arrive later in the decade, the renamed Foundations for Assistance to Foreign Workers lost their denominational character and became targeted exclusively at immigrant workers. An extensive subsystem of public, semi-public, and private organizations developed to deal with the housing and welfare needs of the non-Dutch population.

This approach was in keeping with the "pillarization" system that the Dutch had institutionalized in the nineteenth century to manage their own diversity. Based on a vertical build-up of interest groups in all spheres of public life, this power-sharing arrangement required cooperation among different confessional and secular groups. The major cultural communities—Christian Reformed, Catholic, and Humanist/Liberal—developed their own trade unions, political parties, schools, social work agencies, and broadcasting associations. Many tasks that the public sector normally carried out in other countries fell to "para- or quasi-governmental institutions" in the Netherlands (Toonen 1996).

The system facilitated social and political integration. Not surprisingly, therefore, Dutch officials turned to it when migration seemed to jeopardize that integration in the late 1970s. The halt in new labor recruitment earlier that decade had actually encouraged further emigration from Dutch colonies and overseas territories, and family reunification continued, too. Scuffles broke out between ethnic minorities and native Dutch in and around Rotterdam in the 1970s. Some supporters of an independent Moluccan Republic resorted to terrorism. Simultaneously, political mobilization against migrants was emerging: In the early 1970s, the Netherland's People's Union and, after 1980, the Center Party (CP) gradually picked up strength. It won a seat in the national parliament's Lower Chamber in 1982 and was doing well in elections to Rotterdam's neighborhood councils (Entzinger 1984).

The state responded in 1983 by presenting a new policy that targeted ethnic minorities. It applied to "those for whose presence the government feels a special responsibility (because of the colonial past or because they were recruited by authorities) and who find themselves in a minority situation" (MBZ 1983). The list included Sinti and Roma, refugees, caravan dwellers, and members of "non-indigenous communities" down to the third generation and thus encompassing those who naturalized (Penninx, Schoorl, and van Praag 1994). The ethnic minorities policy required that all public services be accessible to them and acquire the expert knowledge needed to help them. A new institutional division of labor became necessary. Municipal officials gained responsibility for spatial planning, building regulations, public order, the subsidization of street-level welfare work with immigrants, and the establishment of houses of worship.

Citing the danger of "foreigner colonies" if these minorities shut themselves up in their own organizations, the government envisioned their "emancipation" and gradual integration through state-supported participation in the economy and sociopolitical institutions (Voogt 1994). The ideal was a cohesive *and* pluralistic society, comprising ethnically bounded but socially, culturally, and economically integrated groups. To that end naturalization would be made easier; schools of all religious denominations would receive state subsidies; consultative bodies at the national and local levels would give minorities a say in policy-making; and local authorities would stimulate and subsidize the organization of representative associations (Heijs 1995).

Immigrants' earlier mobilization had usually been spearheaded by left-wing political and trade union activists opposed to homeland regimes. Many Southern Europeans also maintained close links with the Italian and Spanish Catholic churches. Turkish and Moroccan Muslims quickly organized, and sports and cultural organizations also multiplied. So, too, did associations formed by second-generation immigrants. The new support from Dutch officials nurtured the emergence of associations with looser homeland ties, and their strategies shifted toward integration at the local level.

Resident non-citizens gained the right to vote in local elections in 1985. While they went to the polls in lower numbers than native-stock Dutch, their turnout varied by ethnic community and city. The Labor Party received most of the minority vote, but the Greens and Christian Democrats had their supporters. Several minority communities remained polarized by "imported" regional, religious, and other differences (Buijs and Nelissen 1994).

Pulling Back from Multiculturalism

The country experienced noticeably more harmonious social relations in the 1980s than its neighbors. By decade's end, however, it was clear that some of the ethnic-based organizing stimulated by Dutch officialdom had "perverse" effects, leading to divisiveness (Rath 1991). Official openness to homeland organizations had left the door open to extremist influences from the outside. Moreover, linking the immigrant-origin communities to the welfare state—with a paternalistic accent on social assistance—had unintentionally delinked them from Dutch society (NCB 1993).

In 1989, the Scientific Council for Government Policy (Wetenschappelijke Raad voor het Regeringsbeleid—WRR) argued against initiatives to cultivate ethnic identity within minority groups. Instead, policy was to be scaled back in favor of combating deprivation *à la française* in "concentration areas" suffering from an "accretion of socioeconomic problems" (see Ireland 1996). There was to be freer play for market forces: For example, rental subsidies replaced social housing. Equal access became the goal, to be attained by ensuring complete legal rights for minorities and by improving their access to public institutions. Only when necessary would officials undertake measures aimed specifically at them. Southern Europeans, it was agreed, had done well enough to cease being the targets of such efforts (Lindo 1994).

Christian Democratic Prime Minister Ruud Lubbers was moving to cure "Dutch disease" (skyrocketing social costs and stagnating economic growth) with incentives for flexibility in the labor market, training schemes, and greater decentralization and privatization of social welfare. Whether taking advantage of new opportunities or despairing of a labor market wherein they still faced discrimination, ethnic entrepreneurs grew in number in the early 1990s (Kloosterman, van der Leun, and Rath 1997). Others of the first immigrant generation who managed socioeconomic mobility largely did so as employees of the welfare state, performing "ethnic functions" (Böcker 1994).

Not everyone in the Netherlands was on board, however, nor was everyone prospering. Lingering resentment at the immense social and economic changes rattling Dutch society and the growth in immigrant-origin communities revived the CP's fortunes. By the 1990s, anti-immigrant parties had elected council members in ten large cities.

Islam

The anti-immigrant parties turned Islam's presence in the Netherlands into a special bugbear. The country had a long history of tolerance toward religious minorities and of dealings with Islam through trade and colonization. Dutch officials entered into contact with Islamic organizations in the mid-1980s, in the belief that they could help implement the new minorities policy. The government assisted in setting up the Islamic Broadcasting Foundation and put imams on equal legal footing with other spiritual leaders (Shadid and van Koningsveld 1996).

To Dutch officialdom's chagrin, dramatic ethnic, regional, and political differences were reflected in the Islamic associations whose growth it stimulated (Can and Can-Engin 1997). They resisted pressures and enticements to structure a unified "Dutch" Islam. The Minister of Home Affairs met with the National Islamic Council, established by a broad array of Islamic associations. Unhappily, it soon split into two, and formal consultations with the government ended. The Ministry likewise made unsuccessful attempts to encourage secular and Islamic North African groups to collaborate. As Jan Rath and his colleagues have shown (1996), even in cities with similar immigrant-origin populations and run by the same party, local politics and networks could produce sharply contrasting Islamic associational profiles and cordial or hostile relations between Muslims and city hall.

Toward a Policy Balance

By the early 1990s, the central government was fashioning a Citizenship Program, through which it hoped to construct a more standardized yet locally anchored "mutual integration" policy. These projects, based on contracts with municipal officials, focused on the quality of life at the neighborhood level. In 1996, the Integration Policy for Newcomers pushed the idea further when authorities decided to require "newcomers" to learn Dutch and set up local offices to implement the program (Van Zelm 1996).

By the late 1990s, almost one-third of Turkish and Moroccan residents had dual nationality, and the country has nationalized by far the highest share of its resident foreign population—11 percent in 1996—in Western Europe (Vermeulen 1997). Some 140 candidates of immigrant origin, Turks and Moroccans being the most numerous, won office in March 1998 local elections, while far-right parties lost all but two of their 88 seats won in 1994. Dutch institutional openness and flexibility have worked against the eruption of widespread social disorder and the development of bonafide social movements, even among the young (Distelbrink and Veenman 1994).

Nevertheless, the most recent policy responses have come under criticism for being "one-size-fits-all" strategies that cannot work for an immigrant-origin population that has become more differentiated by ethnicity and occupational category (Asscher 1996). Indicators have suggested worsening social and economic marginalization for many minorities, Moroccans in particular: greater residential concentration, high unemployment and crime rates, low educational achievement, and substandard housing (Niekerk 1993).

The Dutch have worried that poorer neighborhoods in their major urban conglomerations might come to resemble France's suburbs or even America's inner cities. The emerging nexus of youth gang violence, drugs, and petty crime—"the circuit"—has grown into an obsession. The uncovering of nationalist Turkish and Islamist extremist networks as well as the founding of several Islamic political parties has added to the national angst.

Belgium

Belgium, lodged between France and the Netherlands, has reacted to the immigration challenge with policies that recall those in both of its neighbors. Belgian officials have searched for a balance between specific minority policies and more general anti-poverty measures. Distinctive French-style Walloon and Dutch-style Flemish approaches and conditions have partially converged.

Deepening Belgian Federalism

In the immediate postwar period, the emphasis was on family migration, and Belgium called itself a "receiving" society from the start. In practice, it was up to gatekeepers in the voluntary sector, especially Catholic institutions, to assist foreign workers and their families in trying to fit into Belgian society (Deslé 1992). Trade unions played an equally important integrating role. Ideologically divided and decentralized organizations in Belgium, their tactics differed. From 1946, the Catholic unions were active and effective in incorporating Southern European workers, grouping them according to nationality. Socialist unions, strongest in Wallonia, organized multiethnic regional commissions and were characteristically slow to acknowledge national differences. All trade unions backed immigrants' claims to equal socioeconomic and political rights by the late 1970s. Belgian activists long dominated efforts concerning immigrants, since until 1984, they themselves were not allowed to form their own associations or apply for public subsidies unless three-fifths of their members and contributors held Belgian nationality. From the start, the postwar Belgian state relied on consultative bodies to encourage immigrant integration.

After Belgium had halted new immigration in 1974, admissions and asylum policy, nationality law, voting rights, and most social welfare policies remained under federal purview. National authorities placed restrictions on the settlement of non-European immigrants in certain towns and districts, as it was believed that their spatial concentration would result in marginalization and hostile reactions from native-stock residents. Responsibility for "welcoming" policy and labor market issues was transferred to the regions (Wallonia and Flanders). The linguistically defined Cultural Communities (French-, Dutch-, and German-speaking), which gained autonomy in 1971, took over educational and cultural policies. They began to subsidize local centers and other institutions to improve the reception and integration of immigrants. Municipalities gained access to specially earmarked funds to support their own initiatives.

Wallonia

Official Walloon policy drew on the French republican model of citizenship and national identity, which has imposed a "local version of assimilationism" (Martiniello 1995). Flemings who arrived during the early days of Wallonia's industrialization had either returned home or melted in with nary a trace. Many were leaders in the Walloon Socialist Party, which remains dominant in the region. The history of assimilation and the pervasiveness of socialist rhetoric explain the relative neglect of the ethnic dimensions of immigration. Targeted policies for ethnic minorities per se have long been taboo. Initiatives affecting them have been embedded in broader social policies aimed at eliminating inequities in employment, housing, health care, and the like (Rea 1993).

From the mid-1970s on, training in the French language and intercultural exchanges became priorities in Wallonia. French-style, geographically defined Priority Intervention Zones were the centerpiece of urban and housing policy, as were French-style Priority Action Zones in the education and vocational training sector (CRPI 1993). Budgetary restrictions limited their effectiveness and reach (Leman 1991).

Few associations of immigrants, particularly newer ones, existed as such in Wallonia. Spanish and Italian organizations maintained their connections with Belgian and homeland Catholic and labor movements. The organizational panoply resembled that found in France, although institutional channeling nurtured more homeland orientation in Belgium (Vandenbrande 1995). Regional and community leaders were still condemning official use of the term "ethnic minorities," as it did not "capture the reality of the immigrants' experience and situation" (Blaise and Martens 1992).

Flanders

The Dutch community, meanwhile, organized coordinating bodies in the 1970s to provide logistical support for action at all levels and, eventually, to mount anti-racism campaigns and form immigrant-origin leadership. Flanders moved toward a targeted and multicultural model reminiscent of the Netherlands' experiment. Immigrants' ethnic identities became an accepted element of the Flemish approach. Their "democratic" self-organizations began to receive public funding by the early 1990s, and such associations—geared toward Belgium and the homelands—spread at all levels. Similarly echoing developments in the Netherlands, greater reliance on the private sector in housing hastened residential concentration (Zimmer 1996).

In both Wallonia and Flanders policy-makers were well aware of the differences in the two regions' approaches. In the former it was becoming clear by the early 1990s that immigrant origin and ethnicity were markers of social marginalization that did not fade under global policies to fight poverty. The

Flemings were simultaneously realizing that group-specific policies could fuel tendencies toward social balkanization. Instructive in this regard was the case of bilingual Brussels, which demonstrated the institutional complexity and fragmentation and higher costs that characterized the Belgian context (Vandenbrande 1995). The late 1980s witnessed the rise of the nationalist Flemish Bloc (VB) in local elections and the emergence of several small Walloon fellow travelers.

In a 1989 report the government embraced a grab bag of policy aims that contained elements of both the socialist and French-style assimilationist interpretations typical of Wallonia and the more identity-based one found in Dutch-speaking Flanders (Grudzielski 1990). Premier Wilfried Martens created a national advisory institution, the Royal Commission for Immigrant Policy, to help the government define appropriate measures. In line with its advice, officials promoted the participation of immigrants in Belgian society and added greater flexibility to the nationality code. Discussions opened over how to inspire the development of Belgian-style national federations.

Islam

Upping the ante were Islam and young people of non-European backgrounds. Belgium experienced a "scarf affair" reminiscent of France in the late 1980s (see Ireland 1996), and several Brussels neighborhoods erupted into riots pitting police against North African–origin youths in 1991. Islamic references were prominent in the reproaches they leveled against their treatment in Belgium. Preoccupied with homeland language and culture, first-generation associations showed a relatively weak hold on immigrant-origin youths (Deschamps and Pauwels 1992).

Belgium did not have the historical experience with Islam that the Netherlands had. Aping the Dutch nonetheless, Belgians began to talk about setting up a Muslim "pillar" along the lines of the Catholic/Flemish and Social Democratic/Walloon ones as a way to reduce tensions. A common Islamic faith did not supersede national and ethnic differences, but some organizational structuring did take place. Belgium has a system of formal religious recognition that opens the door to many financial advantages, including full state funding for religious education in public schools. Islam won official recognition in 1974. For a religion to activate its status and access the attendant benefits, however, it must put forth a representative executive body. Overcoming decades of conflict and division, Islam finally joined Catholicism, Orthodox Christianity, Protestantism, Anglicanism, and Judaism in acquiring such an entity in December 1998. That the elections to the body proved controversial did not detract from the fillip to consolidation prompted by the process. In the interim, with institutional gridlock at the top, local authorities were largely free to determine the building and location of mosques by means of building permits and safety regulations (Renaerts 1996).

The debate over Islam and Muslim youths put the spotlight on the myriad social problems plaguing Belgium's large cities and accumulating in certain neighborhoods. Belgium's policy-makers responded by steadily moving naturalization laws closer to *jus soli* and fitting respect for cultural diversity into general policies that focused on social harmony and equality (Martiniello 1998). This perspective has motivated both the Royal Commission and its successor, the Center for Equal Opportunity and the Fight against Racism, established in 1993. The Center has earmarked the lion's share of its one-time and limited-term grants for projects to prevent youth delinquency, promote intercultural understanding, and advance youth employment.

Policy Paralysis?

Despite suffering the divisive effects of Belgian federalism, the far-right parties attained their highest scores ever in the European elections of 1994. Unemployment rose seemingly inexorably among immigrant-origin youths, non-Europeans and girls in particular (Leman 1994). There were fresh outbreaks of rioting in Brussels, Liège, and outside Antwerp in the mid-1990s. Although Belgium has not produced any real youth gangs, looser crime "webs" have been active in many cities, involving young people of North African and, occasionally, Turkish origin (Bortolini 1996).

Belgium's baroque institutional structure has hamstrung the state response. Political clans have been free to step into the breach and assure a share of the spoils for their clients. In the niches of this patron-client system, criminals have found room to maneuver. The country's recent pedophilia scandal brutally awakened Belgians to what has happened to their political system. Early in 1997, the discovery of the corpse of a sexually molested nine-year-old Moroccan girl reminded them of the immigrant communities whom its pathologies afflict as well.

Germany

Some five million foreign residents notwithstanding, Germany's leaders have steadfastly refused to accept that it has become a "country of immigration." Germans attribute citizenship largely along bloodlines, "despite its racist overtones and despite the Nazi policies with which it came to be associated" (Safran 1995). The country's closed organizational system and ethnic-based self-identification mean that its institutions have treated immigrants as clients. Outside this control, they have undergone political structuring by groups operating along ethnic, religious, and regional lines and tied more tightly to the homeland than in the other two countries. Local-level variation has been extensive in federal Germany, however, and it has only increased with the restructuring of the social welfare state.

Social Democracy

German social democracy has been firmly rooted in the inclusion of individuals through social and economic rights. Federal courts have consistently upheld non-citizens' civil and legal rights, and the Basic Law promises every resident a life in keeping with human dignity as well as the right to education and the development of one's capabilities. Fear of inviting segregationist tendencies precluded the explicit recognition and protection of ethnic minorities. Social institutions have exercised a powerful social control function that has kept those without a German passport in a clearly subordinate, dependent position (Thränhardt 1988).

Even when the "rotation model" lost its appeal by the mid-1960s, the general assumption was that most of the "guest-workers" would eventually return "home." Any who did not would blend without a trace into German society, just as the "Ruhr Poles" and Italians of an earlier era had done. Trade unions and public officials, accordingly, allowed foreign unions and other organizations to operate freely in the country. Initial misgivings giving way to acceptance, German trade unions insisted that immigrants, as workers, receive the same social and economic entitlements as "native" workers, so as not to undercut their own position. Socialist suspicions of multiculturalism impeded special outreach efforts to immigrant-origin constituencies. To foster assimilation, authorities implemented a dispersal policy. When the percentage of foreigners in a given district grew "too" high—12 percent officially made for "overburdening"—no more could settle there (Cohn-Bendit and Schmid 1993). Success was measured by gains in housing, labor-market, and educational/training position.

The social welfare system prevented the development of true "ghettoes." Immigrant workers first lived in housing provided by employers, before they and their families entered Germany's social housing regime, which has amounted to government intervention in the private market. In most cities immigrants ended up scattered across neighborhoods next to Germans with similar socioeconomic characteristics (Blanc 1991).

A two-pronged strategy emerged toward educating immigrant children: integration into the German educational system and preparation for what was assumed to be their eventual reintegration into their country of origin. German states (*Länder*) are largely autonomous with respect to schooling, and emphases and approaches differed. Generally, policies in northern Germany shifted earlier and more insistently toward teaching German and targeting groups to address educational deficiencies (Iranbomy 1991).

National politicians who attempted to advance expansive integration policies found the way blocked by the ethnically defined citizenship regime and by conservative reservations. Social experts and subnational policy-makers were not as constrained. On the ground policy-makers made "pragmatic adjustments" and were forced to recognize "ethnic minority cultures" (Rex 1996). Social welfare work included an explicit, targeted policy for foreigners. Three major non-profit organizations took charge of specific nationalities: The Roman Catholic *Caritas* worked with Italians, Iberians, and Catholic Croats and Slovenes; the Protestant *Diakonisches Werk*, with Greeks; and the secular, union-linked *Arbeiterwohlfahrt*, with Muslims from Turkey and the former Yugoslavia. Several *Länder* and large cities installed a "foreigners commissioner" to represent immigrants' interests, as did the federal government in 1978.[3]

Hence, in and outside the workplace German institutional gatekeepers held sway over immigrants, who had little choice but to accept the role of "helped" (and thus controlled) populations. Responding to criticism of this paternalistic setup, a number of large cities introduced "foreigners' auxiliary councils," some of them chosen by immigrant associations or by a vote of resident aliens, to advise local authorities. These ersatz participatory structures, almost always organized along ethnic/national lines, may not have offered a true political voice. German supreme court justices in Karlsruhe, however, vetoed efforts by the (city-) state governments of Berlin, Hamburg, Lower Saxony, and Schleswig-Holstein to extend local voting rights to resident foreigners. With explicitly political participation verboten, debates shifted to educational and social policies toward immigrants, "wars by proxy" that raged on the margins of the German neo-corporatist system (Boos-Nünning and Schwarz 1991).

Immigrant associations increased markedly in number and in diversity as their communities sunk deeper roots in Germany. Labor movements, students, and trade unions opposed to homeland regimes were prominent from the beginning, followed by religious organizations (Christian, Greek Orthodox, and Muslim). Funding, available only at the local level, encouraged the development of a social infrastructure reflecting in its richness and, to German eyes, disarray those of the communities themselves. Their focus never shifted to the host society as much as in the Netherlands or even Belgium. In the 1980s, German-style "umbrella" organizations struggled to emerge, initially at the local and regional levels and eventually at the federal level. They represented the only realistic means of exercising influence on the German policy-making system.

By decade's end, educational and training deficiencies still affected immigrant workers' children disproportionately, and immigrant-origin populations still lived in shoddier housing and were more likely to suffer from unemployment than their German co-workers. Yet all things considered, Germans congratulated themselves for having avoided Belgian and Dutch levels of residential concentration. Relatively speaking, structural indicators were positive for the country's millions of immigrant residents.

Unification

The years following the fall of the Berlin Wall shattered that integration illusion. There was an upsurge in anti-immigrant violence as well as legislation that tightened up asylum laws and made it easier to deport "undesirable foreigners" (Ireland 1997). The federal government abandoned any intentions of developing proactive policies as it turned almost exclusively toward the reforming the asylum law. Only ethnic German resettlers (*Aussiedler*) received special treatment.

Reductions in welfare benefits, the decentralization of social policy, and welfare "chauvinism" (an unwillingness to share resources with immigrants) contributed to mobilization around ethnic boundaries (Faist 1994). Poverty itself became "ethnicized," as by 1993, 184 out of every 1000 immigrants— compared to sixty-two Germans—were on social assistance (Kanther 1996). The major cause of this increased caseload was joblessness, provoked by structural change in heavy industry. Training rates climbed steadily among second-generation immigrants but remained below those for German-stock youth. Non-German employment in the public sector stuck at low levels. The Zentrum für Türkeistudien points to one response to limited opportunities on the labor market: the burgeoning of Turkish, Greek, Iberian, Italian, and North African small businesses. There were already 150,000 "foreign entrepreneurs" in Germany by the mid-1990s.

As the immigrant-origin population underwent some class differentiation, a trend toward home ownership developed. Residential concentration was also becoming stronger, though, reducing contacts with people of native stock. In Germany any public financing qualified a building as social housing. Once the normal thirty-five-year loan is paid off, it goes onto the private market. Much of that housing was built in the 1960s. Thus a huge reduction in the supply began in the early 1990s, affecting immigrants most severely.

Multiculturalism and Islam

Arguments in favor of adopting a minorities policy along Dutch or Flemish lines multiplied in the 1990s, although fears remained that it could lead to tension and violence like that between the Kurds and the Turks (Stüwe 1996). Reluctantly, many Social Democrats (SPD) joined Green and church activists in rallying to the ethnic-pluralist camp. Multicultural proponents still had to contend with lingering socialist misgivings and top-level official repudiation. What resulted were often international food festivals and expressions of solidarity that cost little money or effort. Multiculturalism did make inroads in social policy, social work, and education in northern *Ländern* and a number of big German cities north and south.

As elsewhere, Islam has grown into a source of agitation. Islamic lists have outpolled left-leaning ones among Turks and North Africans on some municipal foreigners councils. Germany even had its own "scarf affair": authorities in Baden-Württemberg forbade an Afghan-origin teacher to wear the *hijab*, a "symbol of cultural isolation." Opponents held that the ruling smacked of hypocrisy in light of the public succor given to Christian denominations (Sommer 1998).

In Germany the relationship between the state and religion has been a matter for both the federal and *Länder* governments. The state pays officials of recognized faiths, subsidizes the upkeep of church buildings, and collects taxes for each religious community. Catholicism, Protestantism, Orthodoxy, and Judaism have won recognition as corporate bodies. While a number of Islamic organizations have applied for public law status, none has demonstrated enough reach to speak for the entire faith.

With no consistent policy on mosques, urban planners have wrestled with Muslims' needs. Bremen and Berlin have placed Islamic religious instruction in the hands of the religious communities themselves, virtually guaranteeing homeland influence. Politics and policy networks have combined to make certain cities far more proactive than others.

As integrative forces in Germany's urban centers weakened for the majority of them, young people of immigrant origin have retreated into their own "cocoons," turning to groups of similar ages and ethnic background and shunning the organizations and institutions that used to link their parents to German society. They have turned inward for protection, romanticizing traditional lifestyles. Among Turks this "self-ghettoization" has generated support for movements at both extremes of the political continuum. Ethnic-based political parties have sprung up, and Alevite and Kurdish nationalism have led to attacks against Turkish institutions on German soil. Members of youth gangs have taken part in robberies and confrontations with *Aussiedler*, the police, and each other. Immigrant-origin young people have sung in rock bands and written plays about their ambivalence and despair. It is not just the tabloid press that has started speaking ominously about the "Los Angeles syndrome." The potential for conflict has become clear, although the German institutional setup has retained enough structuring power to prevent widespread social instability.

At the same time, Germany has been changing in small but potentially important ways. Mirroring their counterparts in the Netherlands and Flanders, German social policies and social work have shifted from ethnic-specific to problem-specific policies that accentuate the stabilizing aspects of social networks. Slowly, the immigrant-origin population has become a source of new members, voters, and candidates for mainstream German political parties (Deponti 1999).

Naturalization became easier for the children of guest-workers in 1990, 1993, 1994, and 1999, although rates vary by *Land* and national background (being higher for Europeans). Such reforms may seem paltry compared to developments elsewhere, but they could herald further integration, with significant implications for immigrant political mobilization. The German case adds further proof that striking the right balance between group and individual rights involves more than simply acting on ethnicity.

CONCLUSION

Policies connected with decolonization and immigration have not only produced immigrant-origin populations with discrete constellations of ethnic groups in the Netherlands, Belgium, and Germany. They have also joined with religious, housing, education, urban planning, social, integration, and naturalization policies and the actions of institutional gatekeepers to determine immigrants' collective identities, the state of ethnic and social relations, and subsequent policy responses.

Each case country figuring in this study has offered up its own pattern of (non-) policy, immigrant organizational reaction, and policy response. Wallonia's amalgamation of assimilationism and the socialist rebuff of multiculturalism made for official denial of ethnic identities, even though they were widely accepted and kindled in practice. The Netherlands and, in a milder form, Flanders came to embrace ethnicity, even though their governments found that such multicultural policies generated undesirable side effects that themselves forced policy changes. The influence of homeland governments and movements has diverged across time and space, too, as have the status and organizational contours of Islam.

It is far too facile to hold ethnicity and ethnic capital accountable for the observed differences. Muslims and immigrants of all national backgrounds have adopted forms of participation resembling those adopted by other immigrants in the same host society more closely than those adopted by immigrants of the same origin in another host society. The content, focus, and wording of demands have varied with the nature of the political opportunity structure. Occasionally, groups that have proved particularly resistant to integration in one country have been held up as models in another. Turks, seen as the most challenging community in Germany, have been a relative success story in Belgium and the Netherlands. In German cities like Nuremberg and Berlin, it is high numbers of Italian- and Greek-origin students in special education classes that have provoked concern.

Europeans have not ignored the welfare and poverty dimensions of immigrant-related ethnic challenges (Favell 1998). Yet by decentralizing and delegating policy responsibilities, states have drawn intermediary groups into cooperative, almost symbiotic relationships with program beneficiaries. The formulation of policies has become subject to compromise and coalition building under the aegis of funding agencies. Ethnic identities have been forced out by the shortcomings of social services, which have often left immigrants with no option but self-help. Cozy local policy networks as well as social networks within immigrant-origin populations cannot but be affected in the process. Whether these networks help or hurt integration remains an open question, but policies and institutions certainly mold them. Even residential concentration and segregation are in part politically constructed (Li 1998).

None of the three host societies figuring here has escaped the effects of regional and global forces: everywhere, economic and welfare state restructuring has yielded a harvest of unemployment and disadvantage, and radical Islam has raised warning flags. But governments have responded in different ways and at different levels, and the nature of their responses has mattered. Institutional factors have cultivated or defused ethnic conflict. The nature of government intervention has defined identities and effected changes in their content and their boundaries. If we want to know how the logic of migration affects ethnic identity and maintenance, it is necessary to consider how institutions shape the opportunities for each of them.

Developing appropriate, effective integration policies in Europe has been arduous and painstaking. Nowhere has the clutch point—the proper mix of group-specific and general anti-poverty policies—been found. The Netherlands, Belgium, and Germany have all been seeking that balance. More often than not, new forms of differentiation and exclusion and new patterns of segregation have resulted, forcing further adaptation. Because politics is the struggle over policy, conflict has been the order of the day, even in the consensus-loving Low Countries. The messy, complicated reality of the process bears keeping in mind. Policy and institutional differences remain striking overall. They, more than inherently ethnic or demographic factors, account for ethnic relations in Europe.

NOTES

1. Definitions of integration stress more or less quantifiable structural positions (labor-market activity, educational and job training, housing conditions, residential/ spatial distribution) and/or participation in the social, cultural, and political spheres of the resettlement society, which usually calls for qualitative research techniques. References will be made here to both dimensions.

2. That figure leaves out sizeable numbers of naturalized citizens and former colonials.

3. Most policy-making power remained with the Ministry of the Interior, which consulted frequently with counterpart ministers of the *Länder*.

Commentary

The Need to Take Religion Seriously for Understanding Multicultural Controversies: Institutional Channeling versus Cultural Identification?

Paul Statham

This volume is structured in a discursive way, a commendable format that allows the commentator the liberty to provide an informed opinion, without some of the shackles normally required for a scholarly article. My set task is to review the "institutional channeling" versus "migrants' culture" debate, in short: Do the political and institutional arrangements which countries put in place for migrant populations importantly shape the paths of their political participation, adaptation, and identification; or alternatively, is ethnic and cultural self-identification by migrant groups decisive in influencing their political behavior in their societies of settlement?

The advancement of knowledge in this field has been considerable over last decade, which renders the question somewhat false, artificial, and simplistic. Certainly, a simple opposition between "institutional channeling" and "cultural identification" provides an inadequate framework for categorizing the positions of Patrick Ireland and John Rex. Both have steadfastly advanced more complete sociological positions focusing on the interactions between institutions and culture as a basis for examining the social relationships between migrants and their host states and societies of settlement. Moreover, their scholarly research has been systematic, empirically informed, and based on deep firsthand knowledge, and has drawn on cross-national comparison. I would place Ireland and Rex in a similar pigeon hole rather than opposing courts. While Ireland is a clear "institutionalist," Rex to my knowledge has never expressed a "culturalist" position. Even in this article, where Rex focuses explicitly on "ethnicity," cultural movements, and community organizations, he stresses that these are not "nationalist" cultural expressions but ought to be seen sociologically as deriving from the specific context of the relationships between migrant communities, and their home-land and receiving states, that result from a particular historical migration. Rex's more normatively focused theoretical texts on multicultural theory, such as his classic "the concept of multicultural society" (reproduced in Guibernau and Rex 2003) delivered initially at the founding of his influential Centre for Research in Ethnic Relations at Warwick, also remain strongly grounded in an empirical understanding of the actual conditions and institu-tional contexts facing migrants. This makes my task as reviewer somewhat tricky. There is much to say about the political trajectories of migrants in Eu-ropean societies, and whether host institutions and "top-down" policy dis-courses for migrant incorporation are decisive, or alternatively, whether it is migrants' "bottom-up" mobilization of cultural identities operating relatively independently from these. However, opposing the two texts of Ireland and Rex will provide few opportunities to address directly the most crucial issues at stake on this topic, which arguably occur most significantly within the controversies over "multiculturalism" and the demands by migrants and mi-norities for group specific rights, exemptions and privileges, and recognition of their cultural identities.

In this contribution I therefore take the liberty of commenting generally on the contributions of Ireland on "institutional channeling" and Rex on "ethnic identification" before switching attention directly to multiculturalism and migrants' claims for group demands. After reviewing the multiculturalism debates—and referring to Rex's and Ireland's stances—I will argue that insuf-ficient attention has been given to the role of religion in these controversies. To demonstrate this, I report briefly on some comparative findings in Europe.

LESSONS FROM IRELAND AND REX

Patrick Ireland's (1994) study on France and Switzerland—on which this ar-ticle builds by adding more country cases—was pioneering in attempting to empirically demonstrate the power of political institutions as "opportunity structures" that importantly influence the trajectories of migrant communities in their societies of settlement. Ireland explained the different forms and lev-els of political participation by similar ethnic groups in France and Switzer-land by referring to the different legal and political institutions—residence laws, naturalization procedures, political rights, welfare policies—which shape migrants' involvement in the host polity. His main finding, namely that similar groups act differently in the two countries, showed that "institutional channeling" is a better explanation for patterns of migrant activism than the socio-economic or cultural characteristics of the group itself, that is, "class," "ethnic," or "homeland" identities. If cultural and social background were determinant of political behavior, one would have predicted, counter to his findings, similar patterns of participation by the same ethnic migrant groups in different countries.

Ireland's research demonstrates the importance of national differences in policy approaches (and within countries, regional differences) and the consequences that they have for migrants' political participation. This general position has become "orthodox" in comparative studies of migrants in Europe and is broadly supported by the work of Brubaker, Favell, Joppke, Freeman, and my own research with Koopmans (2000b). Whatever differences may exist in these authors' conceptual approaches, substantive findings, and interpretations of different country cases, the general thrust has been convincing and "institutionalist": Political institutions and policy frameworks matter most in shaping the life opportunities of migrant populations and their trajectories of participation and exclusion in European countries.[1] In this view, each national policy approach not only has its own problems and advantages but also maintains a built-in "path dependency" so that changes take place within a given overall national tradition of citizenship. Such positions are well known and I don't repeat them here.

The special contribution of Ireland merits highlighting. His originality was in focusing attention directly on migrants themselves and their political activities, whereas other research had tended to be overly policy-centric. Furthermore, Ireland introduced a conceptual approach for linking migrants' political activities interactively to host society institutions and organizations dealing with migrants. Another important characteristic of his contribution is that it brings a hands-on narrative, gleaned from trekking across Europe and speaking to a whole range of officials, community leaders, and trade union officials, and by amassing documents and papers. As his piece on Germany, Belgium, and the Netherlands demonstrates, Ireland packages this basic down-to-earth knowledge and understanding of the practical, messy, idiosyncratic, and sometimes contradictory elements within migrant politics within his overall conceptual framework. Whereas many competitors try to work from the conceptual heavens downward, Ireland builds his house on evidence from the ground upward. His sympathy lies with practitioners and activists—i.e., "real people"—rather than academic approaches, which he considers sometimes overly abstract and distant from the actual lives and conditions of migrants (a charge that could be justifiably leveled at a large proportion of scholarship on migrants, and especially that which is not empirically based). Thus he distinguishes himself from other "institutionalists" with amusing sarcasm: "Local officials and immigrant-origin populations have not had the luxury of sitting back and philosophizing about what the ideal society might look like. To understand the *modi vivendi* that they have devised we need a more nuanced treatment than broad 'models of incorporation' can provide."

This knowledge of real lives and conditions away from the ivory tower is a characteristic that Ireland shares with Rex, a founding father of migration studies. At present, sociology in general, but particularly migrations research, is rife with overblown normative theories and identity politics fads, for example, witness the recent upsurge of "diaspora" literature from cultural studies. Here the "diaspora" concept is inflated beyond any analytic utility and simply serves for advancing the normative position that migrants' claims for their cultural identities are the driving force behind a new world order populated by unlimited numbers of "diasporas"—linking migrants across countries in the loosest sense—who celebrate their ethnicity at the gates of postmodernity (Tölöyan 1996). Much migration scholarship would benefit from re-examining the theoretical writings of Rex, which are based on a deep understanding of migrants' life experiences, gained from systematic research, and where his self-conscious and acknowledged standpoint allows his normative position—advocating a form of multiculturalism—to be tied to specific policy goals. He demands that sociology should be of some practical use, by providing meaningful interpretations of the world that can also be applied outside of the academy. Rex's theory acknowledges that his preferred multiculturalism may be an unattainable vision for society, but nonetheless tries to translate insight and understanding into practical formats that relate to the real world, and that may actually then be picked up by decisive actors and thereby have the potential to impact and bring change to social relationships.

Too often in the academy these days, especially in studies of migrants, it is the political preference and standpoint of the researcher that informs the theory, instead of theoretical insight based on empirical knowledge informing the political standpoint of the research. The consequence is serious, with "political correctness" often triumphing over evidence and reasoned argument. In the worst cases, sociology becomes devoid of systematic analysis and reduced to meaningless normative postulating. Such trends are not restricted to the periphery of cultural studies but influence the sociological mainstream too. Thus Saskia Sassen states in *Guests and Aliens* (1999): "I call immigrants and refugees 'today's settlers' to indicate that old concepts do not fit present realities. Migrations are acts of settlement and of habitation in a world where the divide between origin and destination is no longer a divide of Otherness, a world in which borders no longer separate human realities." I doubt that being patronizingly re-branded "today's settlers" would trigger street parties among the Turks of Kreuzberg in Berlin, nor does it provide a meaningful category, either for sociological analysis or that could be politically meaningful or made policy relevant. It is simply academic hot air that makes no attempt to engage meaningfully with the political world where people's life chances are shaped.

Of course, the cultural identification of migrants is important, but the urge within some of the diaspora and transnational communities approaches to define these identification processes as the "bottom-up" driving force of societal transformation needs to be strongly relativized and made more systematic. Here the analytic insights of Rex are useful. For example, in the plea for a historical grounding of migrant communities in the social relationships produced by international migration, he insists that a diaspora is not "any national or ethnic group dispersed across several countries," but specifically "when an *ethnie* or nation suffers some kind of traumatic event which leads to dispersal of its members, who, nonetheless, continue to aspire to return to the homeland," citing Jews seeking a return to Zion, black Americans a return to Africa, and Armenians a return to Armenia, as cases. Study ought also to follow Rex by readopting Weber's "evaluative neutrality," so that analysis has the interpretative power to potentially make a contribution to knowledge. Another way of making the study of migrant communities more systematic is along the lines indicated by Ireland, by applying a conceptual approach that relates such processes to the "top-down" institutional and ideological frameworks that define their significance, meaning and representativeness. In light of these remarks, I now turn specifically to the culture debates in the controversies over multiculturalism.

ATTEMPTS AT EXPLAINING MULTICULTURAL CONTROVERSIES

Perhaps the most important field where migrants' cultural identification has been addressed, along with the normative implications and consequences of their political adaptation to their host societies, is the debate over multiculturalism. In recent years, there has been a strong preoccupation with the position of ethnic minorities and the—beneficial or harmful—effects of the extension of cultural group recognition and rights to minorities (Taylor 1994). At stake in such academic and policy controversies is the nation-state's capacity for maintaining social cohesion as well as the liberal conception of individual rights on which it rests. Problems are seen to arise from the increasing demands that are put forward by migrant minorities for special group rights, recognition, exemption from duties, and support from the state for their cultural identities. These group demands challenge the concept of a unified, undifferentiated citizenship, a development that is viewed by supporters of multiculturalism as a healthy antidote against the prevalent "white" cultural hegemony (Parekh 1996), and by opponents as a serious assault on the shared communal values and solidarity necessary for cohesion (Huntington 2002). Proponents and opponents tend to agree, however, that such "culture clashes" are widespread and deep at the heart of contemporary societies, presenting in Kymlicka's (1995) words "the greatest challenge" to the liberal nation-state.

Even before September 11, the Madrid and London bombings, and the murder of Theo van Gogh, the position of Muslims in European societies was a key reference point in the fiercely contested controversies over multiculturalism. Public controversies have raged in response to Muslims' cultural group demands, which sometimes appear to challenge the very essence of liberal values. High profile cases include British Muslims' demands for Salman Rushdie's *Satanic Verses* to be banned for blasphemy, when they took to the streets to burn effigies of Rushdie and his book. "Headscarf affairs"—conflicts over the wearing of religious symbols in state institutions—have rumbled on across the continent, principally in France, since 1988, when a headmaster first sent girls home from school for wearing headscarves. In addition, there have been problems associated with Islamic cultural practices. Some, such as food requirements, have been easily accommodated, as they were in previous generations for Jews. Others, such as polygamy and female circumcision, clearly contravene most liberal moral understandings of individual and gender equality. Much depends on the extent to which migrants of Islamic faith wish to practice such traditions. Nonetheless, through these "culture clashes," the visible political presence of Muslim minorities has often been depicted by opinion leaders as a challenge to the norms, values, and principles of liberal democracies.

Regarding cultural requirements, state's migrant policies range from *assimilationist* approaches, where migrants receive rights to the extent that they are prepared to adapt themselves fully to the dominant political culture, to *multicultural* approaches, where migrants acquire full political rights and in doing so are permitted to retain some cultural, ethnic, or religious group identification. As we discussed, research including Ireland's and Rex's has demonstrated that countries produced markedly different ways for conferring group rights, built upon their citizenship traditions, which have had strong general impacts on the collective identities and political participation of migrant populations. Among the Western European countries, France is assimilationist, attempting to convert her migrants culturally into "French citizens." Naturalization laws are open, but as a condition for entry to the national community, the state places strong assimilationist pressures on migrants, who must renounce all particular identities in favor of allegiance to secular values of the republic. In contrast, Dutch, and to a lesser extent British, policy traditions come from the multicultural end of the spectrum, where migrants are allowed to publicly express aspects of their particular identities and interests as part of the national political community, receiving sponsorship to do so from core institutions, including local authorities, schools, the military, and the media.

Rex's position on "the concept of a multicultural society" (2003), though expressed two decades ago, still stands up to detailed scrutiny in the light of more recent events and debates. Rex's preferred multiculturalism is a very British formulation. He comes down explicitly on the side of a shared common "civic culture" in the public domain, but one that allows the maintenance of cultural difference in the private domain through "folk" morality, culture, and religion. He believes this "folk" culture can provide important psychological support to individuals, thereby contributing complementarily to the overall framework of a "multicultural society." As he states (2003), "multiculturalism in the modern world involves on the one hand the acceptance of a single culture and a single set of rights governing the public domain and a variety of folk cultures in the private domestic and communal domains." This is close to the British Race Relations formula, which allows some differential group rights to minorities under a broad state-promoted ascriptive identity of "racial and ethnic minorities," toward a goal of individual "equality of opportunity" (especially in the labor market), but which has also restricted the recognition of particular group identities, which are negated to "folk" status. Thus groups defining themselves as "Muslims" and "Rastafarians" are not included within Race Relations provisions as such, but only indirectly as "Asian" or "Black" minorities, the official categories for such groups.

Rex's preferred "multicultural society" can be achieved only if minority groups do not promote themselves in public domain using collective identities that pose a challenge to the civic culture, the cornerstone of public life, and social interaction. In short, "folk" morality, culture, and religion must be self-restricting and not attempt to become a "public" morality, culture, and religion. In his essay reproduced in this volume, this is further underlined by Rex's argument that ethnic minorities have an "implied contract" with the host nation, which means that: "They will have to accept that there is an official language and that they will have to use it in their dealings with public authorities; they will have to recognize the criminal and civil law; they will have to recognize that existing national values will be taught within the educational system; and they may have to accept that there is an established religion which has special privileges." Rex's multiculturalism by "implied contract" is thus conditional in its granting of cultural pluralism, and at the same time the "civic" is prior to the "cultural" in the public domain, which is further expressed in his hope that for ethnic minorities "it is likely that their main concern will be to fight against racism and racial discrimination and for social equality."

Quite clearly, many cases of particularist group demands by Muslims, and especially those who request exemptions and group rights not already granted to other groups, are examples of a form of expression that does not limit itself to "folk" status but challenges the established norms and practices of public life. Nor are they made as anti-racist claims for social equality. Of course, political change occurs through contestation and demands for rights. However, the crucial point is whether the group rights which are demanded can be accommodated within the overall framework of the civic culture, or whether they are based on values which themselves challenge the authority and principles of the established public culture.

Surveying the European experience, there seems to be sufficient anecdotal evidence to suggest that regardless of the different ways in which states attempt to accommodate cultural diversity, Islamic forms of collective identification have an exceptional propensity for group demands and have been the least easily accommodated. This holds across different countries and policies as well as across the different types of homeland and ethnic background of the migrant populations, whether Magrebians in France, Pakistanis and Bangladeshis in Britain, or Turks and Moroccans in the Netherlands. Such a finding challenges or at least offers an exceptional case to the expectations of Ireland's "institutional channeling" approach. Counter to the shaping powers of national policy approaches, for Muslims' demands for group rights and recognition, it seems that cultural identification operates relatively independently from the political context of the host society and is particularly resilient in the face of adaptation pressures. This provides some support for those who have emphasized the importance of migrants' group identities as a "bottom-up" source of claims-making for "multicultural rights" (Kymlicka and Norman 2000). However, it needs noting that such perspectives tend to be philosophical and normative and have made few attempts to provide empirical evidence regarding the scale and representativeness of cases of migrants' group demands. I argue that it is therefore perhaps more prudent to incorporate this phenomenon of a resilient Muslim or Islamic identification as an exceptional case within a framework that acknowledges the power of "institutional channeling" as a general rule for most types of migrants in most countries.[2]

How then do we explain Muslim claims-making as an exception? My position is that the role of religion, both as a form of political accommodation in the host society and as a form of identification and belief that shapes migrants' political behavior, has not been taken account of sufficiently as an explanatory factor for political behavior, and that this is essential for understanding the exceptional resilience of Islam as a source for group demands. To support this stance, I first attempt to explain why the interpretative frameworks of social science have tended not to factor in religion as an important variable, and then I report briefly on some empirical findings that shed further light on this.

WHY RELIGION MATTERS

Much migration research has maintained a built-in interpretative bias that has led scholars to see religious identification as a backward or reactionary form of "false consciousness" simply masking objectives and interests that are really "secular." Migrant religions with strange rituals and odd customs have been particularly vulnerable. They are so far removed from most academics' life-worlds that it is easy to see how they have been dismissed as reactionary relics to be swept away by a superior secular-civic culture. Empirical evidence from around the world, however, shows that religion is not on the wane but on the increase. Here it is worth repeating the most recent position of Peter Berger. Though a founding father of the influential "secularization" thesis, he has more recently argued against this, stating that we are in fact witnessing a "de-secularization" or "counter-secularization" of the world, marked by an upsurge in religion. Berger concludes (1999), "What in fact has happened is that, by and large, religious communities have survived and even flourished to the degree that they have *not* tried to adapt themselves to the alleged requirements of a secularized world. To put it simply, experiments with secularized religion have generally failed; religious movements with beliefs and practices dripping with reactionary supernaturalism . . . have widely succeeded." Berger's insight is especially relevant for migrant religions, because it implies that the more a religion retains its cultural distinction from the environment of the host society, the more it is likely to remain a core of the life of its own community. So religion matters, but how?

First, although European societies see themselves as broadly secular, Christian religions often play important institutional social and political roles, regardless of how many or few people actually believe or practice religion. These institutional arrangements define pre-existing conditions of the political environment into which migrant religions have to find a space for their community. Second, religious identification is a belief system that can shape people's core identity and shape their associational activity and political behavior. This is likely to be enhanced for migrants, because they often live detached from the grasp of core public institutions that promote civic values, and rely on their own religious organizations and family networks as a "community" support system. Also the nature of a religion itself and the demands it makes on its followers' way of life is likely to influence the extent to which migrants' beliefs and understandings adapt or resist when confronted with those of the dominant culture. Following Berger, those religions most different from Christianity, "dripping with reactionary supernaturalism," are most likely to resist adaptation, not least because if they adapt, they run the risk of losing the elements that attracted believers in the first place. Lastly, it needs mentioning that liberal states uphold the freedom of religious practice, and so although policies for migrants attempt to shape political and secular-civic behavior, states make no efforts to seek converts from religious belief.

The position of Muslims in the West cannot be understood without consideration of the nature of the religion. The global Islamic upsurge is not only a political movement but a revival of commitments that have explicitly religious underpinnings. It has led to a restoration of Islamic beliefs and life styles based on ideas about the relation of religion and the state, women, and the moral codes of everyday behavior, which in many ways contradict the modern ideas of European liberal states. This appeal of Islam to migrants is not just a "homeland hangover" of new arrivals and older people but often serves as a source of identification for second- and third-generation youths. It is often sons and daughters of assimilated migrants, both workers and professionals, who choose to wear the dress and accoutrements that symbolize Islam in public life.

Particularly for those religions that make significant cultural demands on the ways believers lead their public lives, I argue that religion needs to be factored into the equation for understanding a migrant group's political adaptation to its society of settlement. How then does this insight on religion contribute to our understanding of the exceptionalism of Muslims' group demands, and the way in which Islam is a purported challenge to community cohesion?

ISLAM IN EUROPE: A THREAT TO COMMUNITY COHESION?

In spite of the resonance of multicultural controversies, systematic empirical evidence is rather thin on the ground. Recently, I undertook a large cross-national study of public debates over immigration and ethnic relations in European countries, with colleagues Ruud Koopmans, Marco Giugni, and Florence Passy. It is possible to use this representative cross-national sample of political claims over immigration and ethnic relations to address questions regarding the extent and form of migrants' group demands.[3]

A striking finding was that political controversies over migrants' cultural group demands were far less prominent than one might expect. In Britain, France, and the Netherlands, they accounted for between 7.7 and 5.5 percent of public debates over immigration and ethnic relations. Included here are those demands by migrants themselves for cultural rights and recognition, which made up only between 3.4 and 2.0 percent. This evidence implies that the scale of the "cultural challenge" of migrants to liberal nation-states has been largely exaggerated. According to our data, European societies do not appear to be tearing themselves apart at the cultural seams, nor do the political demands of migrants appear to be threatening carriers of cultural differentiation.

However, our research did confirm that cultural demands are principally specific to groups using Muslim or Islamic identities. Muslims made 61.4 percent of cultural demands in Britain, 51.0 percent in France, and 46.4 percent in the Netherlands. This indicates that at least for European countries, the issue of migrants' particularist group demands is not about cultural diversity in general but specifically about religious difference, and especially the difficulty in accommodating Islam. How do we explain this exceptional resilience of Muslim identities? Here comparison with the low levels of group demands made by migrants with identities from other non-Christian religions is revealing.

With respect to Judaism, the relative absence—Jews made 2.2 percent of migrants' cultural demands in Netherlands, 6.8 percent in Britain, 8.1 percent in France—could be explained by the longer presence of Jews in the society of settlement, by the greater secularization of belief and practice, and the greater incorporation of special rights and privileges for Jews in state policies, partly in response to the Holocaust. However, such factors do not hold for Hindus, who are equally conspicuous by their absence in public controversies over cultural difference, making only 2.3 percent of migrants' cultural demands in Britain and 6.7 percent in the Netherlands (in France there are few migrants of Hindu faith). Hindus settled in the same waves of postwar migration, hail from the same regions of origin, with the same post-colonial traditions, have the same type of community structure based on familial ties and patron-client relationships, and face the same levels of recognition from minority policies as Muslims. It is in this comparison that we see the importance of the type of religion as an explanatory variable.

The main difference is in the role of institutional religion for the migrant community. Islam is a much more visible and public religion than Hinduism. It places strong demands on the behavior of its followers in public life and in their interactions with the core institutions. Such religious requirements of Islam make the mosque the regular and central focus of most aspects of communal, associational, and collective life for the migrant community. Crucially, the mosque takes on a political role, not only for negotiating with the authorities of the society of settlement and service provision but in providing moral sustenance to the community and defining what political behavior should be. In contrast, there may be no public Hindu temple for collective worship, or the temple may be in the home, the private domain of life, a "folk" religion invisible to the society of settlement. In addition, Hindu faith requires few public collective celebrations and there are a very wide variety of different sects and co-existing interpretations of faith, which makes it unlikely that religious institutions become the key infrastructure for migrant communities in their interactions with the state and society.

To conclude then, it is the difficulty of the separation between politics and religion in Islam, at a time of a revival of Islamic belief, which has led to "cultural conflicts" across Europe. Overall, Muslim migrants appear to be an exceptional case in their cultural resilience to adaptation. Irrespective of policy approaches, conflicts persist, because Islam does not restrict itself to religious faith but advances into the realm of politics, where the state's authority and civic citizenship obligations reign supreme. Conflicts are therefore likely to continue.

It should also be noted though that our research also demonstrated that multicultural conflicts are only a very modest part of the resonant controversies over immigration and ethnic relations politics. In addition, concerning the conflicts over Islam, it is still perhaps better to have conflicts over being part of a national community than to have resident migrants who see themselves apart from the native civil society. What is needed in response to conflicts over Islam are pragmatic, practical policy discourses of accommodation that are based on factual understandings of the scale, type, and nature of the actual problems, away from distortions of public debate. Too often in today's controversies, liberal intellectuals defend a "myth" of unitary national citizenship, which is an historical anachronism or simply based on nostalgia for the nation's past. In cases such as Rushdie's and the headscarf, the facts of the actual problems have often been distorted under a barrage of rhetoric about national values and identity, and the nature of their threat to cohesion overblown in the public imagination.

NOTES

1. For a detailed and critical account of the positions of the key contributors, plus the advancement of a detailed political opportunity approach that takes into account institutional and discursive dimensions, see Koopmans and Statham (2000a).

2. This position is supported by empirical evidence drawn from a five-country study of the political claims-making of migrants, see Koopmans et al. (2005).

3. These findings are reported from Statham et al. (2005).

IV

INFLUENCE: MEMBERS OR CHALLENGERS?

7

Influencing Migration Policy from Inside: Political Parties

Triadafilos Triadafilopoulos and Andrej Zaslove

International migration has emerged as a flourishing research area in the fields of political science and political sociology. Increased attention has produced an array of theoretical positions, analytical frameworks, and insights. Yet, with the exception of work devoted to understanding the rise and impact of the extreme right, political parties have received relatively short shrift among students of the politics of migration. This is a curious development, given parties' central role in representing competing societal preferences and, through participation in government, translating programs into public policy.

Part of the reason for this lack of interest in parties among migration scholars could be the persuasiveness of the "hidden consensus" argument, according to which mainstream parties of the moderate left and right will prefer to diffuse migration as a political issue by entering into formal or informal agreements to manage policy consensually and out of the public's eye. The reasons for such a strategy are deemed to include mass parties' interests in not alienating important constituencies and internal factions, precluding the rise of racial tensions, and maintaining relatively liberal positions despite negative perceptions regarding immigration held by a majority of the population (Freeman 1995). The exception to this rule lies in the emergence of radical right-wing, "anti-system" parties that include immigration as a central element in their ideological orientations and electoral platforms (Perlmutter 1996, 2002). In marked contrast to mainstream parties, extreme right-wing parties show a "willingness to mobilize public opinion during the policy formulation process and to use the issue in electoral campaigns (Perlmutter 2002)."

While there is no gainsaying either the partial validity of the hidden consensus argument or the importance of extreme right-wing parties, we believe there is more to be said about the role of parties in migration policymaking. The shift in party systems and political discourses that affected states in Western Europe and North America during the 1970s and 1980s not only precipitated the rise of "new" parties of the left and right, in many instances it also eroded the longstanding consensus among mainstream parties regarding migration policies, thereby compelling mainstream parties to clarify their positions. As migration emerges as a central political issue in liberal democratic states, it is being seized by both moderate and more ideologically oriented parties on the left and right as a means of marking political space. Parties are therefore likely to become increasingly important players in migration policy and, as such, will require greater scrutiny.

This chapter considers the influence of parties on migration policy by surveying the extant literature and pointing out ways in which it may be expanded to better capture the role of parties. We begin with a brief overview of several competing theories of migration policy-making, noting that in each case the independent variables assigned primary importance—be they traditions of nationhood, international human rights norms, or rights-based liberalism— overlook the role of parties in the policy-making process, thereby leaving certain outcomes unaccounted for. We then review work on extreme right-wing parties. Brief examinations of the Austrian Freedom Party (FPÖ) and Italian Northern League's influence on migration policy-making while in office allow us to weigh the degree to which these parties' ideological preferences shaped migration policy-making in the respective states, both in terms of legislative outputs and long-term consequences.

We then turn our attention to parties of the left, through a discussion of the Green Party's impact on migration policy in Germany. We follow the development of German migration debates through the 1980s and 1990s and analyze the course of policy-making under the SPD-Green coalition government elected in 1998, to gauge the influence of the Greens in this policy area.

The Austrian, Italian, and German cases are particularly useful, in that all three feature the participation of ideologically oriented parties in national government. Given that the FPÖ, Northern League, and Green Party had clearly articulated positions on migration policy before entering into government, we can gauge the degree to which they were able to influence policy-making by considering to what extent each party's core positions were captured in the legislation passed. Our review of the policy-making *process* reveals the degree to which institutional factors, including interactions with coalition partners and opposition forces, acted as breaks on the translation of ideological preferences into policy.

COMPETING EXPLANATIONS OF
IMMIGRATION POLICY-MAKING: WHITHER PARTIES?

In this section we review arguments pertaining to the influence of (1) traditions of nationhood; (2) international human rights norms; and (3) the structures of the liberal state on migration policy. Despite important differences among these positions, each of them largely neglects the role of political parties, either ignoring them altogether (1 and 2), or granting them a peripheral status (3). We argue that this inattention to parties and partisan competition more generally has diminished the ability of these approaches to understand the policy-making process and the specificity of particular policy outcomes.

Traditions of Nationhood

In his seminal study of citizenship and nationhood, Rogers Brubaker argues that the politics of migration policy is informed by "deeply rooted understandings about what constitutes a nation (Brubaker 1992)." Countries with "civic" national traditions are more likely to accommodate immigrants, while nations with more "ethnic" national traditions are less amenable to demands for mutual adaptation between "strangers" and hosts. Once in place, national traditions dictate the likely course of policy-making, as "judgments of what is in the interest of the state are mediated by self-understandings, by cultural idioms, by ways of thinking and talking about nationhood" (Brubaker 1992; Castles 1995).

Brubaker utilizes this insight to explain the variation in France and Germany's approaches to the incorporation of immigrants after World War Two. France's civic nationhood is deemed to have driven its assimilationist citizenship policy, while Germany's ethnocultural tradition stood in the way of the incorporation of its large postwar immigrant population. In Brubaker's words, "[t]he unthinkability of an assimilationist citizenship law in Germany reflects the lack of an assimilationist tradition and self-understanding" (Brubaker 1992).

Yet, what was "unthinkable" in 1992 has, in large measure, come to pass. The SPD-Green coalition elected in 1998 passed a revised citizenship law that includes provisions for attributing citizenship to children of qualified foreign residents via the principle of *jus soli*.[1] Moreover, the Red-Green government proposed Germany's first ever immigration law. This represents a marked departure from the ethnocultural tradition of the past toward a more "civic" conception of membership. The traditions of nationhood argument cannot account for this change, since the independent variable claimed to be driving policy is itself being transformed (Lieberman 2002).

Simon Green has rightly noted that too great an emphasis on putative elite consensus regarding conceptions of nationhood led Brubaker to miss the importance of political processes and partisan competition in shaping policy outcomes (Green 1999; Koopmans and Statham 1999). In his reading, the stalemate that marked debates over citizenship reform in the late-1980s and 1990s had its root in the *fragmentation* of political positions among German parties, with the Greens, FDP, and SPD pushing in an expansive direction and the governing CDU-CSU opting for minor revisions to the status quo and rejecting calls for dual citizenship and *jus soli* (Green 2001a). That the reform of Germany's citizenship law coincided with a change in government and the ascension of the SPD and Greens to power therefore is perfectly comprehensible, given these parties' particular ideological orientations and policy positions.

International Human Rights Norms

According to Yasemin Soysal, post–World War Two developments including the internationalization of labor markets, decolonization, the emergence of multilevel politics, and, most important, the proliferation of global human rights instruments have "undercut the foundational principles of citizenship, and . . . contributed to the expansion of membership beyond the boundaries of national collectivities" (Soysal 1994). Postwar changes in the "organization and ideologies of the global system have increasingly shifted the institutional and normative basis of citizenship to a transnational level and have extended rights and privileges associated with it beyond national boundaries" (Soysal 1994). Consequently, "host states no longer have sole control over migrant populations." Rather

> [p]ostnational citizenship confers upon every person the right and duty of participation in the authority structures of the public life of a polity, regardless of their historical cultural ties to that community. . . . [P]ostnational dictums . . . undermine the categorical restraints of national citizenship and warrant the incorporation of postwar migrants into host polities (Soysal 1994).

Soysal maintains that postnational membership is "legitimated by ideologies grounded in a transnational community, through international codes, conventions and laws on human rights." Similarly, David Jacobson claims, "transnational citizenship is slowly eroding the traditional basis of nation-state membership, namely citizenship. . . . The devaluation of citizenship has contributed to the increasing importance of international human rights codes, with its premise of universal 'personhood'" (Jacobson 1997).

The argument for global human rights norms holds that migrants' status as rights-bearing persons has affected policy-making by facilitating their access to protections and privileges hitherto reserved for nationals. The picture painted by these scholars is one of general consensus: In a world wherein human rights increasingly dictate the course of policy outcomes, partisan politics loses its importance. Indeed, traditional political actors (e.g., parties) and processes (e.g., elections) barely figure in either Soysal or Jacobson's accounts. This is not entirely surprising. If the world culture posited by Soysal, Jacobson, and others were as powerful as they claim, normative contestation should gradually give way to rationally based consensus (Finnemore 1996). Yet, for better or worse, partisanship, contestation, and politics continue to play an important role in determining the status and scope of rights accorded to migrants, as, for example, in the area of family reunification (Cholewinski 2002). Without taking away from the important insights generated by this framework, its singular focus on global norms hinders its ability to peer "inside the state" and unpack the messy business of politics and policy-making (Gurowitz 1999; Checkel 1999).

The Liberal State

Like the argument from international human rights, the liberal state thesis seeks to make sense of the development of migration policy in the post–World War Two era, particularly the broadening of rights for migrants in liberal democratic receiving countries. However, these scholars see the source of change emanating from *within* liberal democratic states themselves. According to Christian Joppke, states with robust liberal infrastructures and traditions need not resort to international norms, as

[a]ll Western constitutions . . . contain a catalogue of elementary human rights, independent of citizenship, which are to be protected by the state and thus limit its discretionary power. Universal human rights are not the invention of the United Nations in 1945, but of liberal nation-states in the late eighteenth century (Joppke 1998c).

Joppke and others have noted that domestic courts have played a decisive role in extending liberal rights to immigrants in the postwar period (Joppke 2001; Joppke 2004). Unlike the executive and legislative branches of government, the judiciary is shielded from political pressures generated by populist sentiments in civil society. As such, the judiciary has stood as the defender of nationals and (select) non-nationals alike. The "decline of sovereignty" diagnosed by globalists is therefore strictly a domestic affair: Sovereignty is "self-limited" through the judiciary's extension of rights to excluded groups such as migrants.

Domestic liberal rights regimes have also been seen as a key to explaining why liberal states have continued to grant entry to migrants despite popular pressure to limit flows and assert greater control over the boundaries of state and nation. While economic "push-pull" forces and migrant networks linking sending and receiving states serve as *necessary* conditions for continued migration, the *sufficient* conditions are political and legal (Hollifield 2000).

In the words of James Hollifield, "a principal factor that has sustained international migration . . . is the accretion of rights for foreigners in the liberal democracies, or what I have called . . . the rise of 'rights-based liberalism'" (Hollifield 1992a, 2000).

Hollifield's argument regarding the effect of domestic liberal principles is echoed in Gary Freeman's claim that liberal democratic states are marked by an "antipopulist norm" that prevents mainstream politicians and parties from explicitly raising racial and immigration issues (Freeman 1995). When combined with the dynamics of client politics, this "constrained discourse" results in immigration policies that "tend to be more liberal than public opinion." Like Joppke and Hollifield, then, Freeman contends that liberal attitudes toward immigration are rooted in domestic sources that are part and parcel of the liberal state.

Here again, an overpowering causal force—rights-based liberalism—is credited with driving migration policy-making in a more open direction. And yet, policy-making in liberal democratic states often exhibits traits that sharply diverge from the picture presented by liberal state theorists. Among the most obvious is the rather illiberal tightening of asylum and refugee policies across virtually all liberal democratic states. As Ted Perlmutter has rightly argued, understanding this trend compels us to look more carefully at political processes and, especially, the influence of parties (Perlmutter 1996).

Like the traditions of nationhood and international human rights arguments, then, the liberal state thesis occludes the role of parties. Consequently, the sources, timing, and content of policies fall outside the theory's purview. Parties enter the story as minor characters with undefined roles—sometimes active in the narrative presentation of empirical evidence but typically not deemed important enough to be theorized in their own right.

EXTREME RIGHT-WING PARTIES AND MIGRATION POLICY

The emergence of the Front National (FN) in France in the mid-1980s catalyzed a growing interest in extreme right-wing xenophobic parties. This research field has expanded rapidly since then and the resulting literature is rich with competing explanations of the origins of these parties, their relation to fascist parties of the past, and the ways in which they resemble and differ from one another (Schain, Zolberg, and Hossay 2002; Kitschelt 1995; Merkl and Weinberg 1997; Betz 1994, 1999). More recently, scholars have turned their attention to weighing the impact of the extreme right on migration policy-making. There is some agreement that extreme right parties have impacted on politics and policy by placing migration on the political agenda and transforming political discourse pertaining to immigration, asylum, and integration (Minkenberg 2002).

Much less research has been devoted to examining the impact of extreme right-wing populist parties on migration policy. The following section examines the participation of the FPÖ and Northern League in coalition governments in Austria and Italy, weighing their influence on migration policymaking.

Austria: Immigration and the Freedom Party in Power

The formation of the ÖVP-FPÖ coalition in February 2000 catalyzed heated controversy over immigration in Austria. The FPÖ's radicalization of discourse on immigration during the campaign and in previous years mobilized civil society groups and contributed to the intensification of debates. The European Union's (EU) decision to impose sanctions on Austria after the FPÖ was invited to form the government also brought a great deal of attention to Austria and put the government's policies under intense scrutiny.

Discussions within the newly elected coalition focused on tightening asylum policy, furthering cultural and linguistic integration, and establishing immigration quotas. Not surprising, the FPÖ demanded tougher asylum laws. The party's leader, Jörg Haider, argued that Austria's adherence to the Geneva Convention on Refugees was being manipulated by new arrivals posing as refugees. In light of the events of September 11, the FPÖ held that asylum laws should be altered to ensure that criminals, murders, and terrorists were not allowed to enter the country. Haider demanded that asylum-seekers be fingerprinted and that asylum claims be processed quickly, so that those who failed to qualify could be deported immediately. The FPÖ insisted that applications should be made outside of Austria and that only European asylum-seekers be able to apply for refuge in Austria.[2]

The Freedom Party argued that the overall number of migrants entering Austria should be lowered and that a seasonal guest-worker model be adopted. Mandatory language and cultural integration courses were also demanded. Failure to successfully complete integration courses should lead to sanctions, beginning with deductions from social assistance benefits and eventually leading to possible deportation.[3]

Heated dialogue ensued between the FPÖ, ÖVP, opposition parties, and civil society organizations such as the Catholic organization Caritas. Initially, the ÖVP declared that the asylum laws would not be changed and that Austria would under no circumstance contravene the Geneva Convention.[4] The ÖVP also held that Austria should not fingerprint asylum-seekers, as the FPÖ demanded. With regard to integration, the ÖVP claimed that it favored integration, but that legislation would apply only to new arrivals and that no penalties would be imposed on those who did not pass the proposed integration course. The ÖVP also stated that the government would pay 90 percent of the course, in contrast to the FPÖ's proposal that the immigrants be responsible for 50 percent of the costs.[5] In defending the call for integration courses, the ÖVP argued that higher proficiency in German would increase the employability of immigrants.[6]

After much internal politicking, a new integration law was passed in October 2001. All immigrants, new and old, who could not demonstrate an adequate level of German would be required to take integration courses, with the state responsible for only 50 percent of the cost. Thus, the FPÖ's request that all immigrants take the course was met, as was its demand that migrants foot half the costs. New arrivals, those without a permanent visa, and unemployed migrants would all have to enroll in the new integration courses. Although those who failed the course would not be penalized, they would be forced to repeat it at a higher cost.[7] Failure to successfully pass the integration course could eventually prevent the renewal of residence and work permits.

Although Austria's asylum law was not fundamentally transformed, it was decided that asylum-seekers should be fingerprinted, thus satisfying a key FPÖ demand.[8] Calls for a twenty-four-hour "fast tracking" of application procedures were also made, with the support of the ÖVP. Indeed, the ÖVP Interior Minister, Ernst Strasser, appeared to relish his ability to take tough line on asylum and integration issues, thereby loosening the FPÖ's grip on these issues and establishing the ÖVP's hard-line credentials among FPÖ voters (Luther 2003).

The Austrian Social Democratic (SPÖ) and Green parties, along with human rights organizations and other civil society groups, objected to the new integration law and to what they claimed was a highly objectionable attitude toward non–Austrian and non–European Union citizens. Opposition forces declared that the new legislation demonstrated that the ÖVP had completely succumbed to the demands of Haider and the FPÖ (Luther 2003). As already noted, this was a fairly accurate accusation, though the ÖVP found it increasingly easy and politically advantageous to "succumb" in the new security environment that characterized the post–September 11 world.

With regard to labor migration, the governing coalition changed the Austrian quota system, declaring that it would increase quotas for highly skilled workers by 50 percent. Quotas for less-skilled workers would be abolished and replaced by the "importation" of temporary laborers. Temporary workers would now be able to work in industries other than tourism and agriculture and would be able to extend their work visas from six to twelve months. However, such workers would be barred from bringing their families to Austria or changing the status of their visas. They would also be unable to seek work from other employers. Once again the SPÖ and the Green Party accused the ÖVP of caving into the FPÖ and acceding to the implementation of a guest-worker model (European Observer 2001).

Thus despite the rapid decline of the FPÖ in office, its impact on migration policy was tangible. While not all of its preferences were translated into policy, several were, despite a highly mobilized opposition that was extremely critical of the government's positions on migration-related issues. Perhaps more important, the ÖVP's strategy of co-opting the FPÖ and protecting its right flank led it to accept a much harder line on migration issues than it had in the past (Luther 2003). This may be an even more important long-term consequence of the ÖVP-FPÖ coalition. With the center-right accepting FPÖ positions, the ideological field of Austrian migration policy is likely to become more polarized and consensus harder to achieve. The ÖVP's recent successes and continuing reliance on the FPÖ as a coalition partner will force the Austrian SPÖ and Greens to either oppose the right more strongly or, as seems to be the case, to shift to the right while trying to maintain credibility among left-wing supporters. Whatever course Austrian politics takes, the impact of the FPÖ on migration policy-making will have been critically important.

The Northern League and Italy's New Immigration Policy

In legislation passed in 1986 (Law 943), 1989 (Martelli Law), and, most important, 1998 (Turco-Napolitano Law), Italy has attempted to strike a balance between regularizing immigration, granting immigrants rights, and improving control over its borders. At the same time, Italian governments have aimed to placate employers' demands for skilled and unskilled labor by increasing the number of foreigners in the workforce (Veugelers 1993; Di Pascale 2002; Perlmutter 1997). The reaction of the Northern League to the course of migration policy-making in Italy has been consistently negative. In its view, Italy's laws encourage uncontrolled migration, threaten Italian national identity, and disrupt social stability.

The Northern League's first brush with power in 1994 proved to be short lived and relatively ineffective, as disagreements with its coalition partners Forza Italia and Alleanza Nazionale (AN) led it to leave the coalition and force the collapse of the government (Perlmutter 2002). After regaining power with its previous coalition partners, the Northern League made the amendment of the Turco-Napolitano Law a primary goal. The ease with which new immigration legislation was passed this time around was striking and can be explained, in part, by a pre-election agreement on the issue between Silvio Berlusconi (prime minister and leader of Forza Italia) and Umberto Bossi, the leader of the Northern League. This agreement focused on themes that would later be included in the Bossi-Fini bill, including the linking of employment and work visas, stronger control of illegal immigration, tougher laws for family reunification, and the granting of financial incentives to neighboring countries to help fight illegal immigration.

The Bossi-Fini Law passed the Italian Senate in February 2002. It included several important amendments to the 1998 law. The new legislation linked employment with the ability to obtain a work permit or a visa. It is now possible to receive a work permit only if the applicant secures employment, a place of residence, and guaranteed return passage to his or her home country, paid for by his or her employer. Labor migration is possible only if an employer, through one of the newly created local immigration centers, makes a request for a specific quantity and/or a type of worker or for a specific individual. When the work permit expires the immigrant must find a new job or return home. Quotas will also be set more rigidly. At the end of the year—depending on demand and levels of unemployment—the quota for the following year will be determined.[9]

The new law also toughens border controls. Anyone caught attempting to enter the country illegally can be subjected to a jail sentence; on the third offence, there is a mandatory jail sentence from one to four years. Penalties for trafficking in migrants have also been toughened, and calls for the military to block boats attempting to smuggle immigrants into the country were sanctioned. Countries willing to help stop illegal immigration will be given priority in the granting of foreign aid. The Bossi-Fini Law also calls for the streamlining of asylum laws and demands that asylum claims be adjudicated speedily. The law also stipulates that claimants not be given temporary work permits until it is assured that their claims for asylum are legitimate. Finally, Italy's already rigid rules on family reunification have been toughened, with third-generation relatives no longer enjoying sponsorship rights.[10]

As already noted, a pre-election agreement between Berlusconi and Bossi ensured that intragovernment opposition would be kept to a minimum. Moreover, AN leader Fini did not want to appear to be weak on immigration and Berlusconi was happy to reap the advantages of appearing tough on immigration without the potential costs associated with having his name on the bill. Passing the new legislation was especially important for Bossi, as it demonstrated that his coalition with Forza Italia and the AN could produce tangible results. Opposition was, however, registered by the two Christian democratic parties, the CCD and the CDU. Rocco Buttiglione, leader of the CCD, demanded that illegal immigrants already working and living in Italy should be legalized, especially those employed in home care.[11] The Northern League strongly objected, claiming that this would only legalize what amounted to illegal immigration. Bossi declared that the legalization of home workers would in reality constitute the legalization of a million prostitutes.[12] In the end, an agreement was reached whereby families that employed illegal home care workers would be permitted to legalize one such worker per family, except in special circumstances, and on the condition that the illegal employee had entered Italy before the beginning of the year.

Not surprising, civil society organizations and industry also objected to the new law. On several occasions, in cities such as Brescia and Rome, immigrants associations, opposition parties, anti-globalization groups and the unions came together and loudly proclaimed that the Bossi-Fini Law was racist.[13] Business was also disturbed by the government's direction. Summing up the criticism of many employers, the president of the Industrialists of the Veneto, Rossi Luciani, proclaimed that the Veneto needed immigrants and that that the new law would merely increase the bureaucracy and rigidity of the system.[14] Livio Turco, the author of the original Turco-Napolitano Law, joined the chorus, arguing that the new amendments would harm the country. Even though the new law did not go as far as either the Northern League or AN would have preferred, Turco has noted that that it succeeded in casting migrants as a precarious visitors lacking sufficient rights.[15]

The high degree of coalition unity helped to deflect these criticisms, as did the power of the government vis-à-vis parliamentary and extra-parliamentary opposition. The coalition's relative insulation from social movements and interests facilitated the rapid revision of Italy's migration policy along lines favored by the right. Thus, the synergy of interests that helped keep the coalition intact also eased passage of the legislation and minimized the number of openings available to opponents of the government.

BRINGING THE LEFT BACK IN:
THE GREENS AND GERMAN MIGRATION POLICY

In this section, we wish to highlight the influence of parties on the left by focusing on the role of the German Green Party and, to a lesser degree, the SPD. It is our contention that the recent course of migration policy-making in Germany cannot be properly understood without reference to the preferences of the Greens and SPD and that the content of recent legislative changes make sense only in light of partisan contestation and party politics. We begin by outlining the emergence of a distinctive position on migration within the German political left, focusing on the breakdown of cross-party consensus in the 1980s and the heightening of partisanship into the 1990s. We then examine the politics accompanying the revision of Germany's citizenship law and efforts to arrive at a new immigration law. As with our discussion of policy-making in Austria and Italy, we emphasize the importance of party political "interaction effects" on the formulation of policy.

The Twilight of Consensus: 1973–1982

Calls for changes to West Germany's citizenship and immigration laws began to be voiced once it became clear that many of the "guest-workers" recruited to temporarily fill labor shortages between 1955 and 1973 were unwilling to return home as planned (Castles 1985; Schönwälder 2001). The recruitment stop put in place by the SPD-FDP government in November

1973 led to a "boomerang effect," whereby labor migrants concerned about being permanently shut out of West Germany decided to stay put and petitioned to have their family members join them (Bade 1994a; Meier-Braun: 1998). Consequently, the number of migrants in Germany increased during the course of the 1970s and 1980s, transforming West Germany into an "undeclared immigration country" (Thränhardt 1992).

Churches, welfare organizations, and unions argued for greater recognition of West Germany's transformation into a country of immigration and demanded improvements in the basic rights accorded to foreign workers and their families (Micksh 1991). Initially, they enjoyed only limited success on this front, particularly with regard to influencing the outlook of the government and political parties. A tacit consensus between the major parties upheld an outright ban on labor migration and the maintenance of restrictive residency and naturalization policies. A commission appointed by the SPD-FDP coalition government to define a framework for "foreigners policy" (*Ausländerpolitik*) in 1977 underscored and formalized these points, reiterating the government's stance that West Germany was "not a country of immigration" (Green 2001b). The commission also recommended that policies be designed to facilitate the integration of foreigners, on the one hand, and assist in their voluntary repatriation, on the other—a schizophrenic policy prescription, to be sure. The government's acceptance of the commission's recommendations heralded the first phase of the "stable contradiction" that would characterize West German immigration policymaking through the 1980s and 1990s (Thränhardt 1992).[16]

Under the surface, differences in thinking began to emerge even within official circles. In 1978, Heinz Kühn, the former minister-president of North Rhine–Westphalia and a prominent member of the SPD, was appointed the first Federal Commissioner for the Integration of Foreign Workers and their Families. In a 1979 memorandum, Kühn rejected past policies and called for the recognition of West Germany's status as an immigration country. He also recommended radical reforms, including granting foreign residents the right to vote in local elections, improving access to all levels of education for immigrant youth, and expediting naturalization procedures to facilitate the integration of first- and second-generation migrants (Geiß 2001; Kühn 1979). Taken together, Kuhn's recommendations formed a coherent vision oriented toward improving the legal status and integration of foreign residents into West German society (Castles 1985). However, the government at the time failed to pursue his vision with any zeal. The one recommendation that was taken up—regarding expedited naturalization for second-generation youth—was written into a draft law that was ultimately rejected by CDU-CSU–dominated Bundesrat. The looming 1980 Bundestag election and CDU-CSU's decision to use immigration as a campaign issue put the SPD on the defensive (O'Brien 1996). Following its narrow victory at the polls, the SPD was "determined to not yield ground to the CDU-CSU on the issue of restricting immigration" (Green 1999). Thus the government continued to try to balance the contradictory goals of restriction, repatriation, and integration, thereby limiting the force of calls for more thoroughgoing reforms.

The Unraveling of Consensus: 1982–1990

The CDU-CSU's entry into government in 1982, following the dissolution of the SPD-FDP coalition, led to a shift in priorities away from integration and more firmly toward restriction and repatriation. To encourage repatriation, the Kohl government passed legislation in 1983 that called for a payment to be granted to migrants who elected to return to their country of origin (Klusmeyer 1993). More important, the government's interior minister, Friedrich Zimmermann, proposed policies that would sharply limit family reunification by lowering the age of entitlement from sixteen to six (Haberland 1983).

Zimmermann's heavy-handedness was an important catalyst in the development of more liberal positions on migration policy, as it led to sharp protests on the part of churches, unions, welfare organizations, and segments of the SPD. Moreover, the new federal commissioner for Foreigners Affairs, Liselotte Funcke (FDP), came out strongly against the government's proposals, as did the Green Party, a new actor on the German political scene that would come to play a critical role in immigration and citizenship politics.

Widespread criticism of the government's proposals eventually led to Zimmermann's replacement by Wolfgang Schäuble. After several revisions, a new "Foreigners Law" (*Ausländergesetz*) was passed in 1990. Although the final version of the law no longer included the most pernicious elements of an earlier draft, it failed to elicit the support of either the Greens or the SPD and had to be pushed through the Bundestag and Bundesrat by the government. In an effort to quell opposition, the new law did include a right to naturalization for second-generation foreign residents aged sixteen to twenty-one (Green 2001a).

More generally, the struggles of the 1980s precipitated the collapse of cross-party consensus on matters pertaining to immigration and citizenship and the emergence of divergent positions among the parties (Fijalkowski 1991). On the left, the Green's call for "open borders" and a "multicultural society" represented a marked departure from previous discourse (Die Grünen 1990; Joppke 1996). Conversely, the growing popularity of radical right-wing parties reflected the range of preferences within German society and led many conservatives in the CDU-CSU to favor tougher policies on immigration and asylum to protect their electoral flank (Chapin 1997). The SPD's position as a party of opposition allowed it to take a more critical position vis-à-vis immigration and citizenship policy, thereby bringing it closer to its progressive wing, which had by now established links to churches, welfare organizations, and other actors active in the immigration field through consultation in working groups. The FDP was forced to balance its liberal principles with political commitments to the CDU-CSU, its coalition partner. This created a fair amount of intra-coalition tension, as evinced by Commissioner Funcke's role during the debate over family reunification (Geiß 2001).

The Hardening of Positions: 1991–1998

The 1990s were marked by the amplification of political debates over immigration and citizenship policy in Germany. Exogenous events, most notably the collapse of the Soviet Union and the unification of the former East and West German states, played an important role in this regard by producing increased migration pressures (Münz and Ulrich 1995). Debates over the free entry and immediate naturalization of ethnic German *Aussiedler* (Levy 1999), the constitutional right to asylum (Schönwälder 1999), and the integration of former guest-workers and their families punctuated partisan politics during the 1990s.

The ongoing question of integration and citizenship for foreign residents provoked important shifts in thinking, particularly within the Green Party and the SPD. During the course of the decade the two main parties of the left came to adopt roughly similar positions regarding how to best reform Germany's antiquated citizenship laws. By the end of the 1990s, the parties were united in their desire to move German citizenship away from the ethnocultural inflections of the past toward a more republican, territorially based model that included *jus soli*, simplified naturalizations procedures, and dual citizenship. For their part, the conservative union parties agreed that something needed to be done to expedite the integration of foreign residents, but rejected both dual citizenship and *jus soli* (Green 2001a). The FDP was closer to the SPD and Alliance 90/Greens in terms of its reigning principles but was forced to qualify its position to ensure the unity of the governing coalition it formed with the CDU-CSU. Hence, the split among parties and political elites that emerged in the 1980s widened and differences in policy positions on questions of nationality and citizenship hardened.

The convergence of positions among the parties of the left was partly a consequence of shifts in thinking within the Green Party. Although the party had long championed a territorially based membership that decoupled citizenship from nationality, its distaste for policies that facilitated "forced Germanization" (*Zwangsgermanisierung*) led it to favor proposals "geared toward granting [foreign residents] political rights without requiring them to obtain German nationality" (Murray 1994). This opinion was shared by many on the left and reflected a deep-rooted antipathy toward German national-ism. The force of contingent events and the emergence of new ideas con-cerning national identity enabled the Greens, and the Left more generally, to move away from multicultural "differentialism" toward civic republicanism over the course of the 1990s.

Proposals for granting resident foreigners local voting rights—and laws passed to that effect in Hamburg and Schleswig-Holstein—were struck down by the Federal Constitutional Court in 1990, thereby dampening a major "post-nationalist" policy proposal pursued by the left throughout the 1980s (Joppke 1999). More important, the brutal murder of foreign residents in Mölln and Solingen by right-wing thugs and growing incidences of right-wing violence convinced many that legally enforced divisions between "Germans" and "foreign co-citizens" (*ausländische Mitbürger*) were no longer sustainable. Rather, the way forward seemed to lie in transforming German society itself, to make it more amenable to cultural difference. This dove-tailed with theoretical proposals advanced by leading German intellectuals that advocated a German national identity based upon constitutional patri-otism and civic republicanism (Habermas 1993, 1996; Orberndörfer 1993). The experiences of countries such as the United States and Canada were also evoked to illustrate that open, multicultural republics could be built upon a shared culture, so long as that culture was purged of ethnocultural criteria and reinforced by civic principles. This position stood in contrast to conser-vative proposals that placed the burden of adaptation squarely on the shoul-ders of migrants (von Dirke 1994).

The intersection of new ideas regarding nationhood, on the one hand, and immigration and citizenship policy-making, on the other, was facili-tated by the work of scholars and intellectuals (Bade 1994b). Intellectuals worked alongside politicians to translate theories and ideas into concrete policy proposals. The increased salience of migration and citizenship issues in the German media and the emergence of more liberal voices among journalists and opinion leaders added to the legitimacy of the reform pro-posals. A functional dynamic emerged: Whereas journalists came to rely on migration experts for their facts and analysis, intellectuals recognized that they could use the press as a means of voicing their positions to the broader public (Interview with Klaus J. Bade, Osnabrück, March 19, 2002). This fa-cilitated the diffusion of what had been rather esoteric positions into the broader public sphere.

The triumph of the "Realo" wing of the Green Party over the "Fundis" in the mid-1990s helped to secure this shift in positions within the Greens, as proponents of open borders and postnational citizenship gave way to advo-cates of controlled migration and nationality reform. The rise of high-profile politicians such as Cem Özdemir and their leadership on matters of immigra-tion and citizenship also ensured that the more moderate proposals initially drafted by intra-party working groups in the early-1990s would be adopted as the official policies of the party. The experience of governing in coalitions with the SPD at the local and state levels during the 1990s also taught the Greens the value of seeking out political compromise and tempering their ideological commitments (Lees 2000).

For its part, the SPD had also shifted considerably during its years in opposition. Many of the party's members had come to accept the need for fundamental reforms to German citizenship and immigration policies and had come to accept the principles underlying constitutional patriotism (SPD-Bundesfraktion 1995). Furthermore, a key ally, organized labor, was by now firmly in favor of reforming citizenship and immigration policies and had established itself as a leading player in the immigration/citizenship reform coalition. Unlike the Greens, however, the SPD's identity as a catchall party compelled it to continue to balance the pursuit of principled objectives with the imperative of winning office. That the two parties had come to rely on each other to form coalition governments in Germany's post-unification politico-institutional configuration improved the likelihood of reforms being implemented, if and when a change in government at the federal level occurred. Reforms would depend on a combination of the "vision" of the Greens and the political clout of the SPD.

Contested Reforms: 1998–2002

The victory of the SPD in the 1998 federal election and its selection of the Alliance 90/Greens as its coalition partner created a window of opportunity for the transformation of German citizenship and immigration policy. The new government made the reform of Germany's citizenship law a central plank in its coalition agreement and immediately set about drafting a legislative proposal based on common objectives. There was, however, a marked difference of opinion concerning whether to proceed with an immigration law. The SPD preferred to limit the scope of reforms to citizenship and avoid the immigration issue altogether during the governments' first mandate (Prantl 1999). This provoked a strong negative reaction among the Greens (Interview with Cem Özdemir, Berlin, March 15, 2002). The difference of opinion between the SPD and Greens on the question of whether to proceed with a new immigration law highlighted the tension generated by the collision of political and principled interests within the new government.

The new citizenship law called for the reduction of the residency requirement for naturalization from fifteen to eight years for foreign-born applicants and from eight to five years for individuals born or raised from childhood in Germany. Furthermore, dual citizenship would be accepted in order to facilitate the naturalization of longtime foreign residents. The most significant reform addressed the attribution of citizenship for children born of foreign residents: According to the new law, citizenship would be granted through the principle of *jus soli*; that is, children of qualified foreign residents born in Germany would be conferred German citizenship at birth. Moreover, the children could maintain their parents' nationality, thereby becoming dual citizens. In its original form, the new law promised to fundamentally transform the institutional grounding of German nationhood.

The proposal generated a strong negative reaction among conservatives in the CDU-CSU. In January of 1999, the Union parties organized a petition campaign against dual nationality, which accumulated over 3.5 million signatures in six weeks. More important, opposition generated by the campaign helped the CDU win the February state election in Hesse, shifting the balance of power in the Bundesrat in the CDU-CSU's favor (Cooper 2002; Götz 2000; Hansen 2000). Without a majority in the German upper house, the government was forced to amend its citizenship proposal to gain the necessary votes. Ultimately, the SPD adapted elements of an FDP proposal (the so-called *Optionsmodell*) that limited the scope of dual citizenship (Fietz 1999). According to the revised draft of the law, children attributed German citizenship under the principle of *jus soli* would maintain their parents' nationality until they reached the age of eighteen, at which time they would have until their twenty-third birthday to choose between the two. Dual nationality would be discouraged in the conferring of citizenship via naturalization, and criteria pertaining to language competence and loyalty to the constitution would be required of applicants. Thus, the scope of the law was constrained by the politicization of the issue by the CDU-CSU.

Despite this setback, the government continued to pursue innovations in immigration policy. The impetus for further reform was initially driven by business (Scheidler 2000). German employers found that they were ill prepared to meet challenges generated by the revolution in information and communication technologies and petitioned the government to facilitate the recruitment of foreign-born "computer experts." Acting independently of his cabinet colleagues, Chancellor Gerhard Schröder responded by introducing an American-style "green card" visa initiative that envisioned the recruitment of up to 20,000 qualified applicants from non–EU countries. This time, attempts by some in the CDU to politicize the issue failed and the initiative went forward.[17]

The success of the Green Card initiative and mounting pressure from the Greens persuaded the SPD to move forward with a new immigration law. In July 2000, Interior Minister Otto Schily announced the formation of an independent commission on immigration and asylum policy to be chaired by former Bundestag president and senior CDU member Rita Süssmuth. The twenty-one-member commission, which included representatives from churches, unions, industry, local government, and academia, was instructed to come up with concrete proposals for the reform of all facets of Germany's immigration policies. After nine months of extensive hearings, the commission tabled its report. It recommended radical changes. Its opening statement noted that

> Germany needs immigrants. An overall plan defining clear goals is needed to structure immigration to Germany as well as integration: in order to meet its humanitarian responsibilities, to contribute to the safeguarding of economic prosperity, to improve the co-existence of Germans and immigrants to Germany as well as to foster integration (Federal Ministry of the Interior 2001).

In a marked departure from past practices, the report also recommended a yearly immigration quota to help address labor market needs. A portion of the yearly intake would be selected according to a "points system" that ranked applicants according to their education, skills, knowledge of the German language, and other objective criteria.

Shortly after the Commission tabled its report, the government produced a draft law that mirrored several of its recommendations (Scheidler 2001). After a series of ambiguous reactions, the CDU-CSU turned sharply against the proposal. Efforts by the coalition to broker cross-party compromise were denied and the Union parties' new candidate for chancellor in the 2002 election, Edmund Stoiber (CSU), made a point of criticizing the law.[18] After several revisions aimed at mollifying opposition critics were rejected, the government sent the bill forward and the Bundestag passed a version of the law on March 12, 2002. In a historic vote preceded by intense politicking, the law cleared the Bundesrat by the narrowest of margins. Citing irregularities in the vote, the Union parties claimed that the Bundesrat sanction was unconstitutional and brought the case before the Federal Constitutional Court.

Chancellor candidate Stoiber and the CDU/CSU invoked the threat of mass migration during the end-run of the September 2002 election campaign, precisely one day after the Union parties fell behind the SPD for the first time in the campaign. Coming as late as it did, the tactic failed to mobilize the sort of reaction generated by the 1999 signature campaign in Hesse. Given the SPD's slight margin of victory, it is possible that the Union's decision to play the immigration card so late in the game cost it the race by alienating moderate voters and mobilizing immigrants to come out strongly in favor of the Greens and SPD on election day.

The Union parties did however enjoy something of a victory in December 2002, when the Constitutional Court ruled that the Bundesrat vote contravened constitutional guidelines and suspended application of the law. Thus, what was to be a major turning point in Germany's immigration policy was postponed until the passage of a significantly altered law in July 2004. The period preceding the passage of the law were marked by often-strained efforts to carve out a compromise that captured each side's key positions (Kruse, Orren, and Angenendt 2003). This clumsy balancing act helps explain the rather restrictive tone of what was to be a policy instrument for *facilitating* immigration (Schönwälder 2004).

The CDU/CSU's ability to take advantage of the various "veto points" in the German political system made significant reform of Germany's immigration policy along the lines envisioned by the Red-Green coalition difficult, despite the support of key stakeholders, including employers, unions, churches, and NGOs. The interplay of factors in the political process had a direct impact on the course of policy-making and determined both the scope of Germany's new citizenship policies and the fate of the immigration law.

CONCLUSION

Our intention in this chapter has been to point out the importance of political parties on migration policy. We do not believe that parties are the sole determinants of migration policies and recognize the importance of broader forces, including traditions of nationhood, international human rights, and liberal norms and procedures. Rather, we maintain that parties are critical nodes connecting these and other factors to political processes. A focus on parties reveals the contested nature of concepts such as nationhood and rights, and reflects the increasingly deep cleavages on migration-related issues in contemporary liberal democratic states. Attention to political processes allows us to recognize how "interaction effects" generated by partisan conflict influence the content of legislation. Thus, party politics has an important role in determining the course of policy-making. A party-focused approach helps us to understand the importance of changing preferences, their relation to strategic interests, and the means by which they are activated in policy-making processes and transformed into legislation.

While our case studies demonstrate that preferences are not easily translated to policy, the more important challenge lies in understanding why this is the case. Future research can take this insight further by focusing on how differing institutional configurations help or hinder the translation of preferences to policies among governments with clear partisan identifications. More comparative work might also provide clues as to why cross-party consensus persists in some cases but not in others, despite similar pressures and challenges. Our case studies suggest that immigration is an issue which parties of the left and right can use to define their identities, engender coalitions, or co-opt rivals. More work is needed however to better understand the circumstances that trigger such strategies. Structured comparisons of a small number of carefully selected cases may help us understand these processes.

Clearly, there is much room for innovative research on the role of parties—right and left, extreme and moderate—in the migration politics field. We hope this chapter has demonstrated the advantages bringing parties into the study of migration policy and provided some clues as to how further research might be structured.

NOTES

1. The principle of *jus soli* holds that citizenship is conferred to anyone born in a state's territory. Conversely, the principle of *jus sanguinis* holds that citizenship is based on "blood ties."

2. "Ein gemeinsamer Schritt," *Der Standard*, June 7, 2001; "FPÖ will schärferen Integrationsvertrag," *Der Standard*, September 28, 2001; "Integrationsvertrag als politisches Suchfeld," *Der Standard*, September 28, 2001; "Asylverfahren nur im Inland möglich," *Der Standard*, October 3, 2001; "Asylwerber in Drittstaaten deponieren," *Der Standard*, September 28, 2001; "FPÖ fordert Kurse für alle Ausländer," *Der Standard*, September 28, 2001; "FPÖ-Vorschläge zur Verschärfung des Asylrechts werden vom Koalitionspartner vernichtet," *Der Standard*, September 29, 2001; "Asyl: FP wünscht Verbesserung," *Der Standard*, October 3, 2001; "FPÖ verschärft Druck auf ÖVP," *Der Standard*, October 19, 2001; "Kurse und Sanktionen," *Der Standard*, November 28, 2001.

3. "FPÖ will schärferen Integrationsvertrag," *Der Standard*, September 28, 2001.

4. Ibid.

5. Ibid.

6. "Integrationsverträge im internationalen Vergleich," *Der Standard*, October 4, 2001.

7. "Deutschkurse für Ausländer beschlossen," *Der Standard*, October 3, 2001; "Kurse und Sanktionen," *Der Standard*, October 3, 2001.

8. Ibid.

9. See Law 795 as passed by the senate. "Senato dello Repubblica, xiv Legislatura N. 795" and also articles "Legge sull'immigrazione, i punti del DDL," *La Repubblica*, March 1, 2002; "Immigrazione, via libera al Senato," *Il Corriere della Sera*, March 1, 2002; "Il permesso di soggiorno sarà legato al lavoro e alla sua durata," *La Repubblica*, March 1, 2002.

10. Ibid.

11. "Regolarizzare tutti gli immigrati che già lavorano," *Il Corriere della Sera*, December 20, 2001.

12. "Bossi polemizza: così regolarizziamo le lucciole," *La Repubblica*, February 8, 2002.

13. "Sanatoria, immigrati in piazza," *Il Corriere della Sera*, November 25, 2001; *La Repubblica*, February 16, 2002.

14. "Ora il rischio e' l'eccessiva burocrazia," *La Repubblica*, March 1, 2002.

15. "Il permesso di soggiorno sarà legato al lavoro e alla sua durata," *La Repubblica*, March 1, 2002.

16. The SPD-FDP also implemented a series of "guidelines on naturalization" in December 1977. The move marked another missed opportunity. As Simon Green has pointed out: "Instead of placing the emphasis on swift, unbureaucratic natural-

ization, the guidelines set the standard deliberately high effectively institutionalizing the then prevailing situation that naturalization was an exception, not the rule" (Green 1999).

17. Jürgen Rüttgers, the CDU's nominee for minister-president in the *Land* election in North Rhine–Westphalia, campaigned on the slogan "*Kinder staat Inder*" ("children instead of Indians"). The president of the Association of German Industries, Hans-Olaf Henkel, came out strongly against such tactics, noting that Germany could no longer afford such provincial behavior. The Associated Press, "Foreign Workers Plan Criticized,"April 1, 2000.

18. Joachim Käppner and Jeanne Rubner, "Union und Zuwanderung: Edmund Stoiber bleibt bei seiner Ablehnung des Regierungsentwurfs," *Süddeutsche Zeitung*, March 1, 2002.

8

Influencing Migration Policy from Outside: The Impact of Migrant, Extreme-Right, and Solidarity Movements

Marco Giugni and Florence Passy

After having been neglected for years in favor of analyses of the rise and forms of protest activities, the study of the outcomes and consequences of social movements has received a strong boost in recent years. The number of systematic works—both case studies and, though less often, comparative analyses—that focus on movement impact is growing at a sustained pace, thus contributing to filling an important gap in our knowledge of social movements and, more generally, contentious politics (see Giugni 1998 for a review). Yet this gap remains very large in the field of immigration politics. In this specific field, scholars have largely avoided studying protest behavior and collective mobilizations (for exceptions concerning the mobilization of migrants and minorities, see e.g., Blatt 1995; Fibbi and Bolzman 1991; Giugni and Passy 1999; Ireland 1994; Koopmans 2004; Koopmans and Statham 1999; Martiniello and Statham 1999), and even when they did focus on protest, they have been interested in explaining its rise (in particular, that of the extreme right) rather than its effects on policy-making. As a result, we still know very little about the impact of protest activities on the decision-making process in the field of immigration and ethnic relations.

Given this state of affairs, this chapter pursues three goals that are all related to the study of the policy impact of protest activities. Our first aim is empirical and consists in assessing the impact of the mobilization of three social movements that are directly implicated in immigration politics: (1) migrants and ethnic minorities, (2) the extreme right, and (3) pro-migrant or solidarity organizations and groups. We focus on the substantive effects of these three collective actors on migration policy, intended as their ability to influence political decisions on issues pertaining to immigration and ethnic relations. Furthermore, we focus on a specific historical period, namely the 1990s. This is a period during which (1) discussions of the role of minorities in Western Europe, especially in regard to the actual or supposed "multi-culturalization" of society, have been brought to the fore of public debates; (2) the extreme right has witnessed a growth both in terms of electoral strength and in terms of racist or violent actions; and (3) the solidarity movement has consolidated its position within the civil society and become increasingly active in the field of migration politics. To have an empirically grounded assessment of the impact of these three collective actors is therefore all the more important today.

Our second aim is theoretical and follows two lines of reasoning. On the one hand, we draw from the literature on citizenship and integration regimes to explore the hypothesis that models of citizenship—that is, prevailing conceptions and shared understandings of the criteria of membership in a nation—provide a framework for explaining the varying impact of challenging groups that mobilize in the field of immigration and ethnic relations. Following a theoretical perspective recently put forward, we conceive of models of citizenship as a structure of political opportunities for the impact of collective actors on migration policy (Koopmans and Statham 2000a; Koopmans et al. 2005). Our choice to focus on France and Switzerland, two countries that have two distinct models of citizenship, follows from this opportunity approach. On the other hand, we continue an avenue of research we explored elsewhere (Giugni 2001, 2004; Giugni and Passy 1998), suggesting that we take into account the possibility that the policy impact of these movements is determined by the joint presence of protest activities and certain contextual factors.

Our third and final aim is methodological. Since the literature on social movements still lacks systematic and empirically grounded studies of their consequences, we propose an analysis of the effects of migrant, extreme-right, and solidarity movements on migration policy following a longitudinal approach, more precisely by means of time-series analysis techniques, which are particularly well suited to establish causal relationships among variables of interest. We should note, however, that in this respect our study is largely exploratory, sensitizing to an approach rather than testing a theory.

MODEL OF CITIZENSHIP, POLITICAL OPPORTUNITIES, AND THE IMPACT OF SOCIAL MOVEMENTS

Recent comparative work on social movements and contentious politics points to the decisive role of political opportunity structures for explaining the emergence of protest, the forms it takes, and its potential impact (e.g., Brockett 1991; Kitschelt 1986; Kriesi et al. 1995; McAdam 1996; McAdam et al. 2001; Tarrow 1998; Tilly 1978). Typically, scholars identify political opportunities with certain aspects of the institutional context of movements, most notably the degree of access to the political system for challenging groups, the capacity and propensity towards repression by the political authorities, and the configuration of power in the polity.

The underlying assumption in this approach is that the political opportunity structure thus defined applies to all kinds of movements and challenging groups, regardless of the nature of their claims and the policy field they are targeting. This is debatable both on theoretical and empirical grounds. Some authors have shown that different movements react differently to the same political opportunities (Kriesi et al. 1995) and that different policy areas yield different sets of opportunities to challengers (Kriesi et al. 1995). Even a cursory look at actual mobilizations by different movements suggests that some movements are more radical than others. While this might in part depend on the propensity to radicalization by certain groups, certain movements and policy areas have specific opportunity structures that impinge on the mobilization of actors who address issues pertaining to those areas.

Following the lead of recent comparative work on national regimes for the incorporation of migrants and on citizenship rights (Brubaker 1992; Castles 1995; Favell 1998; Freeman 1995; Joppke 1999; Koopmans and Kriesi 1997; Koopmans and Statham 1999, 2000b; Safran 1997; Smith and Blanc 1996; Soysal 1994), we look at the ways in which prevailing citizenship and integration regimes provide different sets of opportunities for the claim-making of collective actors in this field. We suggest that collective action in this field is enabled or constrained not only by political institutions but also by shared understandings and collective definitions of the groups involved and the ways in which their members should be included in or excluded from the national community, in other words by the historically and culturally embedded shared understandings of the rights and duties of migrants and, conversely, of nationals toward migrants (Koopmans and Statham 2000a; Koopmans et al. 2005).

Models of citizenship can be conceptualized as a combination of two main dimensions: an individual dimension referring to the formal criteria for obtaining citizenship rights or membership in the national community, and a collective dimension referring to the cultural obligations posed on migrants for obtaining such rights. On the first dimension, we may distinguish between an ethnic and cultural conception which on the legal level becomes the *jus sanguinis* rule, on the one hand, and a civic and territorial conception of citizenship which translates into the *jus solis* rule, on the other (Brubaker

1992). On the second dimension, we may distinguish between a monist or assimilationist view of the cultural group rights according to which migrants are supposed to assimilate to the norms and values of the host society, on one side, and a pluralistic view in which the state grants and sometimes even promotes the recognition of ethnic difference, on the other.

Combining these two dimensions, we obtain four ideal-types of citizenship and integration regimes (Koopmans and Statham 2000a; Koopmans et al. 2005): an ethnic-assimilationist (or differentialist) model, an ethnic-pluralist (or segregationist) model, a civic-assimilationist (or republican) model, and a civic-pluralist (or multicultural) model. Germany and Switzerland are examples of the first type, South Africa under apartheid of the second type, France of the third type, and Britain and the Netherlands of the fourth type.[1] Thus, according to this typology, France and Switzerland have two distinct models of citizenship. In France, there is a civic and political definition of the nation together with a tendency toward imposing the republican values and norms upon migrants. In Switzerland, the assimilationist view of cultural group rights combines with an ethnocultural conception of citizenship.

In this perspective, the specific structure of political opportunities provided by citizenship and integration regimes channels the claim-making in the field of immigration and ethnic relations. It therefore should favor claims that have greater visibility, resonance, and legitimacy in terms of discursive opportunities within the larger cultural framework provided by the prevailing model of citizenship (Koopmans et al. 2005). Specifically, the shared understanding of the ideal-type of the nation as a civic and political community in France, which has an inclusive definition of citizenship and where all citizens must conform to the principles of the republican state, should provide larger opportunities to actors who mobilize around issues pertaining to the integration of migrants in the host society. Since migrants in France are considered as belonging to the national community, the larger share of their claims bears on the rights and position of resident migrants (i.e., immigrant policy) rather than the regulation of flows (i.e., immigration policy). In contrast, the more exclusive, ethnic-based conception of citizenship in Switzerland should favor actors and claims concerning immigration control and the regulation of immigration flows, as this kind of issues is more visible, resonant, and legitimate.

Table 8.1 shows that this is indeed the case.[2] For all three collective actors under study, the share of claims concerning the situation of resident migrants (minority integration politics and antiracism and xenophobia) is higher in France. In contrast, claims pertaining to the regulation of immigration flows (immigration, asylum, and aliens politics) are more important in Switzerland. To be sure, immigration control claims by migrants are more frequent in France, but even in this case the ratio between immigration policy and im-

Table 8.1. Thematic Focus of Migrant, Extreme-Right, and Solidarity Movement Claims in France and Switzerland (1990–1998)

	Migrants	Extreme Right	Solidarity Movement
France			
Immigration, asylum, and aliens politics	26.6	4.0	36.4
Minority integration politics	40.8	8.1	15.3
Antiracism and xenophobia	21.6	22.7	47.7
Other claims (not in the migration field)	11.0	65.3	0.7
Total	100%	100%	100%
N	473	856	426
Switzerland			
Immigration, asylum, and aliens politics	11.9	24.8	53.0
Minority integration politics	11.5	10.5	15.9
Antiracism and xenophobia	15.3	32.0	27.2
Other claims (not in the migration field)	61.3	32.7	4.0
Total	100%	100%	100%
N	261	153	151

migrant policy is clearly in line with our hypothesis. Furthermore, we have to take into account the fact that in Switzerland most migrant claims deal with homeland politics issues rather than host society ones, which is also a result of the more exclusive conception of citizenship in this country.

The main goal of this chapter, however, is not to explain the thematic focus of migrant, extreme-right, and solidarity movement claims but rather to assess the impact of these actors on migration policy and to determine to what extent their policy impact depends on the dominant definition of the nation and of citizenship. We hypothesize that claims addressing immigrant policy have more chances to find a political space and to be successful in France, for they better fit this country's civic-based model of citizenship. In contrast, we think the terrain should be more favorable to claims directed at immigration politics in Switzerland, which are more visible, resonant, and legitimate in the context of an ethnic-based definition of the nation.

POLITICAL, ECONOMIC, AND SOCIO-DEMOGRAPHIC RESOURCES FOR THE IMPACT OF SOCIAL MOVEMENTS ON MIGRATION POLICY

As the social movement literature has shown, movements are relatively powerless collective actors. Therefore, their potential impact is likely to become greater to the extent that they can exploit certain resources which are available in the larger environment and which may facilitate their task. Political, economic, and socio-demographic resources are certainly among the major ones, and the ones on which we would like to focus in our analysis, in addition to the cultural resources coming from the prevailing models of citizenship.

To begin with, students of social movements have often stressed the contribution of political alliances to the movements' cause. Political opportunity theorists, in particular, argue that the presence of powerful allies within the institutional arenas largely facilitates the task of social movements (Amenta et al. 1992; Burstein et al. 1995; Jenkins and Perrow 1977; Kriesi et al. 1995; Lipsky 1968; Tarrow 1993, 1998). Established parties play an especially important role in this respect (Tarrow 1993), as they can take up movement claims within the institutional arenas and translate them into policy changes.

Political opportunity theory suggests a number of hypotheses regarding the impact of social movements and claim-making in the field of immigration and ethnic relations. Concerning in particular the role of political alliances, the aspect of political opportunity structures which interests us here, migrant, extreme-right, and solidarity movements should be more successful when their potential institutional allies are in power and, more generally, when political alignments are favorable to them. The left (in particular, the Socialist party) is traditionally the most important ally for migrants and the solidarity movement, which therefore should have greater chances of success when the left is gaining power. Furthermore, their impact should go in the direction of liberalizing the admission policy or granting more rights to resident migrants and minorities, as this reflects their interests and demands.

The picture is somewhat more complicated for the extreme right, as established parties (including those of the right) often do not support far-right positions and groups. Nevertheless, at least when it comes to migration policy, the traditional right can still be considered as a potential ally of the extreme right, in spite of their often ambivalent relationship. As a result, extreme-right mobilization should have greater chances of success when the right gains power and, of course, even greater when extreme-right parties themselves benefit from an electoral growth. Furthermore, its impact should consist in tightening both immigration policy and immigrant policy, the typical demand of the extreme right. However, as some have argued in particular for the French case (Favell 1998; Hollifield 1994; Weil 1995), in the migration political field there is often a "hidden consensus" among political parties which results in similar positions of left and right parties, especially regarding immigration control. Therefore, at least in the case of immigration policy, political alignments should not matter that much. The question is open to empirical scrutiny.

Institutional allies are a political resource for migrants, extreme-right, and solidarity movements. However, students of immigration politics have often underscored the role of other contextual factors such as economic (e.g., unemployment), socio-demographic (e.g., immigration flows), cultural (e.g., models of citizenship), and legal-normative (e.g., the existence of domestic or international courts and the emergence of transnational normative frameworks) factors. All these aspects represent external resources that can be exploited by the movements under study to increase their chances of successfully influence migration policy. Here, in addition to models of citizenship and political alliances, we look at economic and socio-demographic resources, two aspects that are likely to strongly affect short-term changes in migration policy at the domestic level.

The economic situation of the host country is among the most significant factors affecting migration policy (Hollifield 1992a; Straubhaar and Weber 1994). A good or bad economic situation can provide crucial resources to social movements that try to influence policy-making in the field of immigration and ethnic relations. When the economy is bad and unemployment high, governments typically respond with restrictive policies. In contrast, in times of economic growth and low levels of unemployment, liberal measures are more likely to occur. This argument applies in particular to immigration policy and much less to immigrant policy, that is, it concerns above all the regulation of immigration flows as well as the criteria of admission of foreigners to the country in general and to the labor market in particular. In this respect, we can make different predictions as to chances of success of the three movements under study. On the one hand, liberalizing immigration policy is not a feasible option in periods of high unemployment. Immigrant policy, on the other hand, is relatively independent of the situation of the labor market. We therefore expect both migrant and solidarity movements to have an impact on immigrant policy (but not on immigration policy) when unemployment increases. Such impact, furthermore, should manifest itself in measures favorable to the situation of migrants in the host society, as in periods of economic recession or stagnation states typically close the borders and, at the same time, are more willing to act to improve the integration of resident migrants. On the other hand, even in a civic-assimilationist context such as France's, which tends to channel the claim-making of collective actors toward minority integration politics, during times of rising unemployment the extreme right should have a restrictive impact on immigration policy (but not on immigrant policy), as claims for such measures may take advantage of the general policy orientation in times of bad economic conditions.

The pressure coming from immigration flows and ethnic diversity is a further potential determinant of policy change in the field of immigration and ethnic relations (Miller 1981; Rex and Tomlinson 1979; Richmond 1988), and, therefore, another external resource that may increase the chance of success of social movements aiming to influence policy-making in this field. This factor is partly linked to the previous one, as the impact of immigration flows generally depends on the economic health of a country, in the sense that the pressure coming from immigration tends to diminish when the labor market is unfavorable to recruiting new labor force. Therefore, the predictions we make about socio-demographic factors follow a reasoning similar to those concerning economic factors. On the one hand, high levels of immigration express a strong socio-demographic pressure that tends to lead to a stricter border control. At the same time, however, measures for the integration of resident migrants are more likely to be taken. We therefore expect that when immigration flows are perceived as being too high, both migrant and solidarity movements will have an impact on immigrant policy (but not on immigration policy). Such impact, furthermore, should be favorable to the migrants' situation in the host society, as a strong socio-demographic pressure in terms of increasing immigration flows pushes state authorities to restrict the access to the country and makes measures for the integration of resident migrants more likely. On the other hand, in a similar situation, we expect the extreme right to have a restrictive impact on immigration policy (but not on immigrant policy), as policy-makers often respond to extreme-right mobilization in the simplest possible way: by tightening immigration control.

DATA RETRIEVAL AND METHODS

To assess empirically the impact of the mobilization of the three movements under study on migration policy we use a technique based on time-series analysis. This approach allows us to incorporate time into the explanation of the effects of protest activities on public policy. In spite of the obvious fact that political and decision-making processes are time-dependent, only rarely has previous work analyzed the effects of social movements and other collective actors with a method that takes time into account (Burstein and Freudenburg 1978; Costain and Majstorovic 1994; Giugni 2001; Giugni 2004; Giugni and Passy 1998). Yet an approach that allows the researcher to capture the dynamic nature of movement outcomes has clear advantages over a static approach. Specifically, the chronological ordering of observations in time-series analysis yields a stronger case for causal inference than cross-sectional approaches (Janoski and Isaac 1994), especially if a temporal lag is introduced in the models. This is all the more important when one is studying the outcomes of protest, as establishing the causal relationship that links social movements to their alleged outcomes is one of the major reasons that have hindered previous research in this field.

The unit of analysis consists in three-month periods that aggregate the observations on the variables of interest concerning the political claim-making (both by the three movements under study as well as other actors), the economic situation (unemployment rate), and the socio-demographic pressure (immigration flows). The data on claim-making come from the MERCI research project.[3] Claims were retrieved by content analyzing every second issue of one national newspaper in each country for the period from 1990 to 1998.[4] From the original, event-based file, the data were then aggregated into three-month counts of claims and stored into a new file specifically organized for time-series analysis (i.e., with chronologically ordered observations).

Appendix 8.1 gives the description of all the variables used in the analyses that follow. We use claim-making data to measure most of the variables concerning the intervention of collective actors in the public space on issues pertaining to immigration and ethnic relations: the mobilization of migrants (MINACT), that of the extreme right (ERACT), and that of the solidarity movement (SOLACT); pro-minority and anti-minority claims (PROMIN, ANTIMIN);[5] and pro-minority and anti-minority claims by parties (PROPART, ANTIPART), as a way to operationalize the political alliances of the three movements under study. In addition, our indicators of changes in migration policy are also based on the claim-making data, specifically on the subset of claims represented by political decisions: one measure of migration policy in general (MIGRPOL); two measures for the two more institutionalized issue fields, that is, immigration control policy (IMMPOL) and minority integration policy (INTPOL);[6] and finally two measures for the position of policy, regardless of the issue field to which they refer, that is, pro-minority and anti-minority political decisions (PROMP, ANTIMP).[7]

In addition to the indicators of claim-making, we have two variables that allows us to control for the effect of the economic situation and the socio-demographic pressure: the unemployment rate (UNEMP) and the immigration rate (IMMRATE).

The time-series analysis performed here aims to find significant relationships between various independent variables measuring the mobilization or claim-making of collective actors, the economic situation, and the socio-demographic pressure, on the one hand, and various indicators of migration policy, on the other. This analysis has three important features. First, it is longitudinal, that is, we look at the impact of changes over time in the variables of interest on policy changes. This allows us to take into account the inherently dynamic nature of the political process. Second, we look at lagged dependent variables. Including a temporal lag (in this case, a three-month time unit) is a way to strengthen causal inference. Third, in some of the analyses, we include a number of interactive terms. We do so with the aim of gauging the role of certain external resources (political, economic, socio-demographic) that might facilitate the movements' task jointly with their mobilization. In other words, we want to determine if the impact of the three movements under study is facilitated by the simultaneous presence of their action and by the external resources provided by the claim-making of political allies, the economic situation, and socio-demographic pressure. Appendix 8.2 lists all the interactive terms used in the analyses. These interactive terms were created by multiplying, for each movement, the variables concerning their mobilization with the variables referring to the claim-making by parties (favorable to migrants in the case of migrants themselves and the solidarity movement, unfavorable to migrants in the case of the extreme-right, so as to capture the action of the political allies of the three movements), the unemployment rate, and the immigration rate. Thus we obtain three variables for migrants (MINPART, MINIMM, MINUNEM), three for the extreme right (ERPART, ERIMM, ERNUNEM), and three for the solidarity movement (SOLPART, SOLIMM, SOLUNEM).

THE POLICY IMPACT OF MIGRANT, EXTREME-RIGHT, AND SOLIDARITY MOVEMENTS

In this section, we try to answer three interrelated questions: (1) What is the impact of migrant, extreme-right, and solidarity movements on migration policy, controlling for political, economic, and socio-demographic contextual factors? (2) Which of the three movements was more successful in its attempt to influence political decisions on issues pertaining to immigration and ethnic relations? (3) Which factors better predict changes in migration policies in France and Switzerland? To answer these questions, we perform a number of regression analyses that test for the existence of a significant relationship between the indicators of claim-making, economic situation, and socio-demographic pressure, on the one hand, and the various measures of changes in migration policy, on the other.[8]

Table 8.2 shows the impact of migrant mobilization on migration policies in France and Switzerland, controlling for four other factors: pro-minority claims by parties (political allies), anti-minority claims by parties (political opponents), the unemployment rate (economic situation), and the immigration rate (socio-demographic pressure). The upper section of the table refers to France, the lower section to Switzerland. The results are clearly unfavorable to an impact of migrants on migration policy, as none of the coefficients for this collective actor are statistically significant. This holds for migration policy in general (MIGRPOL), for the two institutionalized issue fields—immigration control policy (IMMPOL) and minority integration policy (INTPOL)—and both for policy favorable (PROMP) or unfavorable (ANTIMP) to migrants. In contrast, we have some evidence of an effect of

Table 8.2. Impact of Migrant Mobilization on Migration Policy in France and Switzerland

	MIGRPOL (t_1)	IMMPOL (t_1)	INTPOL (t_1)	PROMP (t_1)	ANTIMP (t_1)
France					
MINACT (t_0)	.14	.24	−.13	−.02	.31
PROPART (t_0)	−.03	−.14	−.03	.29	−.38*
ANTIPART (t_0)	.37*	.19	.43**	.32	.18
UNEMP (t_0)	.12	.50*	−.20	−.11	.32
IMMRATE (t_0)	.21	.48*	−.11	.04	.23
R^2	.21	.22	.18	.31	.24
Durbin-Watson	1.86	1.83	2.13	1.88	2.04
Switzerland					
MINACT (t_0)	.07	−.04	−.01	.10	−.01
PROPART (t_0)	−.08	−.07	.12	−.07	.25
ANTIPART (t_0)	−.28	−.08	−.36*	−.30	−.05
UNEMP (t_0)	.81***	.49*	−.00	.64**	.30
IMMRATE (t_0)	.68**	.40	−.06	.81***	.19
R^2	.33	.13	.11	.34	.13
Durbin-Watson	2.10	2.02	1.69	2.06	2.00

$*p < .10; **p < .05; ***p < .01$

NOTE: Standardized regression coefficients generated with a generalized least-squared method of estimation (Prais-Winsten) assuming a first-order autoregressive process. All variables are time series with a three-month period as the unit of time (n=35). All independent variables include a three-month lag. See Appendix 8.1 for variable labels and the number of cases in each original variable.

the claim-making by parties. Both in France and Switzerland, this effect seems to be on decisions concerning minority integration rather than immigration control. Yet, as we can see in the second line of the table, only in France it goes in the same direction as the parties' demands, for pro-minority claims at time t_0 are related to a decline in anti-minority decisions at time t_1. Finally, both the unemployment rate and the immigration rate have a positive effect on migration policy, attesting that both the situation on the labor market and incoming flows of immigrants play an important role in the decision process in the field of immigration and ethnic relations.

Table 8.3 shows the impact of extreme-right mobilization on migration policy, again controlling for political, economic, and socio-demographic factors. Judging from our data, the effectiveness of the extreme right does not seem to be much stronger than that of migrants. However, here we have some evidence of an impact as the coefficient concerning changes in minority integration policy in Switzerland is statistically significant. Furthermore, even though none of the regression coefficients for the case of France are significant, we find a negative effect on pro-minority decisions if we include in the measure of the latter also repressive measures against the extreme

Table 8.3. Impact of Extreme-right Mobilization on Migration Policy in France and Switzerland

	MIGRPOL (t_1)	IMMPOL (t_1)	INTPOL (t_1)	PROMP (t_1)	ANTIMP (t_1)
France					
ERACT (t_0)	−.25	−.22	.25	−.40	−.07
PROPART (t_0)	.15	−.01	−.22	.60**	−.36
ANTIPART (t_0)	.46**	.32	.33	.39**	.36*
UNEMP (t_0)	.06	.38	−.16	−.18	.22
IMMRATE (t_0)	.15	.41	−.07	−.07	.23
R^2	.21	.17	.17	.36	.17
Durbin-Watson	1.79	1.73	2.13	1.90	1.99
Switzerland					
ERACT (t_0)	−.04	.11	−.44**	.03	−.07
PROPART (t_0)	−.03	−.13	.30	−.04	.27
ANTIPART (t_0)	−.29	−.09	−.23	−.34*	−.04
UNEMP (t_0)	.79***	.50*	.06	.60**	.32
IMMRATE (t_0)	.65***	.40	.08	.74***	.21
R^2	.32	.15	.23	.33	.13
Durbin-Watson	2.08	2.04	1.81	2.04	1.99

*p < .10; **p < .05; ***p < .01

NOTE: Standardized regression coefficients generated with a generalized least-squared method of estimation (Prais-Winsten) assuming a first-order autoregressive process. All variables are time series with a three-month period as the unit of time (n=35). All independent variables include a three-month lag. See Appendix 8.1 for variable labels and the number of cases in each original variable.

right (results not shown). Once again, the role of more institutionalized actors such as parties appears to be stronger than that of outsiders, especially in France and when they address anti-minority claims.[9] Finally, the impact of the economic situation and socio-demographic pressure is confirmed, although the significant effects of these variables disappear in the case of France (but the value of the coefficients concerning immigration control policy remains strong).

Table 8.4 shows the impact of the solidarity movement on migration policy, always controlling political, economic, and socio-demographic factors. If migrants had no impact at all and the extreme right only a limited one, at least in the period under study, the solidarity movement apparently was somewhat more successful, particularly so in France. However, in the French case, the sign of all statistically significant coefficients is negative. This means that political decisions at time t_1 have decreased when the mobilization of the movement at time t_0 has increased (or vice versa). As far as the indicator of pro-minority decisions is concerned, this suggests that the movement was clearly unsuccessful, for a decline in decisions favorable to migrants has followed a growth of the mobilization of the solidarity movement (or vice

Table 8.4. Impact of Solidarity Movement Mobilization on Migration Policy in France and Switzerland

	MIGRPOL (t_1)	IMMPOL (t_1)	INTPOL (t_1)	PROMP (t_1)	ANTIMP (t_1)
France					
SOLACT (t_0)	−.49**	−.36*	−.34	−.32*	−.31
PROPART (t_0)	.20	−.01	.18	.45**	−.25
ANTIPART (t_0)	.52***	.34*	.47**	.39**	.42**
UNEMP (t_0)	.19	.49*	−.06	.01	.43
IMMRATE (t_0)	.21	.48*	−.07	.09	.36
R^2	.35	.21	.26	.38	.20
Durbin-Watson	1.49	1.58	2.13	1.78	1.94
Switzerland					
SOLACT (t_0)	.21	.24	−.01	.43***	−.11
PROPART (t_0)	−.06	−.10	.12	−.04	.25
ANTIPART (t_0)	−.26	−.02	−.36*	−.24	−.07
UNEMP (t_0)	.67***	.42	.00	.38*	.36
IMMRATE (t_0)	.52**	.33	−.05	.53**	.24
R^2	.36	.19	.11	.51	.15
Durbin-Watson	2.00	2.02	1.70	2.03	2.04

$*p < .10; **p < .05; ***p < .01$

NOTE: Standardized regression coefficients generated with a generalized least-squared method of estimation (Prais-Winsten) assuming a first-order autoregressive process. All variables are time series with a three-month period as the unit of time (n=35). All independent variables include a three-month lag. See Appendix 8.1 for variable labels and the number of cases in each original variable.

versa). In contrast, the Swiss solidarity movement seems to have been able to produce a real substantial improvement in the rights and position of migrants (as measured through the number of pro-minority political decisions by state actors). Yet we cannot say which specific issue field (immigration control or minority integration) is affected by this improvement. The general impact of parties, especially in France, is once again confirmed, yet with the ambivalence mentioned earlier concerning the direction of the relationship for anti-minority claims by parties in France, while the real effect of pro-minority claims by parties remains. The same holds for the real effect of anti-minority claims by parties on minority integration policy in Switzerland. Similarly, the findings regarding the impact of the unemployment rate and the immigration rate are consistent with those observed above.

Tables 8.2, 8.3, and 8.4 focus on the mobilization of three specific collective actors (migrant, extreme-right, and solidarity movements), controlling for the effect of certain aspects of their political, economic, and social environment that are plausibly related to changes in migration policy. Generally speaking, these three movements express either a favorable (migrants, solidarity) or unfavorable (extreme right) position toward migrants. Yet other

Table 8.5.   Impact of Pro-minority and Anti-minority Claims on Migration Policy in France and Switzerland

	MIGRPOL (t_1)	IMMPOL (t_1)	INTPOL (t_1)	PROMP (t_1)	ANTIMP (t_1)
France					
PROMIN (t_0)	−.25	−.21	−.28	.18	−.54**
ANTIMIN (t_0)	.59***	.26	.72***	.29	.65***
UNEMP (t_0)	.25	.48*	.04	−.04	.57**
IMMRATE (t_0)	.29	.48*	−.00	.14	.40
R^2	.27	.13	.38	.24	.29
Durbin-Watson	1.67	1.66	2.09	1.94	1.91
Switzerland					
PROMIN (t_0)	−.06	−.10	.06	.03	.15
ANTIMIN (t_0)	−.21	.01	−.31	−.36*	.08
UNEMP (t_0)	.73***	.47*	-.03	.55**	.30
IMMRATE (t_0)	.68***	.40	.02	.88***	.13
R^2	.27	.12	.09	.32	.11
Durbin-Watson	2.06	2.02	1.71	1.98	2.01

$*p < .10; **p < .05; ***p < .01$

NOTE: Standardized regression coefficients generated with a generalized least-squared method of estimation (Prais-Winsten) assuming a first-order autoregressive process. All variables are time series with a three-month period as the unit of time (n=35). All independent variables include a three-month lag. See Appendix 8.1 for variable labels and the number of cases in each original variable.

collective actors, in addition to these three movements and in addition to political parties, may have either a pro-minority or an anti-minority stance. One may therefore want to ascertain the policy impact of these two political "camps" in their entirety. The results are shown in table 8.5. Taken as a whole (i.e., including parties as well as any other collective actor) and net of the effect of economic and socio-demographic constraints, political claim-making in the field of immigration and ethnic relations appears to have been successful. This holds for both France and Switzerland, attesting to the preference of a certain degree of policy responsiveness in these two democracies. The only difference, yet a significant one, is that, while in France pro-minority claims have produced a decrease in political decisions that basically deteriorates the rights and position of migrants, in Switzerland anti-minority claims have caused a decrease in decisions that improve their situation. Thus, in a way, a similar path has led to two substantially opposed outcomes: one favorable and the other unfavorable to migrants.

In sum, our analysis so far suggests a number of tentative conclusions about the impact of migrant, extreme-right, and solidarity movements on migration policy in France and Switzerland. First, migrants do not seem to have any substantial impact on political decisions concerning immigration and ethnic relations. Second, the extreme right is somewhat more successful in

Switzerland, but not in France. However, we do not have evidence allowing us to ascertain the direction of its impact. We know that its mobilization tends to produce a decrease in the number of political decisions concerning minority integration policy. This may indicate a deterioration of the situation of migrants, as usually minority integration measures aim at creating better living conditions for resident migrants, but we cannot draw a firm conclusion in this respect. Third, the solidarity movement displays ambivalent results. On the one hand, immigration control policy is affected by its mobilization, yet in a direction apparently opposed to the movement's goals. On the other hand, the movement seems to be able to obtain a real positive impact, but we do not know which specific issue field is affected by its mobilization. Fourth, our analysis underscores above all the important role played by institutional actors such as political parties to produce changes in migration policy. Fifth, the claim-making by all types of actors in the field of immigration and ethnic relations seems to influence the political decision-making in this field. However, while in France both pro-minority and anti-minority claims have an impact (especially on minority integration policy), in Switzerland only anti-minority claims matter. Sixth, we have shown the strong impact of economic and socio-demographic constraints (as measured through the unemployment rate and the immigration rate) on migration policy. Furthermore, this impact concerns above all immigration control policy.

THE ROLE OF POLITICAL, ECONOMIC, AND SOCIO-DEMOGRAPHIC RESOURCES

Thus far, the claim-making by political parties, the economic situation (unemployment rate), and the socio-demographic pressure (immigration rate) have been treated as other factors, in addition to the mobilization of the three movements under study, that may affect migration policy or, to use the social science jargon, as control variables. In this section, we consider them as potential resources for migrant, extreme-right, and solidarity movements, and would like to test the hypothesis that the chances of success of these movements are greater when they can exploit such resources. In other words, here we test the hypothesis that their impact on migration policy is facilitated by the joint presence of their mobilization and one or the other of these resources. Accordingly, the questions we try to answer are the following: (1) Is the impact of migrant, extreme-right, and solidarity movements on migration policy facilitated by the resources provided by the presence of parties as political allies, by the economic situation as measured through the unemployment rate, and by the socio-demographic pressure as measured through the immigration rate? (2) Which of these three types of external resources are more likely to improve the chances of success of the three movements under study? (3) Which of the three movements was more ready to exploit these resources to influence political decisions in the field of immigration and ethnic relations?

Table 8.6 allows us to give an answer to these questions, though a very tentative one. This table shows the results of regression analyses with the interactive terms combining the mobilization of the three movements with the indicators of, respectively, the political, economic, and socio-demographic resources. The results for France and Switzerland are very different. The most important finding concerning France is that migrants seem to take great advantage of all three types of resources, as all three coefficients on pro-minority political decisions had positive significance. The other two movements, in contrast, have not benefited from the resources available in their environment. The significant coefficients for the extreme right could suggest that there is an interactive effect with the claim-making by parties and the economic situation, but the positive sign of the relationships prevents us from speaking of a real effect, for an increase in the mobilization of the extreme right produces an increase in pro-minority decisions, which in principle goes against the movement's goals. Finally, no significant coefficient is observed for the interactive terms referring to the solidarity movement.

The picture is in a way reversed in Switzerland. Here migrants do not seem to have taken any advantage of the resources available in their political, economic, and social environment. The most straightforward findings, however, are those referring to the extreme right. All three regression coefficients for this collective actor on minority integration policy are statistically significant. Furthermore, the sign of the coefficient is negative. If, as we mentioned earlier, this does not allow us to conclude that the impact of the extreme right goes in the direction of its goals, a decline in political decisions concerning the integration of resident migrants could well result in a deterioration of their rights and position. Finally, we observe a positive effect of the solidarity movement in combination with changes in the unemployment rate and the immigration rate.

In sum, our analysis of the role of external resources in facilitating the policy impact of the three movements under study suggests that the presence of institutional allies, which share the goals of the movements, the situation on the labor marker, and the pressure coming from immigration flows, are all important resources that the movements can exploit to become more successful in their attempt to influence migration policy. In other words, the impact of migrant, extreme-right, and solidarity movements seems indeed to be facilitated by political, economic, and socio-demographic resources. Furthermore, all three types of resources have contributed, in combination with mobilization, to policy change in the migration political field. Yet the answer to the question, which of the three movements was more ready to exploit these resources, depends on the country: migrants and the extreme right in France, the extreme right and the solidarity movement in Switzerland.

Table 8.6. Interactive Effects of Migrant, Extreme-right, and Solidarity Movement Mobilization on Migration Policy in France and Switzerland

	MIGRPOL (t_I)	IMMPOL (t_I)	INTPOL (t_I)	PROMP (t_I)	ANTIMP (t_I)
France					
MINPART (t_0)	.29 (1.84)*	.09 (1.71)	.19 (2.17)	.52 (1.95)***	−.09 (1.97)
MINUNEM (t_0)	.25 (1.96)	.19 (1.80)	.05 (2.13)	.31 (1.96)*	.28 (1.97)
MINIMM (t_0)	.38 (1.99)**	.34 (1.86)*	.07 (2.13)	.48 (1.98)***	.25 (1.96)
ERPART (t_0)	.35 (1.75)**	.09 (1.69)	.43 (2.15)**	.50 (1.89)***	.03 (1.96)
ERUNEM (t_0)	.10 (1.78)	−.08 (1.65)	.22 (2.16)	.24 (1.97)	−.13 (1.98)
ERIMM (t_0)	.16 (1.77)	.01 (1.67)	.26 (2.13)	.35 (1.94)**	−.14 (1.98)
SOLPART (t_0)	.04 (1.80)	−.09 (1.63)	−.09 (2.11)	.27 (1.97)	−.24 (1.98)
SOLUNEM (t_0)	−.15 (1.74)	−.21 (1.52)	−.15 (2.10)	.06 (1.98)	−.16 (1.95)
SOLIMM (t_0)	−.04 (1.78)	−.03 (1.64)	−.10 (2.12)	.19 (1.97)	−.12 (1.96)
Switzerland					
MINPART (t_0)	−.00 (1.93)	−.08 (1.99)	.17 (1.65)	−.08 (1.84)	.16 (1.95)
MINUNEM (t_0)	.05 (1.92)	−.04 (1.99)	.15 (1.68)	−.10 (1.84)	.14 (1.94)
MINIMM (t_0)	−.18 (1.94)	−.20 (1.99)	.08 (1.68)	−.07 (1.83)	−.10 (1.94)
ERPART (t_0)	−.23 (1.93)	−.09 (1.98)	−.31 (1.75)*	−.21 (1.83)	.01 (1.93)
ERUNEM (t_0)	−.03 (1.92)	.06 (2.00)	−.30 (1.76)*	−.04 (1.83)	.16 (1.97)
ERIMM (t_0)	.07 (1.94)	.16 (2.03)	−.37 (1.80)**	.19 (1.88)	.04 (1.94)
SOLPART (t_0)	.07 (1.93)	.05 (1.99)	.08 (1.66)	.01 (1.83)	.22 (1.94)
SOLUNEM (t_0)	.42 (1.87)**	.27 (2.00)	.06 (1.67)	.38 (1.74)**	.08 (1.93)
SOLIMM (t_0)	.37 (1.86)**	.34 (1.99)**	−.10 (1.70)	.66 (1.87)***	−.05 (1.94)

*p < .10; **p < .05; ***p < .01

NOTE: Standardized regression coefficients (bivariate) generated with a generalized least-squared method of estimation (Prais-Winsten) assuming a first-order autoregressive process. Durbin-Watson test for serial correlation in brackets. All variables are time series with a three-month period as the unit of time (n=35). All independent variables include a three-month lag. See Appendix 1 for variable labels and the number of cases in each original variable. See Appendix 8.2 for component variables of the interactive terms.

However, some caution must be taken in interpreting these findings. First of all, unlike the previous ones, they are based on bivariate regressions. This calls for wariness in the interpretation of results, as we do not control for the effect of other factors. We therefore cannot exclude that at least some of the relationships may be spurious. Second, additional bivariate analyses using the same variables, but with the indicators of the mobilization by the three movements instead of the interactive terms, suggest that in most cases the latter have only a reinforcing effect (results not shown). This holds particularly in the Swiss case.

CONCLUSION

The analysis presented in this chapter is very much exploratory. It was aimed at sensitizing to a time-series approach to the study of the policy impact of social movements rather than testing a theory of the effect of migrant, extreme-right, and solidarity movements on migration policy. In order to obtain more robust and consistent findings, we will certainly need to complement it with other methods as well as new data. In spite of this cautionary remark, our analysis suggests a number of interesting insights about the impact of social movements within the political field of immigration and ethnic relations.

Previous work on the outcomes and consequences of social movements have pointed to the powerlessness of these collective actors and the difficulty for them to obtain substantive policy gains in the absence of external opportunities and resources. Similarly, specific studies of the mobilization in the migration political field have shown the poor policy impact of protest activities, especially those carried by migrants themselves, which often have difficulties to organize and mobilize (Blatt 1995; Ireland 1994; Miller 1981). Our time-series analysis confirms this weakness. Migrants, in particular, seem to reflect quite well the label of "poor people's movements" (Piven and Cloward 1979) which have scarce resources to intervene in the political process and to influence policy making. Neither in France nor in Switzerland have migrants been able to produce substantial policy changes. Extreme-right and solidarity movements, the two movements formed by "full citizens," score a little better, but only in Switzerland and only to a limited extent.

If, on the one hand, our study confirms the lack of political influence of social movements, especially those formed by migrants, who are to a large extent excluded from the political game, it shows, on the other hand, that political, economic, and socio-demographic factors intervene in important ways in the process leading to changes in migration policy. Not only do these factors impinge on the political decision-making on their own but they provide to some extent external resources that the movements can exploit to reach their policy goals. Although, as we said, the results in this respect should be taken with some caution, sometimes the claim-making by parties, the economic situation, and the pressure coming from immigration flows can improve the chances of success of the three movements we have examined.

The impact of the unemployment rate and the immigration rate shows that political elites take the situation on the labor market and growing immigration into account. Furthermore, these two factors have their effect above all on immigration control, which is the policy aspect that must be modified in order to respond to such economic and socio-demographic "threats." The most consistent finding of our study, however, lies perhaps in the crucial role played by political parties. Quite unsurprisingly given their political status and legitimacy, these institutional actors are often able to influence policy-making in the field of immigration and ethnic relations, and sometimes they can also contribute to the impact of challenging groups.

Finally, contrary to our predictions, we have not found consistent evidence that the prevailing models of citizenship affect the chances of success of movements mobilizing in the migration political field. The influence of citizenship and integration regimes should be felt on three levels. First, the more inclusive civic-based French model should favor the impact of migrants, as compared to the more exclusive ethnic-based model of Switzerland. This does not occur. However, as can be seen in the analyses with the interactive terms, migrants in France apparently have a positive impact when political, economic, or socio-demographic resources are available, whereas in Switzerland they remain unsuccessful even in the presence of such external resources. The more favorable environment in terms of the collective definition of citizenship in France might therefore play an indirect role, at least in regard to the impact of migrants on migration policy. Second, we should observe a greater impact of claim-making in general on minority integration policy in France and on immigration control policy in Switzerland, as claims pertaining to these two issues have greater visibility, resonance, and legitimacy in the respective countries. We did not find evidence of this. It rather appears that both in France and Switzerland claim-making is more likely to influence minority integration policy (whereas economic and socio-demographic factors mostly affect immigration control policy). Third, for the same reason, we expected claim-making in France, to a larger extent than in Switzerland, to influence political decisions that improve the rights and position of migrants. Here there is some evidence pointing to the role of models of citizenship, as in France both pro-minority and anti-minority claims have an impact on migration policy, while in Switzerland only claims that are unfavorable to migrants seem to really matter. This might depend on the different models of citizenship in these two countries, whereby the civic-based model of France gives greater visibility, resonance, and legitimacy to claims that stress the inclusion of migrants in the national community, while the ethnic-based model of Switzerland makes claims that underscore the exclusion of migrants from the national community more visible, resonant, and legitimate.

Appendix 8.1.   Description of Variables Used in the Analyses

Variable Name	Label	N France	N Switzerland
MINACT	Claims by migrants on migration issues	417	101
ERACT	Claims by the extreme right on migration issues	298	109
SOLACT	Claims by the solidarity movement on migration issues	428	151
PROMIN	Pro-minority claims by non-state actors	1601	620
ANTIMIN	Anti-minority claims by non-state actors	390	304
PROPART	Pro-minority claims by parties	546	193
ANTIPART	Anti-minority claims by parties	224	167
MIGRPOL	Political decisions on migration issues	373	370
IMMPOL	Political decisions on immigration and asylum issues	200	271
INTPOL	Political decisions on integration issues	106	79
PROMP	Pro-minority political decisions	182	184
ANTIMP	Anti-minority political decisions	101	136
UNEMP	Unemployment rate	—	—
IMMRATE	Immigration rate	—	—

NOTE: Claim variables come from recodings in the original data. The other variables come from the European System of Social Indicators (Social Indicators Department, ZUMA, Mannheim), except for the unemployment rate in Switzerland for 1990 (Statistical Yearbook of Switzerland). The data on immigration flows and the economic situation are available only on an annual basis. The actual values correspond to the first quarter of each year. The values of the other three quarters are estimates by linear interpolation. The number of cases refers to the number of claims in the original variables, which then have been aggregated in the time series.

Appendix 8.2.   List of Interactive Terms Used in the Analyses

Interactive Term	Component Variables
MINPART	MINACT * PROPART
MINUNEM	MINACT * UNEMP
MINIMM	MINACT * IMMRATE
ERPART	ERACT * ANTIPART
ERUNEM	ERACT * UNEMP
ERIMM	ERACT * IMMRATE
SOLPART	SOLACT * PROPART
SOLUNEM	SOLACT * UNEMP
SOLIMM	SOLACT * IMMRATE

NOTE: All interactive terms have been created by multiplying the two component variables.

NOTES

1. It should be noted that the term *pluralist* here has absolutely no normative meaning and the resulting system can lead to social and political segregation, as the example of the South African apartheid regime attests.

2. See below for information on the data sources and methods. Immigrant politics comprise both minority integration politics and claims regarding racism and antiracism.

3. The MERCI ("Mobilization on Ethnic Relations, Citizenship, and Immigration") project includes the following country studies, in addition to France and Switzerland: Germany (Ruud Koopmans), Great Britain (Paul Statham), and the Netherlands (Thom Duyvené de Wit).

4. *Le Monde* in France and the *Neue Zürcher Zeitung* in Switzerland.

5. Since we want to assess the impact of claim-making on political decisions, pro-minority and anti-minority claims exclude claims by state actors.

6. We exclude racism/antiracism from these analyses, as this is less institutionalized and therefore less policy-oriented an issue than both immigration control policy and minority integration policy.

7. It should be noted that pro-minority and anti-minority claims or decisions here are to be intended in their broader meaning, that is, as claims or decisions that (if realized, in the case of claims) either improve or deteriorate the rights and position of migrants in the host society, not necessarily as claims or decisions that are overtly in favor or against them.

8. The tables below show standardized regression coefficients generated with a generalized least-squared method of estimation (Prais-Winsten) assuming a first-order autoregressive process among the error terms, that is, a model of a time series in which the current value of the series is a linear combination of previous values of the series, plus a random error. The Durbin-Watson statistic is used to test for the presence of first-order autocorrelation (both positive and negative) in the residuals (or error terms) of a regression equation. It ranges between 0 and 4. In the case of a series with 35 observations (such as those we use here) and 4 independent variables in the equation (tables 8.2, 8.3, and 8.4), the null hypothesis that there is no significant correlation in the residuals can be accepted (at the level of significance of 5 percent) if the test statistics ranges between 1.73 and 2.27 (4 − 1.73). With five independent variables (table 8.5), the null hypothesis can be accepted if the test statistics ranges between 1.80 and 2.20 (4 − 1.80). When the test statistics ranges between 1.22 and 1.73 or between 2.27 and 2.78 (four independent variables), and when it ranges between 1.16 and 1.80 or between 2.20 and 2.84 (five independent variables), the null hypothesis can be neither accepted nor rejected (situation of uncertainty). When the test statistics is lower than 1.22 (four independent variables) or 1.16 (five independent variables), the null hypothesis must be rejected and it is likely that there is positive autocorrelation. Finally, when the test statistics is higher than 2.78 (four independent variables) or 2.84 (five independent variables), the null hypothesis must be rejected and it is likely that there is negative autocorrelation.

9. Here, however, we must keep in mind that extreme-right parties are included in the extreme right, not among parties.

Commentary

Political Process as the Key Determinant of Migration Policy

Hanspeter Kriesi

POLITICAL PROCESS AND MIGRATION POLICY

At first sight, these two contributions are quite different from each other. They focus on different actors—social movements versus established political parties—and on different forms of political action—protest politics in the streets versus policy-making in smoke-filled rooms, and they employ contrasting methods—time-series analysis versus qualitative case studies. In spite of these differences, both of these chapters put the political process at center stage of their explanation of migration policy. Both of them study the impact of collective actors on changes in national migration policies over a given period of time—the nineties, essentially—in selected Western European countries: France and Switzerland on the one hand; Austria, Italy, and especially Germany on the other hand.

In putting the emphasis on the political process, both of these contributions turn against more structuralist explanations that have dominated the field in the past. This is most explicit in the case of Triadafilopoulos and Zaslove. They start out by reviewing three competing explanations of immigration policies—explanations referring to traditions of citizenship, international human rights norms, and "rights-based liberalism." They criticize these explanations for their inability to deal with recent developments in European immigration policy—the recent tightening of immigration policy across virtually all liberal democratic states. The first two explanations presuppose too much consensus in this respect—the first at the national and the second at the international level. Both cannot account for the recent break in the anti-

215

populist "hidden consensus" among established political actors and the politicization of the immigration issue. The third explanation may acknowledge this development, but it presumes that the domestic courts continue to protect and enlarge the rights of the immigrants because they are perceived to be shielded from political pressure generated by the mobilization of opposition to immigration.

The driving force behind the illiberal turn in immigration policy in Western liberal democracies has, of course, been the mobilization by the radical populist right. Although its origins varied considerably from one country to the other, everywhere immigration has become the key issue for radical right-wing mobilization. There are good reasons for this (Betz 2004): On the one hand, the increase in international migration has provoked a range of anxieties and resentment which in turn have opened up new opportunities for populist exploitation. On the other hand, there are few issues where the opinions of the population and the political elites diverge as much as with respect to migration, which again provides a unique opportunity for populist mobilization. Indeed, anti-immigration attitudes constitute the most important factor explaining right-wing voting in Western Europe (Lubbers et al. 2002). This does not mean that the radical populist right is nothing more than an opportunistic single-issue movement. As Betz (2004) points out, its position on immigration is increasingly becoming part of a larger program, which poses a fundamental challenge to liberal democracies. For the politicization of migration, however, Triadafilopoulos and Zaslove are right to insist that the mobilization by the radical right has stood in the way of efforts to manage migration policy consensually and that all parties have had to make some effort to stake out a position.

In addition to the radical right, there are other collective actors who have also mobilized in the context of migration issues. They include two movements promoting immigrants' rights—the migrants' and ethnic minorities' own movements and the solidarity movements supporting their cause. While the chapter by Triadafilopoulos and Zaslove focuses on the political process in the party system, Giugni and Passy study the impact of the mobilization by all three collective actors—the movements defending the immigrants' rights and the radical right mobilizing to protect the indigenous population—in their analysis of the development of migration policy.

SHIFTING OPPORTUNITIES

The political process takes place *in a given context*. Thus, Giugni and Passy analyze the impact of the three actors mobilizing from outside in the context of their political, economic, and socio-demographic opportunities. They use the term "resources" instead of "opportunities" to refer to context conditions, but keeping in line with the usual conceptualizations (Koopmans and Statham 2000a), I would prefer to speak of "opportunities" as far as the contextual aspects facilitating or constraining the mobilization and the impact of collective actors are concerned. More specifically, given that they analyze the dynamics of the three actors' impact over time, they consider shifting opportunities, that is, contextual aspects that are liable to change in the short run within a given country context.

With respect to *economic and social-demographic opportunities*, Giugni and Passy focus on unemployment and migration pressures and expect increasing levels of unemployment and increasing migration pressures to constitute favorable conditions for a tightening of admissions policies, while they expect integration policies to be rather unaffected by unfavorable labor market conditions and positively affected by migration pressures.

With regard to the *political context*, Giugni and Passy discuss the role of allies: They expect the left to support the migrants' cause, especially if it is in government; by contrast, the established right is expected to be an ally of the radical right "in spite of their often ambivalent relationship." The hesitation with regard to the relationship between the radical right and the established parties of the right is certainly in order. In fact, the relationship between the left and the solidarity and migrants movements has traditionally been quite different from the relationship between the established parties of the right and the radical right. While the former is typically one of mutual support, the latter has typically been of a much more competitive nature. Contrary to the movements allied with the left, the radical right has usually been organized as a party, which means that it directly competes with the parties of the established right for the citizens' votes. Thus, the established right is not really an "ally" of the radical right. As the chapter by Triadafilopoulos and Zaslove argues, it much rather succumbs to the competitive pressure exerted by the growing electoral success of the radical right, which typically incites it to adopt a more restrictive immigration policy. Under the pressure of the radical right, the established right attempts to preempt its rival by adopting a tough stance with respect to immigration. Betz (2004) even suggests that a growing number of citizens vote strategically for the radical right-wing parties in order to put pressure on the established right in the field of migration policy and that citizens continue to vote for these parties precisely because their pressure on the established right proved to be so effective. According to this line of reasoning the "anti-minority" partisan claims constitute a consequence (and not a precondition) of the mobilization by the extreme right, which in turn contributes to the success of the latter's claims in migration policy.

As Giugni and Passy maintain, much depends, of course, whether or not the left or the right are *in government*. The case studies of the second chapter serve to illustrate this point. But, as they also show, the relationship between government incumbency and movement success is rather complicated. Thus, as is illustrated by the German case, the Schröder government proposed a progressive reform favorable to the migrants' and the solidarity movement's point of view. However, the opposition of the CDU-CSU unexpectedly resorted to movement tactics, transferred the debate to the public sphere where it successfully mobilized for a petition against the reform, and succeeded in watering it down considerably. Moreover, the situation is even more complicated by the possibility that the radical right parties may also be coopted into the government by their established right competitors. In the short run, participation in government coalitions may allow the radical right to push through its restrictive agenda in migration policy even more effectively. In the longer run, however, accepting government responsibility may prove to be highly detrimental to the electoral success of radical right parties, and, it might be argued, for their tough immigration policies. As Betz (2003) argues, radical right populist parties are most successful when in opposition.

MODELS FOR THE IMPACT OF COLLECTIVE ACTORS ON MIGRATION POLICY

The empirical analyses presented by Giugni and Passy, unfortunately, present certain limitations. First of all, the way they have operationalized political decisions makes the evaluation of their hypotheses difficult: They have indicators that distinguish either between decisions in the two branches of migration policy—admissions policy and integration policy—or between pro- and anti-migrant decisions. There are no indicators that combine both distinctions, which would have made the test of the hypotheses with regard to the economic and socio-demographic contexts easier. Second, the incumbency of the left or the right in government has not been operationalized. Third, most of their analyses are limited due to the way they are specified: They present separate analyses for each one of the three movements instead of analyzing the impact of the three actors jointly in one and the same model. Given that the three movements participated in one and the same political process, they are likely to have interacted with each other in producing the policy impact. As Triadafilopoulos and Zaslove observe in their conclusion, "attention to the political processes allows us to recognize how 'interaction effects' generated by partisan conflict influence the content of legislation."

An additional example from Switzerland may illustrate this important point. In the late nineties, organizations of the solidarity movement successfully launched a referendum against measures toughening the refugees' policy. This meant that the citizens had to vote on these measures in June 1999, just a few months before the next federal elections. The referendum proved to be a strategic mistake of the first order for the solidarity movement. Since the massive influx of refugees in the aftermath of the Kosovo war in the spring of the same year, the refugees' issue had been shaping up as the key concern of the Swiss voters. The vote on the referendum provided the radical right with a golden opportunity to campaign not only for a toughening of the admissions policy but also for its own benefit in the election campaign. The overwhelming approval of the referendum foreshadowed its triumph in the federal elections in fall 1999. I admit that such interactions are difficult to model. But even a very rough model would have to include indicators for the mobilization by all three movements.

Fourth, Giugni and Passy have the excellent idea to introduce interactions between each element of the opportunity structure on the one hand and the mobilization effort of a given political actor on the other hand. This idea corresponds to the "logic of value added" that Smelser (1962) recommended for the analysis of social movements forty years ago. Smelser applied this logic to the explanation of the emergence of collective action, but it can also be applied to explain its impact. According to this logic "each determinant is a necessary condition for the next to operate as a determinant of an episode of collective action" (Smelser 1962). In other words, only if there is an economic, socio-demographic, or political opportunity will the mobilization effort of a given collective actor have any impact on migration policy. Alternatively, we may conceive of a given opportunity simply as a facilitating condition, which contributes its share to the policy impact, independently of the collective action of a given actor. I believe that it makes a lot of theoretical sense to expect the impact of collective action on any kind of policy to be conditioned by the opportunities provided by the context. Only if there is a "window of opportunity" (Kingdon 1984) will collective action be of any consequence. In terms of the specification of the model, interaction terms account for such a conditional impact of collective action. The problem with the way these interaction terms (e.g., between the mobilization of the migrants' movement and unemployment) are specified in the models by Giugni and Passy is that they are not introduced together with their original additive components (i.e., the mobilization of the migrants' movement and unemployment), probably due to multi-collinearity problems. As a result, the interaction terms cannot easily be interpreted.

The results that are least affected by these specification problems are those in table 8.5. They show that claims-making does, indeed, have a significant impact on the policy outcomes in both countries. In France the effects are most pronounced on anti-minority decisions, while in Switzerland they are most clear-cut with regard to pro-minority decisions. In France, anti-minority claims significantly contribute to anti-minority decisions, while pro-minority claims counteract them in a significant way. In Switzerland, pro-minority claims do not seem to have any impact on political decisions at all, but anti-minority claims serve to constrain pro-minority decisions. In other words, the mobilization against the minorities is effective in both countries—as expected, given the forceful mobilization by the radical populist right in France as well as in Switzerland. The fact that the effect of the radical right takes on different forms in the two countries is difficult to interpret, however. We would need to know more about the details of the policies concerned in order to give meaning to this difference. The differential effectiveness of the pro-minority claims in the two countries could simply be a result of the relative weakness of the mobilization by the Swiss migrants and solidarity movements. It could, however, also have to do with the fact that the French solidarity and migrant movements could count on a friendly government, while their Swiss equivalents had to face the dire direct-democratic context.

In addition to the claims-making by both camps, increasing levels of unemployment are shown to facilitate anti-minority decisions in France and pro-minority decisions in Switzerland. If the anti-minority decisions in France concern tightening admissions standards, then this result confirms the original hypothesis of the authors. The Swiss result is, however, contrary to expectations. The positive effect of immigration pressures on pro-minority decisions in Switzerland is in line with expectations, as long as the decisions concerned deal with integration policy.

THE LARGER CONTEXT

Giugni and Passy's attempt to put the mobilization by collective actors into a larger social and economic context is, in my view, particularly useful, because it allows us to understand the strategies adopted by the various participants in the interaction context and their differential success. Thus, I believe that in order to understand why the established parties are so susceptible to succumb to the pressure exerted by the radical populist parties, we need to understand why the mobilization for a tightening of the migration policy by the radical right has met with so much resonance among the populations in many, although not all, Western European countries.

Attempting to situate the political process approach adopted by the two chapters in a larger context, I would like to suggest that the astounding success of the populist right (in migration policy and more generally in electoral terms) is ultimately rooted in far reaching *transformations of the cleavage structure* in Western European countries: The program of the radical right, which one might characterize as "a combination of differential nativism and comprehensive protectionism" (Betz 2004), articulates what we could call a new cleavage between the losers and the winners of the process of "denationalization"—the opening up and "unbundling" of national borders. The groups who were protected by these borders and whose life chances are now increasingly threatened by an open, international, cosmopolitan, and deregulated world constitute the core potential for the radical right. This movement seeks to exploit the anxieties and feelings of insecurity provoked by economic globalization and the resentments in response to the sociocultural transformation of Western European societies caused by the presence of a growing resident alien population (Betz 2004, Kriesi 2001). The secret of the populist right's success has been its ability to appeal to a broad range of voters, to the "widespread sentiment of frustration and disaffection with the established political parties, the political process, and, to a certain degree at least, liberal representative democracy in general" (Betz 2004). As already pointed out, migration policy has constituted the main battleground for this new political force.

The country-specific success of the radical right—in politics in general and in migration policy in particular—depends on a number of factors, many of which concern the overall social, cultural, and economic preconditions of the political process. Among these factors we can count the *short-term economic situation* and *the immigration pressure*—the two aspects introduced in Giugni and Passy's model, both of which increase the perceived threat of immigrants among the indigenous population (Quillian 1995): The greater the immigration pressure and the less favorable the economic situation, the greater the perceived threat exerted by immigrants on the resident population. Among these factors we may also count *the tradition of national citizenship* mentioned in both chapters. We can expect that ethnic but also republican models of citizenship serve to exacerbate the new cleavage, while multicultural models tend to appease it. Third, the *strength of the traditional political cleavages* also plays a significant role (Bartolini and Mair 1990, Kriesi and Duyvendak 1995): The stronger the traditional cleavages, the more limited the capacity of the new cleavage to mobilize the citizens. Fourth, the impact of the *overall level of economic development* is important, too, and it is related to the previous point: The new conflict line is likely to be particularly serious in highly developed countries, where the pacification of the traditional class conflicts makes room for the new cleavage. In addition, the economic opportunities in such countries attract large numbers of migrants, which exacerbates the ethnic competition. Moreover, the highly privileged resident populations in such countries are likely to feel particularly threatened by "undeserving" migrants. Fifth, the *traditional national adjustment strategies to international competition* should be taken into consideration, too. Thus, the small Western European nations have a long tradition of economic liberalism and integration into the world markets, the internal consequences of which were alleviated by compensatory internal strategies (Katzenstein 1985). These strategies implied not only the construction of efficient social welfare states but also the protection of sectors focused on the home market. Such protective measures were, for example, especially important for the Swiss adjustment strategies (Mach 2001). The global liberalization has now put strong pressures on these traditional adjustment mechanisms, which contributes to the creation of a broad potential of losers in a country like Switzerland.

As far as the more narrowly *political opportunity structure* is concerned, the *political institutions* constitute a first factor that needs to be taken into account. Lipset and Rokkan (1967) have already pointed out that institutional access constitutes one of the key determinants of political change. Political systems that are difficult to access for newcomers risk a process of radicalization and a highly conflictual restructuration process, while the political process is likely to be more peaceful and gradual in open systems. Second, the *configuration of the established party system* constitutes a key factor for the rise of the radical right and its impact on migration policy. Thus, Kitschelt (1995) has argued that convergence between the major moderate left-wing and moderate right-wing parties opens up the possibility for a radical party to position itself successfully on the extreme at either side. Third, the restructuring of the political space also depends on the *internal structure of the newcomers* on the radical right. Lubbers et al. (2002) point out that such parties, just like other parties, gain support only when they are well-organized, and to the extent that they have created a solid basis for electoral success. Another factor that contributes to their success is the charisma of their leaders. Taggart (1996) has suggested that internal cohesiveness is particularly important in the case of populist parties precisely because they depend so heavily on the charismatic qualities of a single individual to maintain control of the party and to maximize the impact of their relatively small constituency. Finally, their success also depends on *whether they join the government*. Thus, as already mentioned, Betz (2004) argues that radical right-wing parties do better in opposition than in government. While a strategy of isolating them, as the Belgian mainstream parties have done, seems only to enhance their appeal and to increase their electoral potential, their cooptation into a coalition government seems to accelerate their decline, as the recent Austrian, Dutch, and Italian coalition governments serve to illustrate.

I am aware of the fact that the number of factors likely to account for the success of the radical right and, therefore, for the determination of migration policy is rather (too) large. Depending on the aspect of the policy to be explained and depending on the countries compared, the analyst will have to make an informed choice among them. In any case, however, it will be crucial to situate the political process in the context of these factors in order to understand how the migration policy developed in a given country.

References

Aleinikoff, Thomas A., and David A. Martin. 1995. *Immigration Process and Policy*. 3rd ed. St. Paul, MN: West Publishing.

Altermatt, Urs. 1999. "Multiculturalism, Nation State and Ethnicity: Political Models for Multiethnic States." Pp. 73–84 in *Nation and National Identity: The European Experience in Perspective*, edited by Hanspeter Kriesi, Klaus Armingeon, Hannes Siegrist, and Andreas Wimmer. Zurich: Verlag Rüegger.

Amenta, Edwin, Bruce G. Carruthers, and Yvonne Zylan. 1992. "A Hero for the Aged? The Townsend Movement, the Political Mediation Model, and U.S. Old-Age Policy, 1934–1950." *American Journal of Sociology* 98: 308–39.

Angenendt, Steffen. 2003. "Einwanderung und Rechtspopulismus: Eine Analyse im europäischen Vergleich." *Internationale Politik* 58, no. 4 (April): 3–12.

Archdeacon, Thomas. 1983. *Becoming American*. New York, NY: Free Press.

Arendt, Hannah. 1990. *On Revolution*. New York: Viking Press.

Asscher, Ben. 1996. "Integratie minderheden moet anders." *Utrechts Nieuwsblad*, no. 3 (December): 9.

Auer, Andreas. 1996. "Constitution et politique d'immigration: La quadrature des trois cercles (avis de droit)." Berne: Commission fédérale contre le racisme.

Bade, Klaus J. 1994a. *Ausländer, Aussiedler, Asyl: Eine Bestandaufnahme*. München: Verlag C. H. Beck.

———. ed. 1994b. *Das Manifest der 60: Deutschland und die Einwanderung*. Munich: Verlag C. H. Beck.

Bade, Klaus J., and Myron Weiner, eds. 1995. *Migrations Past, Migrations Future*. New York: Berghahn Books.

Balibar, Étienne, and Immanuel Wallerstein. 1988. *Race, nation, classe: Les identités ambigues*. Paris: La Découverte.

Banton, Michael. 1985. *Promoting Racial Harmony*. Cambridge: Cambridge University Press.

———. 2001. "National integration in France and Britain." *Journal of Ethnic and Migration Studies* 27, no. 1: 151–68.

Barth, Fredrik. 1959. *Political Leadership amongst the Swat Pathans*. London School of Economics Monographs in Anthropology, No. 19.

———. 1969. *Ethnic Groups and Boundaries*. London: Allen and Unwin.

Bartolini Stefano, and Peter Mair. 1990. *Identity, Competition and Electoral Availability: The Stabilization of European Electorates 1885–1985*. Cambridge: Cambridge University Press.

Bauman, Zygmunt. 1998. *Globalization: The Human Consequences*. Cambridge: Polity.

Bean, Frank D., et al. 1989. *Mexican and Central American Population and U.S. Immigration Policy*. Austin, TX: University of Texas Press.

Bell, Mark. 1999. "Shifting Conceptions of Sexual Discrimination at the Court of Justice: From P v. S to Grant v. SWT." *European Law Journal* 5: 63–81.

Benarieh Ruffer, Galya. 2002. "Virtual Citizenship: Migrants and the Constitutional Polity." Ph.D. diss., University of Pennsylvania.

Berger, Maria, Christian Galonska, and Ruud Koopmans. 2004. "Political Integration by a Detour? Ethnic Communities and Social Capital of Migrants in Berlin." *Journal of Ethnic and Migration Studies* 30: 491–507.

Berger, Peter L. ed. 1999. *The Desecularisation of the World: Resurgent Religion and World Politics*. Michigan: Eerdmans.

Betts, Katharine. 1999. *The Great Divide*. Sydney: Duffy and Snellgrove.

Betz, Hans-Georg. 1994. *Radical Right-Wing Populism in Western Europe*. New York: St. Martin's Press.

———. 1999. "Contemporary Right-Wing Radicalism in Europe." *Contemporary European History* 8, no. 2: 299–316.

———. 2004. *La droite populiste en Europe: Extrême et démocrate?* Paris: Autrement.

Birnbaum, Pierre. 1998. *La France imaginée*. Paris: Fayard.

Blaise, Pierre, and Albert Martens. 1992. "Des immigrés à intégrer." *Courrier Hebdomadaire*, no. 1358–9. Brussels: Centre de Recherche et d'Information Socio-Politiques.

Blatt, David. 1995. "Towards a Multi-Cultural Political Model in France? The Limits of Immigrant Collective Action, 1968–1994." *Nationalism and Ethnic Politics* 1: 156–77.

Blanc, Maurice. 1991. "Von heruntergekommenen Altenquartieren zu abgewerteten Sozialwohnungen: ethnische Minderheiten in Frankreich, Deutschland und dem Vereinigten Königreich." *Information zur Raumentwicklung* 6–7: 447–57.

Block, James. 2001. *A Nation of Agents: The American Path to a Modern Self and Society*. Cambridge, MA: Harvard University Press.

Böcker, Anita. 1994. *Turkse migranten en sociale zekerheid: Van onderlinge zorg naar overheidszorg?* Amsterdam: Amsterdam University Press.

Boos-Nünning, Ursula, and Thomas Schwarz. 1991. *Traditions of Integration of Migrants in the Federal Republic of Germany*. Berlin: BIVS.

Borjas, George J. 1990. *Friends or Strangers: The Impact of Immigrants on the U.S. Economy*. New York: Basic Books.

————. 1999. *Heaven's Door: Immigration Policy and the American Economy* Princeton: Princeton University Press.

Bortolini, Massimo. 1996. "La presse et les immigrés en Belgique en 1995." *Migrations-Société* 8, no. 44 (March–April): 109–22.

Bousetta, Hassan. 2000. "Political Dynamics in the City: Three Case Studies." Pp. 129–44 in *Minorities in European Cities*, edited by Sophie Body-Gendrot and Marco Martiniello. New York: St. Martin's Press.

Bovenkerk, Fredrik. 1986. *Een eerlijke kans*. Den Haag: Staatsuitgeverij.

Brettell, Caroline, and James F. Hollifield, eds. 2000. *Migration Theory: Talking Across Disciplines*. New York and London: Routledge.

Brockett, Charles D. 1991. "The Structure of Political Opportunities and Peasant Mobilization in Central America." *Comparative Politics* 23: 253–74.

Brubaker, Rogers ed. 1989. *Immigration and the Politics of Citizenship in Europe and North America*. Lanham, MD: The German Marshall Fund of the United States and the University Press of America.

————. 1992. *Citizenship and Nationhood in France and Germany*. Cambridge, MA: Harvard University Press.

Bruno, Michael, and Jeffrey Sachs. 1985. *Economics of Worldwide Stagflation*. Cambridge, MA: Harvard University Press.

Buijs, Frank J., and Carien Nelissen. 1994. "Tussen continuïteit en verandering: Marokkanen in Nederland." Pp. 177–206 in *Het demokratisch ongeduld*, edited by Hans Vermeulen and Rinus Penninx. Amsterdam: Het Spinhuis.

Burstein, Paul, Rachel L. Einwohner, and Jocelyn A. Hollander. 1995. "The Success of Political Movements: A Bargaining Perspective." Pp. 225–35 in *The Politics of Social Protest*, edited by J. Craig Jenkins and Bert Klandermans. Minneapolis: University of Minnesota Press.

Burstein, Paul, and William Freudenburg. 1978. "Changing Public Policy: The Impact of Public Opinion, Anti-War Demonstrations and War Costs on Senate Voting on Vietnam War Motions." *American Journal of Sociology* 84: 99–122.

Calavita, Kitty. 1992. *Inside the State: The Bracero Program, Immigration, and the I.N.S.* New York: Routledge.

Can, Murat, and Hatice Can-Engin. 1997. *De zwarte tulp*. Utrecht: Uitgeverij Jan van Arkel.

Castles, Stephen. 1985. "The Guests Who Stayed—The Debate on 'Foreigners Policy' in the German Federal Republic." *International Migration Review* 19, no. 3: 517–34.

————. 1994. "La sociologie et la peur des 'cultures incompatibles': Commentaires sur le rapport Hoffmann-Nowotny." Pp. 370–384 in *Europe: Montrez patte blanche! Les nouvelles frontières du "laboratoire Schengen,"* edited by Marie-Claire Caloz-Tschopp and Micheline Fontolliet Honoré. Genève: Editions du CETIM.

————. 1995. "How Nation-States Respond to Immigration and Ethnic Diversity." *New Community* 21, no. 3: 293–308.

Castles, Stephen, and Godula Kosack. 1985 [1973]. *Immigrant Workers and Class Structure in Western Europe*. 2nd ed. Oxford: Oxford University Press.

Castles, Stephen, and Mark J. Miller. 1998. *The Age of Migration: International Population Movements in the Modern World*. 2nd ed. Guilford Press.

Cattacin, Sandro. 1987. *Neokorporatismus in der Schweiz: Die Fremdarbeiterpolitik.* Zürich: Forschungsstelle für politische Wissenschaft—Kleine Studien zur politischen Wissenschaft, nos. 243–44.

Cerutti, Mauro. 1994. "Un secolo di emigrazione italiana in Svizzera (1870–1970), attraverso le fonti dell'Archivio federale." *Studi e fonti* 20: 11–141.

———. 2005. "La politique migratoire de la Suisse 1945–1970." Pp. 89–134 in *Histoire de la politique de migration, d'asile et d'intégration en Suisse depuis 1944,* edited by Hans Mahnig. Zurich: Seismo.

Chalmers, Damian. 2000. "The Much Ado about Judicial Politics in the United Kingdom: A Statistical Analysis of Reported Decisions of United Kingdom Courts invoking EU Law 1973–1998." Working paper 2000–2001, Harvard University Press.

Chapin, Wesley D. 1997. *Germany for the Germans? The Political Effects of International Migration.* Westport, CT: Greenwood Press.

Checkel, Jeffrey. 1999. "Norms, Institutions, and National Identity in Contemporary Europe." *International Studies Quarterly* 43: 83–114.

Cholewinski, Ryszard. 2002. "Family Reunification and Conditions Placed on Family Members: Dismantling a Fundamental Human Right." *European Journal of Migration and Law* 4: 271–90.

Cohn-Bendit, Daniel, and Thomas Schmid. 1993. *Heimat Babylon.* Hamburg: Hoffmann und Campe Verlag.

Commissariat Royal à la Politique des Immigrés (CRPI). 1993. *Rapport final: Desseins d'égalité.* Brussels: CRPI.

Commission d'experts en migration. 1997. *Une nouvelle conception de la politique en matière de migration: Rapport de la commission d'experts en migration.* Berne: Office fédéral des réfugiés.

Cooper, Alice Holmes. 2002. "Part-Sponsored Protest and the Movement Society: The CDU/CSU Mobilizes Against Citizenship Law Reform." *German Politics* 11, no. 2: 88–104.

Cornelius, Wayne A., Philip L. Martin, and James F. Hollifield, eds. 2004. *Controlling Immigration: A Global Perspective.* Stanford, CA: Stanford University Press.

Cose, Ellis. 1992. *A Nation of Strangers: Prejudice, Politics, and the Populating of America.* New York: William Morrow and Company.

Costain, Anne N., and Steven Majstorovic. 1994. "Congress, Social Movements and Public Opinion: Multiple Origins of Women's Rights Legislation." *Political Research Quarterly* 47: 111–135.

Cross, Malcolm. ed. 1992. *Ethnic Minorities and Industrial Change in Europe and North America.* Cambridge: Cambridge University Press.

Danese, Gaia. 1998. "The European transnational collective action of migrants: The case of Italy and Spain." *Journal of Ethnic and Migration Studies* 24, no. 4: 715–734.

Daniels, Roger. 1990. *Coming to America: A History of Immigration and Ethnicity in American Life.* New York: HarperCollins.

Département fédéral de justice et police. 2001. *Compte rendu des résultats de la procédure de consultation relative à l'avant-projet de loi fédérale sur les étrangers.* Berne: Office fédéral des étrangers.

Deponti, Luisa. 1999. "Politique d'immigration et droit de la nationalité en Allemagne." *Migrations Société* 11, no. 61 (January-February): 121–36.

Deschamps, Luk, and Koenraad Pauwels, eds. 1992. *Eigen organisaties van migranten*. Brussels: Ministerie van de Vlaamse Gemeenschap.

Deslé, Els. 1992. *Grenzen aan de racisme bestrijding*. Brussels: Vrije Universiteit Brussel, Interuniversitaire Attractiepool 37.

Dhima, Giorgio. 1991a. *Politische Ökonomie der schweizerischen Ausländerregelung: Eine empirische Untersuchung über die schweizerische Migrationspolitik und Vorschläge für ihre künftige Gestaltung*. Chur [etc.]: Rüegger.

————. 1991b. *Wie viele Südeuropäer würden im Falle eines EG-Beitritts in die Schweiz einwandern? Eine empirische Schätzung gestützt auf Migrationsdaten des Jahres 1988 zwischen 5 Gast- und 9 Entsendeländern*. Basel: Wirtschaftswissenschaftlich.

Die Grünen. 1990. *Die Multikulturelle Gesellschaft*. Bonn: Die Grünen.

Di Pascale, Alessia. 2002. "The New Regulations on Immigration and the Status of Foreigners in Italy." *European Journal of Migration and Law* 4: 1–11.

Distelbrink, Marjolijn Julia, and Justus Veenman. 1994. *Hollandse nieuwe: Allochtone jongeren in Nederland*. Utrecht: De Tijdstroom.

Dudziak, Mary L. 2000. *Cold War Civil Rights: Race and the Image of American Democracy*. Princeton: Princeton University Press.

Dummett, Ann, and Andrew Nicol. 1990. *Subjects, Aliens, and Others*. London: Weidenfeld and Nicolson.

Eatwell, Roger. 1995. "Why Has the Extreme Right Failed in Britain?" In *The Extreme Right in Europe and the USA*, edited by Paul Hainsworth. New York: St. Martin's Press.

Emirbayer, Mustafa, and Anne Mische. 1998. "What Is Agency?" in *American Journal of Sociology* 103: 962–1023.

Entzinger, Han B. 1984. *Her et minderhedenbeleid; dilemma's voor de overheid in Nederland en zes andere immigratielanden in Europa*. Meppel/Amsterdam: Boom.

Étienne, Bruno. 1989. *La France et l'islam*. Paris: Hachette.

European Observer on line. August 13, 2001.

Faist, Thomas. 1994. "Immigration, Integration, and the Ethnicization of Politics." *European Journal of Political Research* 25: 439–59.

Favell, A. 1998. *Philosophies of Integration: Immigration and the Idea of Citizenship in France and Britain*. London: Macmillan Press.

————. 2000. "L'européanisation ou l'émergence d'un nouveau "champ politique": Le cas de la politique d'immigration." Pp. 153–85 in *Sociologie de l'Europe: Élites, mobilizations et configurations institutionelles, Cultures et conflits*, no. 38–39 (été-automne).

————. 2001a. "Integration Policy and Integration Research in Europe: A Review and Critique." Pp. 349–399 in *Citizenship Today: Global Perspectives and Practices*, edited by Aleinikoff, Alexander and Klusmeyer, Douglas. Washington, D.C.: Brookings Institute/Carnegie Endowment for International Peace.

————. 2003a. "Games Without Frontiers? Questioning the Transnational Social Power of Migrants in Europe." *Archives Européennes de Sociologie* XLIV, no. 3 (Winter): 106–36.

————. 2003b. "Integration Nations: The Nation-State and Research on Immigrants in Western Europe." *Comparative Social Research Yearbook* 22: 23–62.

Favell, Adrian, and Andrew Geddes. 2000. "Immigration and European integration: New Opportunities for Transnational Political Mobilization?" Pp. 407–28 in *Challenging Ethnic Relations Politics in Europe: Comparative and Transnational Perspectives*, edited by Ruud Koopmans and Paul Statham. Oxford: Oxford University Press.

Favell, Adrian, and Randall Hansen. 2002. "Markets Against Politics: Migration, EU Enlargement and the Idea of Europe." *Journal of Ethnic and Migration Studies* 28, no. 4 (October): 581–601.

Federal Ministry of the Interior. 2001. *Structuring Immigration, Fostering Integration*. Berlin.

Fennema, Meindert. 2004. "The Concept and Measurement of Ethnic Community." *Journal of Ethnic and Migration Studies* 30: 429–47.

Federal Ministry of the Interior. 2001. *Structuring Immigration, Fostering Integration*. Berlin.

Fennema, Meindert, and Jean Tillie. 1999. "Political Participation and Political Trust in Amsterdam: Civic Communities and Ethnic Networks." *Journal of Ethnic and Migration Studies* 25: 703–26.

Fennema, Meindert, and Jean Tillie. 2001. "Civic Community, Political Participation and Political Trust of Ethnic Groups." *Connections* 24: 26–41.

Fetzer, Joel S. 2000. *Public Attitudes Toward Immigration in the United States, France, and Germany*. Cambridge: Cambridge University Press.

Feuille fédérale. Bern: Centre des publications officielles (CPO) de la Chancellerie fédérale, <http://www.admin.ch/ch/f/ff>.

Fibbi, Rosita, and Claudio Bolzmann. 1991. "Collective Assertion Strategies of Immigrants in Switzerland." *International Sociology* 6: 321–41.

Fibbi, Rosita, and Sandro Cattacin. 2000. "Vers une internationalisation de la politique migratoire suisse?" *Revue Européenne des Migrations Internationales* 16, no. 3: 125–46.

Fietz, Martina. 1999. "Doppelpaß: Schily strebt Kompromß an." *Die Welt* (March 5).

Fijalkowski, Jürgen. 1991. "Nationale Identität versus multikulturelle Gesellschaft: Entwicklungen der Problemlage und Alternativen der Orientierung in der politischen Kultur der Bundesrepublik in den 80er Jahren." In *Die Bundesrepublik in den achtziger Jahren: Innenpolitik, Politische Kultur, Aussenpolitik* edited by Werner Süss. Opladen: Leske und Budrich.

Finnemore, Martha. 1996. "Norms, Culture, and World Politics: Insights from Sociology's Institutionalism." *International Organization* 50, no. 2 (Spring): 325–48.

Foner, Nancy. 1997. "The Immigrant Family: Cultural Legacies and Cultural Changes." *International Migration Review* 31, no. 4 (Winter): 961–74.

Freeman, Gary P. 1986. "Migration and the Political Economy of the Welfare State." *Annals of the American Academy of Political and Social Sciences*, no. 485: 51–62.

———. 1995. "Modes of Immigration Politics in Liberal Democratic States." *International Migration Review* 29, no. 4: 881–902.

———. 1998. "The Decline of Sovereignty? Politics and Immigration Restriction in Liberal States." Pp. 86–108 in *Challenge to the Nation-State*, edited by Christian Joppke. Oxford: Oxford University Press.

———. 2001. "Client Politics or Populism? Immigration Reform in the United States." Pp. 31–64 in *Controlling a New Migration World*, edited by Virginie Guiraudon and Christian Joppke. London: Routledge.

Freeman, Gary P., and James Jupp, eds. 1992. *Nations of Immigrants: Australia, the United States, and International Migration.* Melbourne: Oxford University Press.

Fuchs, Lawrence. 1990a. *The American Kaleidoscope: Race, Ethnicity, and the Civic Culture.* Hanover and London: Wesleyan University Press.

———. 1990b. "The Corpse That Would Not Die: The Immigration Reform and Control Act of 1986." Pp. 111–27 in *L'Immigration aux Etats-Unis.* Special issue of the *Revue Europeenne des Migrations Internationales*, edited by J. F. Hollifield and Yves Charbit.

Gamson, William A. 1990 [1975]. *The Strategy of Social Protest.* 2nd ed. Belmont, CA: Wadsworth Publishing.

Garcia, Juan Ramon. 1980. *Operation Wetback: The Mass Deportation of Mexican Undocumented Workers in 1954.* Westport: Greenwood Press.

Garcia y Griego, Manuel. 1989. "The Mexican Labor Supply, 1990–2010." In *Mexican Migration to the United States: Origins, Consequences, and Policy Options W.A.*, edited by Wayne A. Cornelius and Jorge A. Bustamente. San Diego, CA: Center for U. S. Mexican Studies, University of California, San Diego.

Geddes, Andrew, and Adrian Favell, eds. 1999. *The Politics of Belonging: Migrants and Minorities in Contemporary Europe.* Aldershot: Ashgate.

Geertz, Clifford. 1963. *Old Societies and New States: The Quest for Modernity in Asia and Africa.* Glencoe, IL: Free Press.

Geiß, Bernd. 2001. "Die Ausländerbeauftragten der Bundesregierung in der ausländerpolitischen Diskussion." *Deutschland – ein Einwanderungsland? Rückblick. Bilanz and neue Fragen*, edited by Edda Currie and Tanja Wunderlich. Stuttgart: Lucius & Lucius.

Gellner, Ernest. 1983. *Nations and Nationalism.* Oxford: Blackwell.

Gibney, Matthew J. 2001. "The state of asylum: Democratization, judicialization and evolution of refugee policy in Europe." *New Issues in Refugee Research*—UNHCR Working Paper 50.

Giugni, Marco. 1998. "Was it Worth the Effort? The Outcomes and Consequences of Social Movements." *Annual Review of Sociology* 24: 371–93.

———. 2001. "L'impact des mouvements écologistes, antinucléaires et pacifistes sur les politiques publiques: Le cas des Etats-Unis, de l'Italie et de la Suisse, 1975–1995." *Revue Française de Sociologie* 42: 641–68.

———. 2004. *Social Protest and Policy Change.* Lanham, MD: Rowman and Littlefield.

Giugni, Marco, and Florence Passy. 1998. "Social Movements and Policy Change: Direct, Mediated, or Joint Effect?" *American Sociological Association Section on Collective Behavior and Social Movements Working Paper Series*, vol. 1, no. 4, <http://www.nd.edu/~dmyers/cbsm>.

———. 2000. "Resistance to Europeanization: National Barriers to Supranational Changes in Migration Policy." *La Lettre de la Maison Française d'Oxford* 12: 183–206.

———. 2002. "Le champ politique de l'immigration en Europe: Opportunités, mobilisations et héritage de l'État national" Pp. 443–60 in *L'action collective en Europe*, edited by Richard Balme, Didier Chabanet, and Vincent Wright. Paris: Presses de Sciences Po.

———. 2004. "Migrant Mobilization Between Political Institutions and Citizenship Regimes: A Comparison of France and Switzerland." *European Journal of Political Research* 43: 51–82.

Götz, Irene. ed. 2000. *Zündstoff doppelte Staatsbürgerschaft: Zur Veralltäglichung Nationalen*. Münster, Hamburg and London: Lit Verlag.

Green, Simon. 1999. "The Politics of Exclusion: Immigration, Residence and Citizenship Policy in Germany, 1955–1998." Ph.D. diss., University of Birmingham.

———. 2000. "Beyond Ethnoculturalism? German Citizenship in the New Millennium." *German Politics* 9, No. 3 (December): 105–24.

———. 2001a. "Citizenship Policy in Germany: The Case of Ethnicity over Residence." In *Towards a European Nationality? Citizenship, Migration and Nationality Law in the European Union*, edited by Randall Hansen and Patrick Weil. Houndmills: Palgrave

———. 2001b. "Immigration, Asylum and Citizenship in Germany: The Impact of Unification and the Berlin Republic." *West European Politics* 24, no. 4 (October). 82–106.

Greenwald, Rachel Toby. 2000. "The German Nation is a Homogeneous Nation? Race, the Cold War, and German National Identity, 1970–1993." Ph.D. diss., University of California, Irvine.

Grudzielski, Stany. 1990. *Immigrés et égalité des chances en Europe: Immigration et politiques sociales en Europe*. Brussels: European Centre for Work and Society, (September).

Guibernau, Montserrat, and John Rex. 2003. "The Nature of Ethnicity in the Project of Migration." *The Ethnicity Reader: Nationalism, Multiculturalism, and Migration*, edited by Montserrat Guibernau and John Rex. Cambridge: Polity Press.

Guiraudon, Virginie. 1998. "Citizenship Rights for Non-Citizens: France, Germany and the Netherlands (1974–1994)." Pp. 272–318 in *Challenge to the Nation-State*, edited by Christian Joppke. Oxford: Oxford University Press.

———. 2000a. *Les politiques d'immigration en Europe: Allemagne, France, Pays-Bas*. Paris: L'Harmattan.

———. 2000b. "European Integration and Migration Policy: Vertical Policy-Making as Venue Shopping." *Journal of Common Market Studies* 38, no. 2: 249–69.

Guiraudon, V., and G. Lahav. 2000. "A Reappraisal of the State Sovereignty Debate: The Case of Migration Control." *Comparative Political Studies* 33, no. 2: 163–95.

Gurowitz, Amy. 1999. "Mobilizing International Norms: Domestic Actors, Immigrants, and the Japanese State." *World Politics* 51 (April): 413–45.

Haberland, Jürgen. 1983. "Die Vorschläge der Kommission Ausländerpolitik" *Zeitschrift für Ausländerpolitik* 2: 55–61.

Habermas, Jürgen. 1993. "Die Festung Europa und das neue Deutschland." *Die Zeit* (May 28).

———. 1996. "The European Nation-state—Its Achievements and Its Limits: On the Past and Future of Sovereignty and Citizenship." In *Mapping the Nation*, edited by Gopal Balakrishnan and Benedict Anderson. London: Verso.

Hainsworth, Paul, ed. 1995. "Why Has the Extreme Right Failed in Britain?" *The Extreme Right in Europe and the USA*. New York: St. Martin's Press.

Hammar, Tomas, ed. 1985. *European Immigration Policy: A Comparative Study*. Cambridge: Cambridge University Press.

Hansen, Randall. 2000. "The Problems of Dual Nationality in Europe." *ECPR News* 11, no. 2 (Spring).

———. 2001. *Towards a European Nationality? Citizenship, Migration and Nationality Law in the European Union*. Houndmills: Palgrave.

Hatton, Timothy J., and Jeffrey G. Williamson. 1998. *The Age of Mass Migration: Causes and Economic Impact.* New York: Oxford University Press.

———. 2002. "What Fundamentals Drive World Migration?" Working Paper 9159. Cambridge, MA: National Bureau of Economic Research.

Haug, Werner. 1980. *". . . und es kamen Menschen": Ausländerpolitik und Fremdarbeit in der Schweiz 1914–1980.* Basel: Z-Verlag.

Heijs, Eric. 1995. *Van vreemdeling tot Nederlander.* Amsterdam: Het Spinhuis.

Heinisch, Reinhard. 2003. "Success in Opposition—Failure in Government: Explaining the Performance of Right-Wing Populist Parties in Public Office." *West European Politics* 26, no. 3 (July): 91–130.

Heisler, Martin O. 1992. "Migration, International Relations and the New Europe: Theoretical Perspectives from Institutional Political Sociology." *International Migration Review* 26: 596–621.

Higham, John. 1985. *Strangers in the Land: Patterns of American Nativism, 1860–1925.* New York: Atheneum.

Hoffmann-Nowotny, Hans-Joachim. 1985. "Switzerland." Pp. 206–36 in *European Immigration Policy: A Comparative Study,* edited by Tomas Hammar. Cambridge: Cambridge University Press.

———. 1992. *Chancen und Risiken multikultureller Einwanderungsgesellschaften.* Bern: Schweizerischer Wissenschaftsrat.

———. 1995. "Switzerland: A non-immigration immigration country." Pp. 302–7 in *The Cambridge Survey of World Migration,* edited by Robin Cohen. Cambridge: Cambridge University Press.

Hollifield, James F. 1990. "Immigration and the French State." *Comparative Political Studies* 23 (April): 56–79.

———. 1992a. *Immigrants, Markets, and States: The Political Economy of Postwar Europe.* Cambridge, MA: Harvard University Press.

———. 1992b. "Migration and International Relations: Cooperation and Control in the European Community." *International Migration Review* 26: 568–95.

———. 1994. "Immigration and Republicanism in France: The Hidden Consensus." In *Controlling Immigration,* edited by Wayne A. Cornelius, Philip L. Martin, and James F. Hollifield, Stanford, CA: Stanford University Press.

———. 2000. "The Politics of International Migration: How Can We Bring the State Back In?" In *Migration Theory: Talking Across Disciplines,* edited by Caroline Brettell and James F. Hollifield. New York: Routledge.

Huntington, Samuel P. 1996. *The Clash of Civilizations and the Remaking of World Order.* New York: Simon and Schuster.

———. 2002. *The Clash of Civilizations and the Remaking of World Order.* London: Free Press.

Hutchinson, Edward P. 1981. *Legislative History of American Immigration Policy, 1798–1965.* Philadelphia: University of Pennsylvania Press.

Interdepartementale Strategiegruppe. 1989. *Strategie für eine Flüchtlings- und Asylpolitik der 90er Jahre.* Bern: Interdepartementale Strategiegruppe für eine Flüchtlings- und Asylpolitik der neunziger Jahre EJPD, EDA, EVD [Bundesamt für Flüchtlinge].

Iranbomy, Seyed Shahram. 1991. "Die juristischen Rahmenbedingungen für Ausländer in der gegenwärtigen deutschen transkulturellen Industriegesellschaft." Pp.

77–109 in *Einwanderbares Deutschland*, edited by Daniel Cohn-Bendit, Liselotte Funcke, Heiner Geissler, and Dorothee Sölle. Stuttgart: Horizonte Verlag.

Ireland, Patrick. 1994. *The Policy Challenge of Ethnic Diversity.* Cambridge, MA: Harvard University Press.

———. 1996. "Vive le Jacobinisme: Les Étrangers and the Durability of the Assimilationist Model in France." *French Politics and Society* 14, no. 2 (Spring): 33–46.

———. 1997. "Socialism, Unification Policy, and the Rise of Racism in Eastern Germany." *International Migration Review* 31, no. 119 (Fall): 541–68.

Jacobs, Dirk, and Jean Tillie. 2004. "Introduction: Social Capital and Political Integration of Migrants." *Journal of Ethnic and Migration Studies* 30: 419–27.

Jacobson, David. 1996. *Rights Across Borders: Immigration and the Decline of Citizenship.* Baltimore, MD: Johns Hopkins University Press.

———. 1997 reprint. *Rights Across Borders: Immigration and the Decline of Citizenship.* Baltimore, MD: Johns Hopkins University Press.

———. 1998–1999. "New Border Customs: Migration and the Changing Role of the State," in *UCLA Journal of International Law and Foreign Affairs* 3, no.2 (Fall/Winter): 443–62.

Jakubowicz, Andrew, Michael Morrissey, and Joanne Palser. 1984. *Ethnicity, Class, and Social Welfare in Australia.* Sydney: Social Welfare Research Center, University of New South Wales.

Janoski, Thomas, and Larry W. Isaac. 1994. "Introduction to Time-Series Analysis." In *The Comparative Political Economy of the Welfare State*, edited by Thomas Janoski and Alexander M. Hicks. Cambridge: Cambridge University Press.

Jenkins, Craig, and Charles Perrow. 1977. "The Insurgency of the Powerless: Farm Workers' Movements (1946–1972)." *American Sociological Review* 42: 249–68.

Jöhr, Walter Adolf, and Robert Huber. 1968. "Die konjunkturellen Auswirkungen der Beanspruchung ausländischer Arbeitskräfte: Untersuchungen mit Hilfe eines Simulationsmodelles der schweizerischen Volkswirtschaft." *Schweizerische Zeitschrift für Volkswirtschaft und Statistik* 104, no.4: 365–610.

Joppke, Christian. 1996. "Multiculturalism and Immigration: A Comparison of the United States, Germany, and Great Britain." *Theory and Society* 25, no. 4 (August): 470–71.

———. 1998a. "Why Liberal States Accept Unwanted Immigration." *World Politics* 50: 266–93.

———. ed. 1998b. *Challenge to the nation-state: Immigration in Western Europe and the United States.* Oxford: Oxford University Press.

———. 1998c. "Immigration Challenges the Nation-State." In *Challenge to the Nation-State: Immigration in Western Europe and the United States*, edited by Christian Joppke. Oxford: Oxford University Press.

———. 1999. *Immigration and the Nation-State: The United States, Germany, and Great Britain.* Oxford: Oxford University Press.

———. 2001. "The Legal-Domestic Sources of Immigrant Rights: The United States, Germany, and the European Union." *Comparative Political Studies* 34, no. 4 (May): 339–36.

———. 2002. *Place and Belonging in America.* Baltimore, MD: Johns Hopkins University Press.

Joppke, Christian, and Elia Marzal. 2004. "Courts, the New Constitutionalism and Immigrant Rights: The Case of the French *Conseil Constitutionnel.*" *European Journal of Political Research* 43: 823–44.

Kanther, Manfred. 1996. "Deutschland ist kein Einwanderungsland" *Frankfurter Allgemeine Zeitung*, no. 265 (November 13): 11.

Käppner, Joachim, and Jeanne Rubner. 2002. "Union und Zuwanderung: Edmund Stoiber bleibt bei seiner Ablehnung des Regierungsentwurfs." *Süddeutsche Zeitung* (March 1).

Kastoryano, Riva. 1997. *La France, l'Allegmagne et leurs immigrés: Négocier l'identité.* Paris: Armand Colin.

———. 1998. *Quelle identité pour l'Europe? Le multiculturalisme à l'épreuve.* Paris: Presses de Science Po.

Katzenstein, Peter J. 1985. *Small States in World Markets.* Ithaca, NY: Cornell University Press.

Kessler, Alan E. 1999. "International Trade, Domestic Coalitions, and the Political Economy of Immigration Control." Doctoral diss. University of California, Los Angeles.

Kettner, David. 1978. *The Development of American Citizenship, 1608–1870.* Chapel Hill, NC: University of North Carolina Press.

King, Desmond. 2000. *Making Americans: Immigration, Race, and the Origins of the Diverse Democracy.* Cambridge, MA: Harvard University Press.

Kingdon, John W. 1984. *Agendas, Alternatives, and Public Policies.* Boston: Little, Brown.

Kitschelt, Herbert. 1986. "Political Opportunity Structures and Political Protest: Anti-Nuclear Movements in Four Democracies." *British Journal of Political Science* 16: 57–85.

Kitschelt Herbert (in collaboration with Anthony J. McGann). 1995. *The Radical Right in Western Europe: A Comparative Analysis.* Ann Arbor, MI: University of Michigan Press.

Kloosterman, Robert, Joanne van der Leun, and Jan Rath. 1997. *Over grenzen.* Amsterdam: Instituut voor Migratie- en Etnische Studies.

Klusmeyer, Douglas. 1993. "Aliens, Immigrants, and Citizens: The Politics of Inclusion in the Federal Republic of Germany." *Daedalus* 122, no. 3: 81–114.

Kohli, Ulrich R. 1979. "Niveau de l'emploi et exportation du chômage." *Wirtschaft und Recht* 4: 315–21.

Koopmans, Ruud. 2004. "Migrant Mobilization and Political Opportunities: Variation Among German Cities and Regions in Cross-National Perspective." *Journal of Ethnic and Migration Studies* 30: 449–70.

Koopmans, Ruud, and Hanspeter Kriesi. 1997. "Citoyenneté, identité nationale et mobilisation de l'extrême droite: Une comparaison entre la France, l'Allemagne, les Pays-Bas et la Suisse." In *Sociologie des nationalismes*, edited by Pierre Birnbaum, Paris: Presses Universitaires de France.

Koopmans, Ruud, and Paul Statham 1999. "Challenging the Liberal Nation-State? Post-Nationalism, Multiculturalism and the Collective Claims Making of Migrants and Ethnic Minorities in Britain and Germany." *American Journal of Sociology* 105, no. 3: 652–96.

————. 2000a. "Migration and Ethnic Relations as a Field of Political Contention: An Opportunity Structure Approach." Pp. 13–56 in *Challenging Immigration and Ethnic Relations Politics: Comparative European Perspectives*, edited by Ruud Koopmans and Paul Statham. Oxford: Oxford University Press.

————. eds. 2000b. *Challenging Immigration and Ethnic Relations Politics: Comparative European Perspectives*. Oxford: Oxford University Press.

Koopmans, Ruud, Paul Statham, Marco Giugni, and Florence Passy. 2005. *Contested Citizenship: Immigration and Cultural Diversity in Europe*. Minneapolis: University of Minnesota Press.

Krell, Gert, Hans Nicklas, and Aenne Ostermann. 1996. "Immigration, Asylum, and Anti-Foreigner Violence in Germany." *Journal of Peace Research* 33, no. 2 (May): 153–70.

Kriesi, Hanspeter. 1982. "The Structure of the Swiss Political System." Pp. 133–61 in *Patterns of Corporatist Policy-Making*, edited by Gerhard Lehmbruch and Philippe C. Schmitter. London: Sage.

————. 2001. "Nationaler politischer Wandel in einer sich denationalisierenden Welt." Pp. 23–44 in *Globalisierung, Partizipation, Protest*, edited by Ansgar Klein, Ruud Koopmans, and Heiko Geiling. Opladen: Leske und Budrich.

Kriesi, Hanspeter, and Jan-Willem Duyvendak 1995. "National Cleavage Structures." Pp. 3–25 in *New Social Movements in Western Europe: A Comparative Analysis*, by Hanspeter Kriesi, Ruud Koopmans, Jan-Willem Duyvendak, and Marco G. Giugni. Minneapolis: University of Minnesota Press.

Kriesi, Hanspeter, Ruud Koopmans, Jan Willem Duyvendak, and Marco G. Giugni. 1995. *New Social Movements in Western Europe: A Comparative Analysis*. Minneapolis: Univesity of Minnesota Press.

Kruse, Imke, Henry Edward Orren, and Steffen Angenendt. 2003. "The Failure of Immigration Reform in Germany." *German Politics* Vol. 12, no. 3 (December): 129–45.

Kühn, Heinz, 1979. *Stand und Weiterentwicklung der Integration der ausländischen Arbeitnehmer und ihrer Familien in der Bundesrepublik Deutschland*. Memorandum des Beauftragten der Bundesregierung, Bonn.

Kuhn, W. E. 1978. "Guest Workers as an Automatic Stabilizer of Cyclical Unemployment in Switzerland and Germany." *International Migration Review* 12, no. 2: 210–24.

Kymlicka, Will. 1995. *Multicultural Citizenship: A Liberal Theory of Minority Rights*. Oxford: Oxford University Press.

Kymlicka Will, and Wayne Norman, eds. 2000. *Citizenship in Diverse Societies*. Oxford: Oxford University Press.

Lambelet, Jean-Christian. 1994. *L'Economie Suisse*. Paris: Economica.

Lees, Charles. 2000. *The Red-Green Coalition in Germany: Politics, Personalities and Power*. Manchester: Manchester University Press.

Leman, Johan. 1991. "The Education of Immigrant Children in Belgium." *Anthropology and Education Quarterly* 22, no. 2 (June): 140–153.

————. 1994. *Kleur bekennen*. Tielt: Uitgeverij Lannoo.

Levy, Carl, and Alice Bloch, eds. 1999. *Refugees, Citizenship and Social Policy in Europe*. Houndmills: Palgrave.

Levy, Daniel. 1999. "Coming Home? Ethnic Germans and the Transformation of National Identity in the Federal Republic of Germany." In *The Politics of Belonging:*

Migrants and Minorities in Contemporary Europe, edited by Andrew Geddes and Adrian Favell. Aldershot: Ashgate

Li, Wei. 1998. "Anatomy of a New Ethnic Settlement: The Chinese 'Ethnoburb' in Los Angeles." *Urban Studies* 35: 479–501.

Lieberman, Robert C. 2002. "Ideas, Institutions, and Political Order: Explaining Political Change." *American Political Science Review* 96, no. 4 (December): 697–712.

Lindo, Flip. 1994. "Het stille succes: De sociale stijging van Zuideuropese arbeidsmigranten in Nederland." Pp. 117–44 in *Het demokratisch ongeduld*, edited by Hans Vermeulen and Rinus Penninx. Amsterdam: Het Spinhuis.

Lipset, Seymour M., and Stein Rokkan, eds. 1967. *Party Systems and Voter Alignments: Cross-national Perspectives*. New York: Free Press.

Lipsky, Michael. 1968. "Protest as a Political Resource." *American Political Science Review* 62: 1144–58.

Lubbers, Marcel, Mérove Gijsberts, and Peer Scheepers. 2002. "Extreme Right-Wing Voting in Western Europe." *European Journal of Political Research* 41, no. 3: 345–78.

Luther, Kurt Richard. 2003. "The Self-Destruction of a Right-Wing Party? The Austrian Parliamentary Election of 2002." *West European Politics* 26, no. 2 (April): 136–52.

Mach, André. 2001. "Entre internationalisation et changements politiques internes: La révision de la loi sur les cartels et l'évolution des relations industrielles en Suisse dans les années 1990." Doctoral thesis. University of Lausanne.

Mahnig, Hans. 1996. *Konturen eines Kompromisses? Die migrationspolitischen Positionen schweizerischer Parteien und Verbände im Wandel*. Neuchâtel: Forum suisse pour l'étude des migrations—Rapport de recherche 4.

———. 1999. "La question de 'l'intégration' ou Comment les immigrés deviennent un enjeu politique: Une comparaison entre la France, l'Allemagne, les Pays-Bas et la Suisse." *Sociétés Contemporaines*, nos. 33–34: 15–38.

Mahnig, Hans, and Andreas Wimmer 2000. "Country Specific or Convergent? A Typology of Immigrant Policies in Western Europe." *Journal of International Migration and Integration* 1: 177–204.

Mahnig, Hans, and Andreas Wimmer. 2003. "Integration without Immigrant Policy: The Case of Switzerland." Pp. 235–66 in *The Integration of Immigrants in European Society*, edited by Friedrich Heckmann, and Dominique Schnapper. Stuttgart: Lucius & Lucius.

Mahnig, Hans, and Etienne Piguet. 2003. "La politique d'immigration suisse de 1948 à 1998: Evolution et effets." Pp. 67–203 in *Les Migrations et la Suisse*, edited by Rosita Fibbi, Werner Haug, and Hans-Rudolf Wicker, Zurich: Seismo.

Marshall, Thomas H. 1950. *Citizenship and Social Class*. Cambridge: Cambridge University Press.

Martin, Philip L., and Elizabeth Midgley. 1994. "Immigration to the United States: Journey to an Uncertain Destination." *Population Bulletin* 49, no. 2 (September): 2–45.

Martiniello, Marco. 1995. "The National Question and the Political Construction of Immigrant Ethnic Communities in Belgium." Pp. 131–44 in *Racism, Ethnicity, and Politics in Contemporary Europe* edited by Alec G. Hargreaves, and Jeremy Leaman. Aldershot: Edward Elgar.

———. 1998. "Les élus d'origine étrangère à Bruxelles: Une nouvelle étape de la participation politique des populations d'origine immigrée." *Revue Européenne des Migrations Internationales* 14, no. 2: 123–49.

Martiniello, Marco, and Paul Statham. 1999. "Ethnic Mobilisation and Political Participation in Europe." *Journal of Ethnic and Migration Studies* 25 (special issue).

Masi, Paula de, and S. G. B. Henry. 1996. *Aspects of the Swiss Labor Market*. Geneva: International Monetary Fund.

Massey, Douglas S., Rafael Alarcon, Jorge Durand, and Humberto Gonzalez. 1987. *Return to Azatlan*. Berkeley, CA: University of California Press.

Massey, Douglas, et al. 1998. *Worlds in Motion: Understanding International Migration at the End of the Millennium*. Oxford: Oxford University Press.

Massey, Douglas S., Jorge Durand, and Nolan J. Malone. 2002. *Beyond Smoke and Mirrors: Mexican Immigration in an Era of Economic Integration*. New York: Russell Sage Foundation.

McAdam, Doug. 1996. "Conceptual Origins, Current Problems, Future Directions." Pp. 24–40 in *Comparative Perspectives on Social Movements: Political Opportunities, Mobilizing Structures, and Cultural Framings*, edited by Doug McAdam, John D. McCarthy, and Mayer N. Zald. Cambridge: Cambridge University Press.

McAdam, Doug, Sidney Tarrow, and Charles Tilly. 2001. *Dynamics of Contention*. Cambridge: Cambridge University Press.

Meier-Braun, Karl-Heinz. 1998. "Aus 'Gastarbeitern' wurden Einwanderer: Geschichte und Perspektiven der Ausländerpolitik in der Bundesrepublik Deutschland." Pp. 223–32 in *40 Jahre "Gastarbeiter": Deutschland auf dem Weg zur multikulturellen Gesellschaft.* Edited by Karl-Heinz Meier-Braun, Martin A. Kilgus and Wolfgang Niess. Tübingen: Stauffenburg Verlag.

Merkl, Peter, and Leonard Weinberg, eds. 1997. *The Revival of Right Wing Extremism in the 90s*. London: Frank Cass.

Meyer, John, John Boli, George M. Thomas, and Francisco O. Ramirez, 1997 "World Society and the Nation State." *American Journal of Sociology*, no. 103: 144–81.

Micksh, Jürgen. 1991. *Deutschland – Einheit in kultureller Vielfalt*. Frankfurt am Main: Otto Lemback.

Miller, Mark J. 1981. *Foreign Workers in Western Europe*. New York: Praeger.

Milward, Alan. 1992. *The European Rescue of the Nation State*. London: Routledge.

Minister van Binnenlandse Zaken (MBZ). 1983. *Minderhedennota*. The Hague: MBZ.

Mink, Gwendolyn. 1986. *Old Labor and New Immigrants in American Political Development: Union, Party, and State, 1875–1920*. Ithaca: Cornell University Press.

Minkenberg, Michael. 2001. "The Radical Right in Public Office: Agenda-Setting and Policy Effects." *West European Politics* 24, no. 4 (October): 1–22.

———. 2002. "The New Radical Right in the Political Process: Interaction Effects in France and Germany." In *Shadows Over Europe: The Development and Impact of the Extreme Right Wing in Western Europe*, edited by Martin Schain, Aristide Zolberg, and Patrick Hossay. Houndmills: Palgrave.

Misteli, Roland, and Andreas Gisler. 1999. "Überfremdung: Karriere und Diffusion eines fremdenfeindlichen Deutungsmusters." Pp. 95–120 in *Vom kalten Krieg zur Kulturrevolution: Analyse von Medienereignissen in der Schweiz der 50er und 60er Jahre*, edited by Kurt Imhof, Heinz Kelger, and Gaetano Romano. Zürich: Seismo Verlag.

Money, Jeannette. 1999. *Fences and Neighbors: The Political Geography of Immigration Control*. Ithaca, NY: Cornell University Press.

Moore, Robert 1975. *Racism and Black Resistance in Britain*. London: Pluto Press.

Moravcsik, Andrew. 1998. *The Choice for Europe: Social Purpose and State Power from Messina to Maastricht.* Ithaca, NY: Cornell University Press.

Morelli, Anne. 1994. "Cent ans d'immigration belge." Pp 18–20 in *L'annuaire de l'émigration—Maroc* edited by Kacem Basfao and Hinde Taarji. Rabat: Fondation Hassan II Pour les Marocains Résidents à l'Étranger.

Moulin, Jean-Pierre. 1985. *Enquête sur la France multiraciale.* Paris: Calmann-Lévy.

Münz, Rainer, and Ralf Ulrich. 1995. "Changing Patterns of Immigration to Germany, 1945–1995." In *Migrations Past, Migrations Future,* edited by Klaus J. Bade and Myron Weiner. New York: Berghahn Books.

———. 1998. "Deutschland: Rot-Grün bringt Reform des Staatsbürgerschaftsrechts, aber kein Einwanderungsgesetz." *Migration und Bevölkerung* (November).

Murray, Laura. 1994. "'Einwanderungsland Bundesrepublik Deutschland?' Explaining the Evolving Positions of German Political Parties on Citizenship Policy." *German Politics and Society* 33 (Fall): 23–56.

Myrdal, Gunnar. 1962. *An American Dilemma: The Negro Problem and American Democracy.* New York: Harper and Row.

Nederlands Centrum Buitenlanders (NCB). 1993. *Het jaar van de omslag.* Utrecht: NCB.

Newland, Kathleen, and Demetrios Papademetriou. 1998–1999. "Managing International Migration." *UCLA Journal of International Law and Foreign Affairs* 3 (Fall/Winter).

Ngai, Mae M. 2004. *Impossible Subjects: Illegal Aliens and the Making of Modern America.* Princeton: Princeton University Press.

Niederberger, Josef Martin. 1982. "Die politisch-administrative Regelung von Einwanderung und Aufenthalt von Ausländern in der Schweiz: Strukturen, Prozesse, Wirkungen." Pp. 11–123 in *Ausländer in der Bundesrepublik Deutschland und in der Schweiz: Segregation und Integration: Eine vergleichende Untersuchung.* Frankfurt: Campus Verlag.

Niekerk, Miles van. 1993. *Kansarmoede: Reacties van allochtonen op achterstand.* Amsterdam: Het Spinhuis.

O'Brien, Peter. 1996. *Beyond the Swastika.* London: Routledge.

OECD. 2001. *Trends in International Migration.* Paris: Organization for Economic Cooperation and Development.

OFDE. 1991. *Rapport sur la conception et les priorités de la politique suisse des étrangers pour les années 90.* Berne: Office fédéral du développement économique et de l'emploi.

Orberndörfer, Dieter. *Der Wahn des Nationalen.* Freiburg: Herder, 1993.

Papademetriou, D., et al. 1989. *The Effects of Immigration on the U.S. Economy and Labor Market.* Immigration Policy and Research Report 1. Washington, D.C.: U.S. Department of Labor.

Parekh, Bhikhu. 1996. "Minority Practices and Principles of Toleration." *International Migration Review* 30, no.1: 251–84.

Parini, Lorena. 1997. *La politique d'asile en Suisse: Une perspective systémique.* Paris: L'Harmattan.

Penninx, Rinus, Jeannette Schoorl, and Carlo van Praag. 1994. *The Impact of International Migration on Receiving Countries: The Case of the Netherlands.* The Hague: Netherlands Interdisciplinary Demographic Institute.

Perlmutter, Ted. 1996. "Bringing Parties Back In: Comments on 'Modes of Immigration Politics in Liberal Democratic Societies'." *International Migration Review* 30, no. 1: 375–88.

———. 1997. "Immigration Politics Italian Style: The Paradoxical Behavior of Mainstream and Populist Parties." *South European Politics and Society* 1, no. 2: 229–52.

———. 2002. "The Politics of Restriction: The Effect of Xenophobic Parties on Italian Immigration Policy and German Asylum Policy." In *Shadows Over Europe: The Development and Impact of the Extreme Right Wing in Western Europe*, edited by Martin Schain, Aristide Zolberg, and Patrick Hossay. Houndmills: Palgrave.

Phillips, Anne. 1991. *Engendering Democracy*. University Park, PA: The Pennsylvania State University Press.

Piguet, Etienne. 2005. *L'immigration et intégration en Suisse depuis 1948—Une Analyse des Flux Migratoires*. Zurich: Seismo.

Piguet, Etienne, and Hans Mahnig. 2000. "Quotas d'immigration: L'expérience suisse." *Cahiers de Migrations Internationales (ILO/BIT)*, no. 37: 1–42.

Piguet, Etienne, and Jean-Hughes Ravel. 2002. *Les demandeurs d'asile sur le marché du travail suisse 1996–2000*. Neuchâtel: Forum suisse pour l'étude des migrations—Rapport de recherche 19.

Piore, Michael J. 1979. *Birds of Passage: Migrant Labor in Industrial Societies*. Cambridge: Cambridge University Press.

Piven, Frances Fox, and Richard A. Cloward. 1979. *Poor People's Movements*. New York: Vintage Books.

Portes, Alejandro. 1996 "Transnational Communities: Their Emergence and Their Significance in the Contemporary World-System." Pp. 151–68 in *Latin America in the World Economy*, edited by Roberto P. Korzeniewicz and William C. Smith. Westport, CT: Greenwood Press.

———. 1997. "Immigration Theory for a New Century: Some Problems and Opportunities." *International Migration Review* 31: 799–825.

Portes, Alejandro, and Robert Bach. 1985. *Latin Journey: Cuban and Mexican Immigration to the United States*. Berkeley, CA: University of California Press.

Portes, Alejandro, and Ruben G. Rumbaut. 1990. *Immigrant America: A Portrait*. Berkeley, CA: University of California Press.

Prantl, Heribert. 1999. *Rot-Grün: Eine erste Bilanz*. Hamburg: Campe Paperback.

Quillian, Lincoln. 1995. "Prejudice as a Response to Perceived Group Threat: Population composition and anti-immigrant and racial prejudice in Europe." *American sociological review* 60: 586–611.

Radtke, Franz-Olaf. 1990. "Multikulturell—das Gesellschaftsdesign der 90er Jahre?" *Informationsdienst zur Ausländerarbeit* 4: 27–34.

Rath, Jan, Rinus Penninx, Kees Groenendijk, and Astrid Meijer. 1996. *Nederland en zijn islam*. Amsterdam: Het Spinhuis.

Rath, Jan. 1991. *Minorisering: De sociale constructie van etnische minderheden*. Amsterdam: Sua.

Rea, Andrea. 1993. "La politique d'intégration des populations d'origine étrangère." In *Migrations et minorités ethniques dans l'espace européen*, edited by Marco Martiniello and Marc Poncelet. Brussels: De Boeck Université.

Reimers, David. 1985. *Still the Golden Door*. New York: Columbia University Press.

Reimers, David M. 1992. *Still the Golden Door: The Third World Comes to America*. New York: Columbia University Press.

Reisler, Mark. 1976. *By the Sweat of Their Brow: Mexican Immigrant Labor in the United States, 1900–1940*. Westport: Greenwood Press.

Renaerts, Monique. 1996. "L'historique de l'Islam en Belgique et la problématique de sa reconnaissance." *Cahier* no. 3: 51–63. Brussels: Institut de Philologie et d'Histoire Orientales, Université Libre de Bruxelles.

Rex, John. 1995. "Ethnic Identity and the National State: The Political Sociology of Multicultural Societies." *Social Identities: Journal for the Study of Race, Nationality and Culture* 1.

———. 1996. *Ethnic Minorities in the Modern Nation State*. Houndmills/Basingstoke: Macmillan.

Rex, John. 2003. "The Concept of a Multicultural Society." Pp. 205–20 in *The Ethnicity Reader: Nationalism, Multiculturalism and Migration*, edited by Montserrat Guibernau and John Rex. Reprinted ed. Cambridge: Polity Press.

Rex, John, and Beatrice Drury, eds. 1995. *Ethnic Mobilisation in a Multi-Cultural Europe*. Aldershot: Avebury.

Rex, John, and Sally Tomlinson. 1979. *Colonial Immigrants in a British City*. London: Routledge and Kegan Paul.

Richmond, Anthony H. 1988. *Immigration and Ethnic Conflict*. New York: St. Martin's Press.

Rohner, Kurt. 1991. *Main d'oeuvre et population étrangère: Politique suisse des étrangers des années '90, rapprochement de l'Europe-Espace économique européen*. Lausanne: Institut des Hautes Études en Administration Publique.

Roosens, Eugeen. 1989. *Creating Ethnicity*. London: Sage.

Royce, Anya Peterson. 1982. *Ethnic Identity*. Bloomington: Indiana University Press.

Safran, William. 1995. "Ethnicity and Citizenship: The Canadian Case—Conclusions" *Nationalism and Ethnic Politics* 1, no. 3 (Autumn): 107–11.

Safran, William. 1997. "Citizenship and Nationality in Democratic Systems: Approaches to Defining and Acquiring Membership in the Political Community." *International Political Science Review* 18: 313–35.

Sandmeyer, Elmer C. 1973. *The Anti-Chinese Movement in California*. Urbana: University of Illinois Press.

Sassen, Saskia. 1988. *The Mobility of Labor and Capital: A Study in International Investment and Labor Flow*. Cambridge: Cambridge University Press.

———. 1991 (2nd ed. 2001). *The Global City*. Princeton: Princeton University Press.

———. 1996. *Losing Control? Sovereignty in an Age of Globalization*. New York: Columbia University Press.

———. 1998. "The de facto Transnationalizing of Immigration Policy." In *Challenge to the Nation-State*, edited by Christian Joppke. Oxford: Oxford University Press.

———. 1999. *Guests and Aliens*. New York: The New Press.

———. 2002. "Global Cities and Diasporic Networks: Microsites in Global Civil Society." In *Global Civil Society Yearbook 2002*, edited by the Center for the Study of Global Governance.

Schain, Martin. 1987. "The National Front in France and the Construction of Political Legitimacy." *West European Politics* 10: 229–52.

Schain, Martin A. 1994. "The Development of the American State and the Construction of Immigration Policy (1880–1924)." Unpublished paper delivered at the annual meeting of the American Political Science Association, New York.

————. 1997. "The National Front and the Politicization of Immigration in France: Implications for the Extreme Right in Europe." Unpublished paper presented at Conference on Citizenship, Immigration and Xenophobia in Europe, Berlin, Wissenschaftszentrum.

Schain, Martin, and Martin Baldwin Edwards, eds. 1994. *The Politics of Immigration in Western Europe.* Essex: Frank Cass.

Schain, Martin, Aristide Zolberg, and Patrick Hossay. 2002. *Shadows Over Europe: The Development and Impact of the Extreme Right Wing in Western Europe.* Houndmills: Palgrave.

Scharpf, Fritz Wilhelm. 1997. *Games Real Actors Play: Actor-Centered Institutionalism in Policy Research.* Boulder, CO: Westview Press.

Scheidler, Antje. 2000. "Deutschland/USA: Ausländische Arbeitskräfte für die Computerbranche." *Migration und Bevölkerung* (February/March).

————. 2001. "Deutschland: Erster Entwurf eines Zuwanderungsgesetzes." *Migration und Bevölkerung* (September).

————. 2001b. "Deutschland: Kabinett verabschiedete Gesetzentwurf zu Zuwanderung und Integration." *Migration und Bevölkerung* (November).

Schiek, Dagmar. 1998. "Sex Equality Law After *Kalanke* and *Marschall,*" *European Law Journal* 4: 148–66.

Schmidt, Manfred G. 1985. *Der schweizerische Weg zur Vollbeschäftigung: Eine Bilanz der Beschäftigung, der Arbeitslosigkeit und der Arbeitsmarktpolitik.* Frankfurt a.M.: Campus Verlag.

Schmitter Heisler, Barbara. 1992. "The Future of Immigrant Incorporation: Which Models? Which Concepts?" *International Migration Review* 26: 623–645.

————. 2000. "The Sociology of Immigration." Pp. 77–96 in *Migration Theory: Talking across Disciplines,* edited by Caroline B. Brettell and James F. Hollifield. New York: Routledge.

Schnapper, Dominique 1994. *La communauté des citoyens.* Paris: Gallimard.

Schönwälder, Karen. 1999. "'Persons Persecuted on Political Grounds Shall Enjoy the Right to Asylum—but not in Our Country': Asylum Policy and Debates about Refugees in the Federal Republic of Germany." In *Refugees, Citizenship and Social Policy in Europe,* edited by Carl Levy and Alice Bloch. Houndmills: Palgrave

————. 2001. *Einwanderung und ethnische Pluralität: Politische Entscheidungen und öffentliche Debatten in Großbritanien und der Bundesrepublik von den 1950er bis zu 1970er Jahren.* Essen: Klartext Verlag.

————. 2004. "Kleine Schritte, verpasste Gelegenheiten, neue Konflikte: Zuwanderungsgesetz und Migrationspolitik." *Blätter für deutsche und internationale Politik* (October): 1205–15.

Schuck, Peter H. 1984. "The Transformation of Immigration Law." *Columbia Law Review* 84 (January): 1–90.

————. "The Politics of Rapid Legal Change: Immigration Policy in the 1980s," in *Citizens, Strangers and In-Between: Essays on Immigration and Citizenship,* by Peter Schuck. Boulder, CO: Westview Press.

————. 1993. "The New Immigration and the Old Civil Rights." *The American Prospect* (Fall): 102–11.

————. 1998. *Citizens, Strangers, and In-Betweens.* Boulder, CO: Westview Press.

Shadid, W. A. R., and P.S. van Koningsveld. 1996. "Islampolitiek en islamonderzoek in Nederland." Pp. 37–54 in *Etnische minderheden en wetenschappelijk onderzoek,* edited by Henk Heeren, Patricia Vogel, and Hans Werdmölder. Amsterdam and Meppel: Uitgeverij Boom.

Simon, Julian. 1989. *The Economic Consequences of Immigration*. Oxford: Basil Blackwell and the Cato Institute.

Smelser, Neil. 1962. *Theory of Collective Behavior*. New York: The Free Press.

Smith, Anthony. 1986. *The Ethnic Origins of Nationalism*. Oxford: Blackwell.

Smith, David M., and Maurice Blanc. 1996. "Citizenship, Nationality and Ethnic Minorities in Three European Nations." *International Journal of Urban and Regional Research* 20: 66–82.

Smith, Rogers M. 1993. "Beyond Tocqueville, Myrdal, and Hartz: The Mutiple Traditions in America." *American Political Science Review* 87, no. 3 (September): 549–66.

———. 1997. *Civic Ideals: Conflicting Visions of Citizenship in U.S. History*. New Haven, CT: Yale University Press.

Somek, Alexander. 1999. "A Constitution for Antidiscrimination: Exploring the Vanguard Moment of Community Law." *European Law Journal* 5: 243–71.

Sommer, Theo. 1998. "Der Kopf zählt, nicht das Tuch." *Die Zeit*, no. 30 (July 16): 3.

SOPEMI (Continous Reporting System on Migration). 1998. *Trends in International Migration*. Paris: OECD.

Soysal, Yasemin. 1993. "Immigration and the Emerging European Polity." Pp. 171–86 in *Making Policy in Europe: The Europeification of National Policy Making*, edited by Svein S. Anderson and Kjell A. Eliasson. London: Sage.

———. 1994. *Limits of Citizenship: Migrants and Post-National Membership in Europe*. Chicago: Chicago University Press.

———. 1996. "Changing Citizenship in Europe: Remarks on Postnational Membership and the National State." In *Citizenship, Nationality and Migration in Europe*, edited by David Ceasarini and Mary Fulbrook. London and New York: Routledge.

Soysal, Yasemin Nuhoglu 1998. "Toward a Postnational Model of Membership." Pp. 189–220 in *The Citizenship Debates*, edited by Gershon Shafir. Minneapolis: University of Minnesota Press.

SPD-Bundesfraktion. 1995. *Dokumentation: Einbürgerung erleichtern—Integration fördern*.

Statham, Paul, Ruud Koopmans, Marco Giugni, and Florence Passy. 2005. "Resilient or Adaptable Islam? Multiculturalism, Religion and Migrants' Claims-making for Group Demands in Britain, the Netherlands and France." *Ethnicities* 5: 427–59.

Storey, Hugo. 1998. "Implications of Incorporation of the European Convention of Human Rights in the Immigration and Asylum Context." *European Human Rights Law Review* 452.

Straubhaar, Thomas. 1984. "The Accession of Spain and Portugal to the EC from the Aspect of the Free Movement of Labour in an Enlarged Common Labour Market." *International Migration* 22, no 3: 228–38.

———. 1986. "The Causes of International Migration—A Demand Determined Approach." *International Migration Review* 20, no. 4: 835–55.

———. 1988. *On the Economics of International Labor Migration*. Bern and Stuttgart: Verlag Paul Haupt.

Straubhaar, Thomas, and Peter A Fischer. 1994. "Economic and Social Aspects of Immigration into Switzerland." Pp. 127–48 in *European Migration in the Late Twentieth Century: Historical Patterns, Actual Trends, and Social Implications*, edited by Heinz Fassmann and Rainer Münz. Aldershot: Edward Elgar Publishing.

Straubhaar, Thomas, and René Weber. 1994. "On the Economics of Immigration: Some Empirical Evidence for Switzerland." *International Review of Applied Economics* 8: 107–29.

Stüwe, Gerd. 1996. "Migranten in der Jugendhilfe." *Migration und Soziale Arbeit* 3–4: 25–29.

Süß, Werner, ed. 1991. *Die Bundesrepublik in den achtziger Jahren: Innenpolitik, Politische Kultur, Außenpolitik.* Opalden: Leske und Budrich.

Taggart, Paul. 1996. *The New Populism and the New Politics.* London: Macmillan.

Tarrow, Sidney. 1993. "Social Protest and Policy Reform: May 1968 and the *Loi d'Orientation* in France." *Comparative Political Studies* 25: 579–607.

———. 1996. "States and Opportunities: The Political Structuring of Social Movements." Pp. 41–61 in *Comparative Perspectives on Social Movements: Political Opportunitites, Mobilizing Structures, and Cultural Framings*, edited by Doug McAdam, John D. McCarthy, and Mayer N. Zald. Cambridge: Cambridge University Press.

———. 1998. *Power in Movement.* 2nd ed. Cambridge: Cambridge University Press.

Taylor Charles. 1994. " The Politics of Recognition." Pp. 25–73 in *Multiculturalism*, edited by Amy Gutmann. Princeton: Princeton University Press.

Teitelbaum, Michael. 1992. "Advocacy, Ambivalence, Ambiguity: Immigration Policies and Prospects in the United States." *Proceedings of the American Philosophical Society* 136, no. 2: 188–206.

Thränhardt, Dietrich. 1988. "Die Bunderepublik Deutschland—Ein unerklärtes Einwanderungsland." *Aus Politik und Zeitgeschichte* 24: 3–13.

———. 1992. "Germany—An Undeclared Immigration Country." In *Europe—An Immigration Continent*, edited by Dietrich Thränhardt. Münster: Lit Verlag.

Tichenor, Daniel J. 1994. "The Politics of Immigration Reform in the United States, 1981–1990." *Polity* XXVI, no. 3 (Spring): 333–62.

———. 2002. *Dividing Lines: The Politics of Immigration Control in America.* Princeton: Princeton University Press.

Tijdelijke Wetenschappelijke Commissie Minderhedenbeleid (TWCM). 1995. *Kaderadvies: Eenheid en verscheidenheid.* Amsterdam: Het Spinhuis.

Tillie, Jean. 2004. "Social Capital of Organisations and Their Members: Explaining the Political Integration of Immigrants in Amsterdam." *Journal of Ethnic and Migration Studies* 30: 529–41.

Tilly, Charles. 1978. *From Mobilization to Revolution.* Reading, MA: Addison-Wesley.

Tocqueville, Alexis de. 1945. *Democracy in America.* Volumes 1–2. New York: Alfred A. Knopf.

Tölölyan, Khachig. 1996. "The Nation-State and Its Others: In Lieu of a Preface." In *Becoming National: A Reader*, edited by Geoff Eley and Ronald Grigor Sunny. Oxford: Oxford University Press.

Toonen, Theo A. J. 1996. "On the Administrative Condition of Politics." *West European Politics* 19, no. 3 (July): 609–32.

Torpey, John. 1999. *The Invention of the Passport.* Cambridge: Cambridge University Press.

Ugur, Mehmet. 1995. "Freedom of Movement vs. Exclusion: A Reinterpretation of the 'Insider'—'Outsider' Divide in the European Union." *International Migration Review* 29: 964–99.

U.S. INS (Immigration and Naturalization Service). Various years. *Annual Report.* Washington, D.C.

———. Various years. *Statistical Yearbook.* Washington, D.C.

U.S. Department of Justice, Immigration and Naturalization Service. 2002. *Annual Report.* Office of Policy and Planning. Washington, D.C.

Van Zelm, E. A. 1996. *Sturen met twaalf kapiteins.* Rijswijk: Ministerie van Volksgezondheid, Welzijn en Sport.

Vandenbrande, Kristel. 1995. *Het Vlaams-Brussels migrantenbeleid bestaat niet.* Brussels: Vrije Universiteit Brussel, Interuniversitaire Attractiepool 37.

Vermeulen, Hans, ed. 1997. *Immigrantenbeleid voor de multiculturele samenleving.* Amsterdam: Het Spinhuis.

Veugelers, John W. P. 1993. "Recent Immigration Politics in Italy: A Short Story." *West European Politics* 17, no. 2: 33–49.

Veugelers, J.W.P. and T.R. Klassen. 1994. "Continuity and Change in Canada's Unemployment-Immigration Linkage (1946–1993)." *Canadian Journal of Sociology* 19 (3): 351–67.

Von Dirke, Sabine. 1994. "Multikulti: The German Debate on Multiculturalism." *German Studies Review* 17 (October): 513–35.

Voogt, Peter W. 1994. *In de buurt: Participatie van migranten bij buurtbeheer.* Rotterdam: Rotterdams Instituut Bewonersondersteuning.

Waldinger, Roger. 1994. "The Making of an Immigrant Niche." *International Migration Review* 28, no.1 (Spring): 3–30.

Warbrick, Colin. 2002. "The Principles of the European Convention on Human Rights and the Response of States to Terrorism," in *European Human Rights Law Review* 3: 287–314.

Webber, Michael J. 1992. "Settlement Characteristics of Immigrants in Australia." Pp. 165–181 in *Nations of Immigrants: Australia, the United States, and International Migration,* edited by Gary P. Freeman, and James Jupp. Oxford: Oxford University Press.

Weil, Patrick. 1995. *La France et ses étrangers.* Paris: Gallimard.

———. 2002. *Qu'est-ce qu'un Français?* Histoire de la nationalité française depuis la Révolution. Paris: Grasset.

Weiler, Joseph H. H. 1999. *The Constitution of Europe: 'Do the New Clothes Have an Emperor?' and Other Essays on European Integration.* Cambridge: Cambridge University Press.

Weiner, Myron. 1985. "International Migration and International Relations." *Population and Development Review* 11: 441–55.

———. 1995. *The Global Migration Crisis.* New York: Harper Collins.

Welch, Susan, and Donley T. Studlar. 1985. "The Impact of Race on Political Behaviour in Britain." *British Journal of Political Science* 15: 528–39.

Williams, Raymond. 1961. *The Long Revolution.* London: Chatto and Windus.

Wimmer, Andreas. 1996. *The Resettlement of Refugees: An Analysis of the Swiss Experience in the International Context.* Neuchâtel: Forum suisse pour l'étude des migrations—Rapport de recherche 5E.

———. 1997. "Ein Zulassungsmodell für Arbeitsmigranten von ausserhalb der EU: Vorschlag zuhanden der Expertengruppe Migrationspolitik." Neuchâtel: Forum suisse pour l'étude des migrations—Discussion paper 2.

———. 2001. "Ein helvetischer Kompromiss: Kommentar zum Entwurf eines neuen Ausländergesetzes." *Schweizerische Zeitschrift für Politikwissenschaft* 7, no. 1: 97–104.

Young, Iris. 1990. *Justice and the Politics of Difference.* Princeton: Princeton University Press.

Zimmer, Pol. 1996. "Le logement social à Bruxelles." *Courrier hebdomadaire* 1521–1522. Brussels: Centre de Recheache et d'Information Socio-Politiques.

Zimmermann, Klaus F. 1996. "European Migration: Push and Pull." *International Regional Science Review* 19, nos. 1–2: 95–128.

Zolberg, Aristide. 1999. "Matters of State: Theorizing Immigration Policy." In *Becoming American, America Becoming,* edited by Douglas S. Massey. New York: Russell Sage.

Index

admission policy, 68, 71, 98
Afghan, 153
Africa, 126–28, 130, 161; Africans, 101;
   North Africa, 137, 145, 148–49, 152
agency, 25–39, 47, 55, 60
Alevite, 153
Alleanza Nazionale (AN), 179–80
Al Qaeda, 27
Amsterdam Treaty. *See* Treaty of
   Amsterdam
Anglicanism, 148
anti-immigrant, 53, 86; decision, 218;
   hostility, 52; movement, 137; parties,
   144; position, 53; violence, 152. *See
   also* immigrant; pro-immigrant
anti-immigration: attitudes, 216; circles,
   79; groups, 78, 87; initiatives, 77;
   lobby, 77; movements, 69. *See also*
   immigration
anti-migrant, 17; decision, 218; position,
   16. *See also* migrant; pro-migrant
anti-minority: claims, 201–7, 211–12,
   213n6, 213n8, 219; decision, 203,
   219–20; political decision, 201, 212.
   See also minority; pro-minority
Armenians, 126, 161

Arubans, 141
Asia, 101, 135, 163; Asians, 101, 135,
   163; Southeast Asia, 127
assimilationist: alternative, 132;
   approach, 13, 162; citizenship law,
   173; countries, 20; model, 19, 196;
   policy, 173; pressures, 162; view, 13,
   148, 196
asylees, 28
asylum, 16, 80, 86, 93, 116, 176, 184,
   196–97, 212; laws, legislation, 28,
   35–36, 152, 177–78, 180; policies, 68,
   81–82, 84, 146, 176–77, 187; request,
   28, 80, 82; seekers, 4, 28, 36, 54, 80,
   84, 89n14, 113, 116, 137, 141,
   177–78; seeking, 4, 9, 28, 116
Asylum and Immigration Appeals Act, 36
Australia, 4, 8, 13, 69, 83–84, 115, 139
Australo-Canadian model, 84
Austria, 22, 172, 177–79, 181, 215
Austrian Freedom Party (FPÖ), 172,
   177–79, 190n2

Belgium, 8, 51, 140–41, 146–49, 151,
   154–55, 159
Berlin Wall, 141, 152

245

About the Contributors

Adrian Favell is Associate Professor of Sociology, UCLA. He is the author of *Philosophies of Integration* (St. Martin's Press, 1998).

Gary P. Freeman is Professor of Government at the University of Texas–Austin and specializes in comparative immigration politics.

Marco Giugni is a researcher and teacher in the Department of Political Science at the University of Geneva. He is the author of several books on social movements and contentious politics as well as various articles in major French-, English-, and Italian-speaking journals. His current research focuses on political claims-making in the fields of immigration and unemployment, on the political participation and integration of migrants at the local level, and on the conceptions and practices of democracy in the global justice movement.

Patrick Ireland earned degrees in modern languages and political science from the University of Notre Dame and Harvard University, and has published extensively on immigrant integration, ethnic relations, and social policy in Europe and North America. He currently teaches comparative and international politics at the American University of Beirut (Lebanon).

James Hollifield is Arnold Professor of International Political Economy and Director of the Tower Center for Political Studies at SMU. He is a member of the Council on Foreign Relations, has worked as a consultant on migration

258 · About the Contributors

and trade for the United Nations and other international organizations, and has published widely on these issues, including *Immigrants, Markets, and States* (Harvard University Press 1992), *Controlling Immigration* (Stanford University Press 1994, 2004) with Wayne Cornelius and Philip Martin, *Migration Theory* (Routledge 2000, 2006) with Caroline Brettell, and *The Emerging Migration State* (forthcoming). His current research looks at the rapidly evolving relationship between trade, migration, and security, and includes an NSF-funded study of immigrant incorporation in the Dallas-Fort Worth metroplex.

Valerie Hunt received her Ph.D. in Political Science from the University of Washington. She also holds a B.A. and an M.A. in International Relations. Dr. Hunt's research includes studies of public opinion with a particular focus on public attitudes toward immigrants and immigration policy. Her second main area of research involves the study of U.S. immigration policy processes, specifically addressing the role of congressional state politics in the U.S. immigration policy process. Dr. Hunt also has substantive expertise in current and historical trends in U.S. immigration policy reforms.

Hanspeter Kriesi holds the Chair in Comparative Politics in the Department of Political Science at the University of Zurich. Previously, he has taught at the universities of Amsterdam and Geneva. He is a specialist in Swiss direct democracy, but his wide ranging research interests also include the study of social movements, political parties and interest groups, public opinion, the public sphere, and the media. He has recently co-edited (together with David Snow and Sarah Soule) *The Blackwell Companion to Social Movements* (Blackwell Publishers, 2004). His books include *Direct Democratic Choice: The Swiss Experience* (Lexington Books, 2005). His articles have appeared in major journals such as *American Journal of Sociology, American Political Science Review, British Journal of Political Science, European Journal of Political Research, European Sociological Review, Politische Vierteljahresschrift*, and *West European Politics*. For eight years, he has been the president of the expert committee for the largest social science program of the Swiss National Science Foundation and he is now the director of a Swiss national research program on the "Challenges to democracy in the twenty-first century."

David Jacobson is the founding director of the School of Global Studies at Arizona State University. His research and teaching are in politics from a global, cultural, and legal perspective, with a particular focus on international law and institutions, human rights, and citizenship issues. His books include *Rights Across Borders: Immigration and the Decline of Citizenship* (Johns Hopkins University Press 1996) and *Place and Belonging in America* (Johns Hopkins University Press 2002).

Florence Passy is Associate Professor of Political Science at the University of Lausanne (Switzerland). She is the author of *L'action altruiste: contraintes et opportunités de l'engagement individuel dans les mouvements sociaux* (Droz 1998), co-author of *Histoires de mobilisation politique en Suisse* (L'Harmattan 1997), *Mouvements sociaux et Etat* (Actes Sud 1997), *Contested Citizenship: Immigration and Cultural Diversity in Europe* (University of Minnesota Press, 2005), *La citoyenneté en débat: Mobilisations politiques en France et en Suisse* (L'Harmattan, 2006). Her current research examines individual representations and understandings of politics and democracy in a comparative perspective.

Etienne Piguet is Professor of Human Geography at the University of Neuchâtel (Switzerland). His publications and research fields cover immigration policy, ethnic and minority business, asylum-seekers and refugees, urban segregation, and integration of migrant populations.

John Rex holds a Ph.D. (Leeds) and a D.Sc. (Plymouth). He has taught at Leeds University, Birmingham University, Durham University, and Warwick University, and has been Professor Emeritus, Department of Sociology, Warwick University since 1990. Rex was the president of the International Sociological Association Research Committee on Racial and Ethnic Minorities. His principal publications include *Key Problems of Sociological Theory* (Routledge and K. Paul 1961), *Race Relations in Sociological Theory* (Schocken Books 1970), *Colonial Immigrants in a British City* (Routledge and K. Paul 1979), *Race and Ethnicity* (Open University Press 1986), *Race Community and Conflict* (Oxford University Press 1987), *Ethnic Minorities in the Modern Nation State* (Palgrave Macmillan 1996), *The Ethnicity Reader* (edited with M. Guibernau, Polity Press 1997), and *The Governance of Multicultural Societies* (edited with G. Singh, Ashgate Publishing 2004).

Galya Ruffer is a visiting researcher at the Transnationalism Project at the University of Chicago. Her current research focuses on immigration and asylum law in transnational legal contexts. She holds a J.D. from Northwestern University and a Ph.D. in Political Science from the University of Pennsylvania.

Saskia Sassen (University of Chicago and London School of Economics) has most recently authored *Territory, Authority and Rights: From Medieval to Global Assemblages* (Princeton University Press 2006). Her comments have appeared in *The Guardian, The New York Times, Le Monde Diplomatique,* the *International Herald Tribune,* and *The Financial Times,* among other journals and newspapers.

Paul Statham is Professor of Social Movements and the Public Sphere and Research Director of the Centre for European Political Communications

(EurPolCom) at the University of Leeds. His research focuses on issues of migration and ethnic relations, Islam and European integration with regard to Britain and in European comparative perspective. He is author of numerous articles published in international journals and collected volumes. Most recently, he is co-author with Koopmans, Giugni and Passy of a five-country comparison: *Contested Citizenship: Immigration and Cultural Diversity in Europe* (Minnesota University Press, 2005).

Daniel Tichenor is Research Professor at the Eagleton Institute of Politics and Associate Professor in the Department of Political Science at Rutgers University–New Brunswick. In addition to various articles and essays on the politics of immigrant admissions and rights, he is the author of *Dividing Lines: The Politics of Immigration Control in America* (Princeton University Press 2002), which received the American Political Science Association's 2003 Gladys Kammerer Award. He has also published scholarly works on the American presidency, civil liberties, interest groups and social movements, and American political development.

Phil Triadafilopoulos is a Social Sciences and Humanities Research Council of Canada Postdoctoral Fellow in the University of Toronto's Department of Political Science. His research focuses on how immigration and citizenship policies intersect with and help define boundaries of national belonging in liberal-democratic states. He earned his Ph.D. in Political Science from the New School for Social Research and conducted extensive field research in Germany as a DAAD Visiting Research Fellow. Triadafilopoulos is the co-editor of *European Encounters: Migrants, Migration and European Societies since 1945* (with Rainer Ohliger and Karen Schönwälder, Ashgate 2003) and has published articles and reviews in the *Journal of Historical Sociology, Citizenship Studies, Migration und Bevölkerung*, the *Journal of Politics*, the *Canadian Journal of Political Science, Canadian Public Administration, East European Quarterly*, and the *Journal of Southern Europe and the Balkans*. He is a contributor to the *Dictionary of the Social Sciences* (Oxford University Press 2002) and the *Ethnopolitical Encyclopaedia of Europe* (Palgrave 2004).

Andrej Zaslove earned an M.A. from the New School for Social Research and a Ph.D. from York University, Toronto, Canada. His areas of research interest are political parties, radical right populism, and immigration. He has published articles on the Lega Nord, the Austrian Freedom Party, and the radical right. He is currently completing a book on the Lega Nord.